MEDITATIONS ON AMERICA

MEDITATIONS ON AMERICA:
JOHN D. MACDONALD'S
TRAVIS MCGEE SERIES
AND OTHER FICTION

Lewis D. Moore

Bowling Green State University Popular Press
Bowling Green, OH 43403

ISBN: 0-87972-663-6 Clothbound
     0-87972-664-4 Paperback

Library of Congress Catalog Card Number: 94-71363

Cover by Gary Dumm

For

Barbara

Acknowledgments

Chapter Two appeared in a slightly different version in *Clues: A Journal of Detection* 11.1 (1990) and Chapter Four appeared in a different version in *Clues* 6.2 (1985). I wish to thank the editor, Pat Browne, for permission to use them.

Chapter Nine was published in an earlier version in *JDM Bibliophile* 46 (Dec. 1990). Authors are assigned all rights to their own material by the editor, Edgar W. Hirshberg, on the first page of that publication.

I wish to thank Ms. Carmen Hurff, Special Collections Division, University Libraries, University of Florida, Gainesville, Florida, for her help in using the John D. MacDonald Collection housed there. In addition, I wish to thank Professor Edgar W. Hirshberg, University of South Florida, Tampa, Florida, and Professor Thomas D. Lane, East Tennessee State University, Johnson City, Tennessee, for sharing their ideas about MacDonald over the years. I gratefully acknowledge the MacDonald material received from Dr. Philip Skerry, Lakeland Community College, Mentor, OH; Dr. W. Russel Gray, Delaware County Community College, Media, PA; and Dr. John Springhall, University of Ulster, Coleraine, Northern Ireland, along with the editing help of Dr. Priscilla Ramsey, Howard University, Washington, DC. Finally, I want to express my appreciation for those Western studies specialists and others who have listened patiently to my ideas on MacDonald over many dinners at the Popular Culture Association conferences. They include Dr. Leonard Engel and Dr. John M. Gourlie, Quinnipiac College, Hamden, CT; Dr. Richard Hutson, University of California, Berkeley, CA; Dr. John W. Bailey, Carthage College, Kenosha, WI; Dr. Daniel Miller, University of South Carolina, Aiken, SC; and Dr. Helen M. Nixon, University of Nebraska, Omaha, NE. It was above the call of duty. Of course, all responsibility for any errors in the book rests with me.

Contents

Chapter 1

Early Fiction

In his 1964 article, "How to Live with a Hero," John D. MacDonald discusses his evolution from a writer of novels of manners and suspense into a writer of a detective series. Appropriately, he focuses on his ability to sustain a believable character through a number of books of which neither he nor his readers will tire. Only when the character achieves a certain degree of independence does he feel that he can continue the series (14-16). Thus, character and plot are dominant features of MacDonald's analysis of his thinking about Travis McGee. However, he indicates another level of concern in this informative article:

I made shameless use of certain conventions: a variation of the Robin Hood *modus operandi*, a houseboat environment, a tropic resort flavor, a capacity for indignation. I discarded other conventions I find restrictive and boring—for example, the idea that the hero must always win. I made him an iconoclast, a critic of the cheapening aspects of his culture, an unassimilated rebel in an increasingly structured society. I gave him a light, wry, amiable touch, partially obscuring the areas of doubt all men have. (16)

Here, MacDonald's suggestive remarks, worked out in the series, reveal the importance of the thematic. Not only will McGee's intriguing, changing personality and the often intricate plots draw readers and critics, but also the exploration of ideas dramatized through the story lines will deepen the significance of the work. And, the dominant theme that includes all others is the complex, struggling nature of late twentieth-century American society. As Michael J. Tolley writes, "He is a serious moral writer who uses the thriller as his vehicle; taken as a whole, his canon represents a monumental indictment of American values: sexual, economic, ecological, social, political, legal" ("Hero" 49). In effect, MacDonald never stops approaching his craft as a novelist of manners and morals even while working within the detective/suspense/adventure fiction formulas.

1

2   Meditations on America

A prolific short story writer, MacDonald also published forty-two novels before he began the Travis McGee series in 1964. While one may disagree on which novel goes into which area, and Edgar W. Hirshberg states that "they are difficult to categorize" ("MacDonald" 237), the works can be divided into four categories: detective, mystery/suspense/adventure, manners and morals, and science fiction or science fantasy. Seven novels, with some qualifications, fit the detective category in whole or part, among them *The Brass Cupcake* (1950), *Deadly Welcome* (1959), and *The Drowner* (1963). Nineteen works go in the second category, including *Judge Me Not* (1951), *All These Condemned* (1954), *The Price of Murder* (1957), *The Executioners* (1958), and *The End of the Night* (1960). Surprisingly, MacDonald wrote thirteen novels of manners and morals before 1964 such as *Cancel All Our Vows* (1953), *A Man of Affairs* (1957), *Clemmie* (1958), *A Key to the Suite* (1962), and *A Flash of Green* (1962). Finally, MacDonald produced three science fiction or science fantasy novels: *Wine of the Dreamers* (1951), *Ballroom of the Skies* (1952), and *The Girl, the Gold Watch & Everything* (1962). The novels in the detective category are a varied group, and several choices need further explanation as to their inclusion. For instance, only four have licensed private investigators: Milton D. Grassman in *A Bullet for Cinderella* (1955), Paul France in *You Live Once* (1956), Adam Fergasson in *On the Run* (1963), and Paul Stanial in *The Drowner*. Of these, only Stanial is a protagonist. The other detective novels feature Cliff Bartells as an insurance adjuster in *The Brass Cupcake*, Alexander Doyle as a government investigator in *Deadly Welcome*, and Sam Brice, with the weakest investigative credentials, as an insurance appraiser in *Where Is Janice Gantry?* (1961). Bartells, Doyle, and Brice also function as protagonists. Bartells and Stanial are the only ex-policemen in this category, and Grassman is the only detective to die. Earl Fitzmartin, violent like Howie Brindle in *The Turquoise Lament* (1973) and Junior Allen in *The Deep Blue Good-by* (1964), kills him. One thing that the detectives have in common is some training or experience in investigation or weighing evidence. Even Brice trains as an appraiser in a firm in Miami before setting up his own business in Florence City, Florida (*Where Is Janice Gantry?* 13). He has no other background that would enhance his detective skills and is similar in this regard to characters from the next category such as Dillon Bryant in *Murder for the Bride* (1951) and Andrew McClintock in *Dead Low Tide* (1953) who become enmeshed in an unfolding series of events and are forced to find out answers to the dangerous situations from which they and those for whom they care must struggle to escape. Each detective shows some competence in looking for answers to the problems he encounters, even Grassman whose death at Fitzmartin's hands is explainable in terms of the latter's cunning and physical power. As a function of the hard-boiled tradition, the detective protagonists often experience danger regardless of their competence. While France, only a minor character, generally serves as the cool professional above the fray in rescuing Clint Sewell from being framed for Mary Olan's murder, Angie Powell nearly kills the equally experienced Stanial.

The mystery/suspense/adventure novels have many elements in common with the former group, except a detective. It should be noted that MacDonald states that "My form of writing is not mystery writing. Of the books I've written I think that probably 60 percent of them are suspense-action. I think the other 40 percent are novels of manners and morals" (qtd. in Shine, "Snippets" 20). Of course, he also writes earlier in "How a Character Becomes Believable" that "There is nothing more dreadful than the 'mystery' novel of action and suspense wherein the characters have that peculiar woodennesss characteristic of the English school of the mystery story, genus 1925" (113). Later in the same article he states, "I am about half through the first draft of a first-person mystery as yet untitled" (115). The term "'mystery' novel of action and suspense" corresponds to my category of mystery/suspense/adventure in that MacDonald includes elements of mystery in his suspense-action novels. Tzvetan Todorov notes the presence of mystery in the thriller (48) and the suspense novel (50).

Some protagonists in this category's novels work at jobs that come close to being included in the rather broad activities listed under the detective label. For example, Teed Morrow in *Judge Me Not*, set in Deron, New York, works as Powell Dennison's assistant city administrator in a trouble-shooting capacity before Felice Carboy, the mayor's wife, is murdered at his lakeside cabin. After her death, he must not only extricate himself from the attempted frame but discover who is behind it while aiding Dennison in reforming the city's corrupt governing structure. Just as the above detectives are not uninvolved in their stories' plots, Morrow ranks high in the number of complications he must unravel. Another similarity between the two categories is the intense emotional involvement of the protagonists. France, Fergasson, and Grassman play minor roles in their respective novels, which, except for containing detectives, belong in the second category. And, only Fergasson gets personally involved and then only toward the end when he offers to help Sidney Shanley avenge Paula Lettinger's death (*On the Run* 143). However, Bartells, Doyle, Brice, and Stanial are just as emotionally entangled as Gevan Dean in *Area of Suspicion* (1954, 1961), Leo Harrison in *The Beach Girls* (1959), and Hugh Darren in *The Only Girl in the Game* (1960). While the latter three characters must solve the tricky problems encountered and avoid the threatening dangers with which their respective antagonists confront them, so must Bartells and the others.

Aside from the similarities, the novels in the second category differ in many instances from the first. Ad hoc detectives like Hugh MacReedy in *Death Trap* (1957) and Lee Bronson in *The Price of Murder*, even though they have dealt with life's rough aspects, do not expect the dangers they experience. They are private citizens unprepared for the investigative roles thrust on them and sometimes only reluctantly accepted. Love (MacReedy) and family (Bronson) involve them in situations that must be faced. There are times when no mystery exists about the villain's identity. Sam Bowden in *The Executioners* is under no illusion that Max Cady is a serious threat to him and his family. Cady clearly demonstrates the truth of R. Gordon Kelly's statement about MacDonald's fictional world: "A central element in MacDonald's fiction is a vivid sense of the precariousness and vulnerability underlying life in American society" (149). Suddenly erupting into Bowden's life after many years, Cady emanates danger; the suspense centers on Bowden's ability to deter him. In some novels in this category, police and/or criminals play the major roles. *One Monday We killed Them All* (1961) opposes Dwight McAran, a recently released convict, to Lt. Fern Hillyer and Meg Hillyer, McAran's sister and Fern's wife. *The End of the Night* actually focuses more on four murderers than the police, FBI, or law-abiding citizens. Most of their victims, except for Helen Wister, have no clear personalities. In *Soft Touch* (1958), the two protagonists, Jerry Jamison and Vincent Biskay, become criminals, and Jamison eventually kills Biskay for the money they stole. Other novels in this group bear no resemblance to those in the first group and only relate to others in the second group in their use of suspense and/or mystery. *The Neon Jungle* (1953), *All These Condemned, April Evil* (1956), and *Slam the Big Door* (1960) have no ad hoc detectives, and while several policemen appear, they play relatively minor roles. Finally, *The Empty Trap* (1957) is an adventure novel overlaid with some suspense elements. This category of novels reveals MacDonald's astonishingly broad range of characters and themes that boded well for the Travis McGee series.

The gap between MacDonald's more traditional novels and the previous groups is sometimes not very great, and this clarifies the role that categories play as interpretive tools that add enlightenment but remain open to further analysis. Two sets of novels especially show the transition from one category to another. *The Neon Jungle* and *Slam the Big Door* function primarily as suspense novels but with concerns that move them close to novels of manners and morals such as *Contrary Pleasure* (1954) and *A Man of Affairs*. MacDonald remarks more than twenty-five years after *Slam the Big Door*'s first publication that "What pleased me most of all was to find that it stands up both as a novel of suspense and a novel of morals and manners in a specific setting. The anti-hero, Mike Rodenska, is three dimensional" ("Introduction to *Slam the Big Door*" 9). In both *The Neon Jungle* and *Contrary Pleasure*, dysfunctional families set the stage for the sometimes violent events that follow. But, it is the greater emphasis on violence in *The Neon Jungle*, centered especially on Vern Lockter, that puts it in the suspense category while in *Contrary Pleasure*, MacDonald's analysis of the various pressures on the Delevan family members stemming from adultery, money, and envy, to name only three themes, clearly outweighs Quinn Delevan's death and other potentially powerful currents moving the novel toward the suspense group. *Slam the Big Door* and *A Man of Affairs* are similar in the roles that Mike Rodenska and Sam Glidden, respectively, play. However, *Slam the Big Door*'s Troy Jamison creates enough tension to dominate the action and place it squarely in the suspense group while Glidden's relationship to the Dodge family and his position in their business is more important than the chaotic and deadly events that occur on Mike Dean's Caribbean island.

In essence, many of MacDonald's early traditional novels have a flavor of suspense and adventure which sharpens and improves them. MacDonald is not alone in using these plot devices to enhance his stories. Many important twentieth-century American novels involve their characters in situations that raise doubts as to their survival. Ernest Hemingway's *For Whom the Bell Tolls* (1940) and F. Scott Fitzgerald's *The Great Gatsby* (1925) are two of the most prominent examples that demonstrate the role that suspense can play when subsumed under larger concerns. And, MacDonald, more capable in writing suspense novels than most other twentieth-century novelists who have combined both types, demonstrates the value of suspense in such novels as *The Deceivers* (1958) and *Clemmie*. *Cancel All Our Vows* and *Contrary Pleasure* set up an analysis of these latter two novels in that all four deal with middle-class marital and family conflicts and the role that illicit passion plays in producing them. *A Key to the Suite* might be seen as a final investigation of these themes in MacDonald's early fiction but with a changed focus since the protagonist Floyd Hubbard is at a convention when he commits adultery with Corinna Barlund while his wife, Jan, although referred to, never appears in the action. *Clemmie*, published immediately after *The Deceivers*, focuses prominently on the wealthy Clemmie Bennet. MacDonald counterposes her unpredictability, along with wealth and a playboy father, against the more stolid Craig Fitz whom she lures into self-destructive behavior with her siren-like appeal. The question that hovers over the novel is whether or not Fitz can survive a relationship with her and what will be left to him and his family if he does. Female predators such as Clemmie are archetypal literary figures, and MacDonald's portrait of her convincingly explores the conflation of sanctioned and forbidden pleasures.

MacDonald's novels of confluence are another type of traditional novel, thematically overlapping others in this category. A device used by Agatha Christie in *And Then There Were None* (1975), this type of work is frequently employed in English country house mysteries. In MacDonald's case, a sense of violence and suspense hovers over the novels, but again these qualities serve to sharpen the tension, not dominate it. *The Damned* (1952), the first of these, portrays a group of people stranded, as Charles Alva Hoyt observes, "in various stages of exasperation and despair" (227) because they cannot cross the Rio Conchos in Mexico. Weaving together elements of many characters' lives, MacDonald portrays a broader range of people than in the above middle-class novels. In three of them, *The Damned*, *Cry Hard, Cry Fast* (1955), and *Murder in the Wind* (1956), some natural or external force (the river, multiple car and truck crashes, and a hurricane, respectively) drives people together. MacDonald then analyzes what other factors bring each person to that place at that particular time. While *Please Write for Details* (1959) investigates the lives and relationships of people at an artist's colony in Mexico, *The Crossroads* (1959) partially inverts this image of people's being drawn together by fate or chance and explores the lives of those who for the most part already live and prosper at a point of confluence. Of course, the highway first attracted Anton Drovek to start his business beside it, but the family, with Charles Drovek's leadership, have stayed and struggled to survive their internal problems as well as the difficulties that flow through their world of restaurants and motels.

Science fiction has certain qualities that separate it from other types of fiction. Setting a work on another planet, in space, or in the future or the past has some effect on how one reads and interprets it. True, the other-worldly or nonrealistic trappings might be only a veneer, dispensed with easily. However, MacDonald's science fiction or science fantasy novels cannot be so easily dismembered. Without the power that Kirby Winter accidentally discovers in his uncle's watch, *The Girl, the Gold Watch & Everything* would be another kind of novel. The powers of the watch are part of the novel's shape. This is not to say that one could not find a novel that substitutes another force for the watch's power and retains the general thrust of the action. But, one needs some source for the power that becomes both a prize and a danger. If it does not matter whether or not the events occur in a space ship or an apartment house on earth or whether or not supernatural forces are significant, then the work partakes little of this subgenre's attributes. Ayn Rand's *Atlas Shrugged* (1957) needs the power source that John Galt discovers as much as William Morris's *News from Nowhere* (1891) needs that unexplained break in space-time that vaults William Guest from the late nineteenth to the late twentieth century. Similarly, the ability to affect others' lives through one's own dreams in *Wine of the Dreamers* and the powers that Dake Lorin develops in *Ballroom of the Skies* are integral to the plots' developments. The former work might be viewed as an allegory of power and responsibility and the latter an analysis of the importance of transnational values, but both integrate the science fiction elements of space travel and superhuman capabilities into their texts.

As interesting as the science fiction qualities are, what strikes one about these novels is the human conflicts and dramas. Bard Lane's and Sharon Inlays's struggles in *Wine of the Dreamers* to complete their space project while, unknowingly, contending with the extraterrestrial dreamers and the earthly bureaucrats parallel Raul Kinson's efforts to open the eyes of his sister Leesa and the other members of their hermetic, dying world to the harm they do through their dreams. These and other themes resemble ones found in the second and third categories, especially, and continue in another literary form MacDonald's interest in the human condition.

Some themes do turn out to be blind allies. For instance, MacDonald generally avoids dramatizing international conspiracies. However, early on he portrays Dillon Bryant in *Murder for the Bride* and Gevan Dean in *Area of Suspicion* successfully overcoming agents for foreign powers. Dake Lorin in *Ballroom of the Skies* succumbs to an aggressively exotic ideology, and although not a communist conspiracy, the power he works for controls the destinies of those on earth, especially focusing on the crumbling Western societies. Joe Sanders asserts that this alien group is "an organization of supermen [who] keep humanity from making too much technological progress" (159). Why does MacDonald portray this vision as a possible future human social development and then abandon it? One answer lies in his focus on individual people in conflict with themselves or others, and while natural disasters as in *Murder in the Wind* or criminal conspiracies as in *April Evil* and *The Only Girl in the Game* powerfully affect the plots, even in those novels what people do, say, think, and feel receives primary attention.

As MacDonald initiated the Travis McGee series, he had a fund of narrative experience which heightened his ability to draw characters and tell stories. In his early fiction, using and reusing character types, plot lines, and themes, MacDonald developed an amazingly rich repertoire which was surely poised, to mix a metaphor, on the "finger tips" of his imagination. Beginning with Cliff Bartells in *The Brass Cupcake*, MacDonald explores the familiar aspects of the hard-boiled character who can both endure punishment and fight back while reaching an accurate conclusion about whatever mystery the novel contains. Not all detectives in terms of the earlier definition, these characters share many attributes with McGee and foreshadow the types of difficulties he will undergo. In addition to Bartells, MacDonald portrays this toughness of spirit in Bill Danton (*The Damned*), Lloyd Westcott (*The Empty Trap*), Sam Bowden (*The Executioners*), Leo Harrison (*The Beach Girls*), Sydney Shanley (*On the Run*), and Paul Stanial (*The Drowner*). Though not the only characters to show these traits, they clearly embody them in ways suggestive of McGee's independent, sometimes quirky personality. For, it is not only the violence that foreshadows the series but the peculiar personality combinations in some of his early protagonists that reveal the direction of MacDonald's work.

Another aspect these characters share with McGee is their generally protective relationships with women. Unlike McGee,

MacDonald's early male protagonists tend to marry as well as become romantically involved. Being a series character, McGee naturally has a greater number of romantic entanglements than the earlier heroes, but MacDonald has prefigured McGee's emotional life clearly enough in the stages of their lives. Paul Stanial feels emotionally and professionally dissatisfied, as McGee frequently does, before Barbara Larrimore hires his firm to investigate her sister Lucille Hanson's death. In the process, Stanial falls in love with Barbara, and this new emotional involvement reawakens him and, after the novel's dangerous events, leads to their planned marriage. MacDonald's theme of renewal through love, while not present in every pre-Travis McGee novel, certainly represents for him a central resolution to the human dilemma. Leo Harrison in *The Beach Girls* initially comes to Elihu Beach, Florida, as Leo Rice to confront Rex Rigsby over the suicide of his wife Lucille Harrison. In the process, he not only falls in love with Christy Yale but also lets go of the anger and rage engendered by Rigsby's callous use of Lucille. This traditional pattern of renewal appears vital in specific situations that MacDonald creates for McGee. In *Blue*, his recovery from the loss of Lois Atkinson through Cathy Kerr's loving response and Nina Gibson's youthfully exuberant acceptance of him in *Nightmare in Pink* (1964) are just two early examples.

A distinct trait of MacDonald's work lies in the opposition between light and dark aspects of human nature. Since evil exists, it has to manifest itself. Chapter Four will explore the amoral character in the series, but like so much in MacDonald, it has its origins in his early work. Being a criminal or committing violent acts does not by itself make one an amoral character. In addition to violence, MacDonald portrays the amoral type as someone indifferent to the sufferings of others and willing to inflict this suffering if an occasion arises. Indifference to others as fellow human beings except as they contribute to some satisfaction or pleasure also distinguishes the amoral characters from other sociopaths. Furness Trumbull in *The Brass Cupcake* is a trial run for this type as he murders Elizabeth Stegman and plans the deaths of Melody Chance and Cliff Bartells to ensure the success of his future financial arrangements. Trumbull does not attempt to avenge some wrong committed against him or protect himself or others against a threatened danger. He is basically indifferent towards those he harms or plans to harm and would probably not kill if he could obtain money more easily. This indifference marks the worst offenders in MacDonald's fiction and leads them to depths of horrors that other killers do not match.

While not completely separate from the amoral characters, even Max Cady in *The Executioners* and Kirby Stassen in *The End of the Night* reveal some reason for their actions though Stassen's is less apparent than Cady's. However dangerous, A. Christy in *Border Town Girl* (1956) works for someone and usually kills when ordered to do so. Prefiguring Junior Allen in *Blue*, Paul Dissat in *A Tan and Sandy Silence* (1971), and Howie Brindle in *Turquoise*, early amoral characters like Vern Lockter in *The Neon Jungle*, Earl Fitzmartin in *A Bullet for Cinderella*, Dwight McAran in *One Monday We Killed Them All*, and Ronald Crown in *April Evil* reveal MacDonald's preoccupation with good and evil and his awareness of the dangerous possibilities confronting all people in the modern world.

In addition to the themes of love, violence, and amorality, a brief analysis of other plots and themes will clearly indicate the rich resources on which MacDonald drew for the McGee series. Like many serious writers, MacDonald does not merely copy himself; instead, one can see distinct preoccupations that he continues to dramatize. For example, while from 1964 on he largely forgoes the police/criminal conspiracy novel of *The Brass Cupcake* and *Judge Me Not*, *Pale Gray for Guilt* (1968), *The Girl in the Plain Brown Wrapper* (1968), *The Long Lavender Look* (1970), and *A Purple Place for Dying* (1964) demonstrate his awareness that the police, whether in whole or part, are susceptible to illegal influences. Novels of obsession such as *Weep for Me* (1951), *All These Condemned*, and *Clemmie* find their counterparts in *Bright Orange for the Shroud* (1965), *Lavender*, and *The Scarlet Ruse* (1973). Revenge novels like *The Beach Girls* and *On the Run* do not appear until late in the series in *The Green Ripper* (1979) and *Cinnamon Skin* (1982). McGee usually works for someone else, thus generally precluding the passionate focus that revenge requires. As McGee hunts in *Green* and *Cinnamon*, so he is hunted in *Free Fall in Crimson* (1981). Early novels like *You Live Once* and *On the Run* use this plot structure and in the process explore the role of deception in staying alive as well as achieving other ends.

Finally, one of the most common plots is the search novel used in *Blue* and *The Lonely Silver Rain* (1985) as well as other novels in the series. Novels such as *A Bullet for Cinderella* and *Where is Janice Gantry?* structure their plots around a search for something or someone. Novels of discovery differ slightly from this in that an element of mystery dominates the search structure. McGee uses this device in *Pink* and *Purple* and earlier in *The Brass Cupcake*, *Murder for the Bride*, *Death Trap*, and *The Price of Murder*. With the understanding that these are dominant plot structures and that, along with a variety of themes, MacDonald frequently employs other types for his subplots, readers of his early fiction develop a greater appreciation for his skills as a novelist and an understanding of his achievements in the series. After seven McGee novels, Charles Willeford writes that "John D. MacDonald . . . is a spokesman for our times: he speaks for the Sixties as Scott Fitzgerald did for the Twenties, Nathaniel West for the Thirties, Raymond Chandler for the Forties, and John Barth for the Fifties" (qtd. in Shine, *Rave*). George Garrett's statement that MacDonald's readers get "a clearly focused picture of the world we're in, and a generous sense of its patterns and process" suggests what one can expect from him as a writer. And, MacDonald seldom fails to explore the complexities and ambiguities that modern society presents him and his readers.

Chapter 2

McGee and Meyer:
The Development of a Detective Duo

MacDonald introduces Meyer early into the Travis McGee series. MacDonald states: "I invented Meyer out of fragments in the vast scrap basket in the back of my head, vowing that I would not have a clown on scene, nor would I have someone dependent upon McGee emotionally, financially or socially" ("Introduction and Comment" 67). Meyer's consciousness, supportive of McGee's, adds depth to McGee's characterization and variety to the perceptions of the dilemmas that they face. Although Meyer helps McGee considerably in *Darker than Amber* (1966) and *Pale Gray for Guilt,* he plays his first major role in *Dress Her in Indigo* (1969). Thereafter, Meyer both advises and acts in ways that make their arrangement an unstated partnership. Although developed, as Edgar W. Hirshberg notes, as "contrasting personalities" (*MacDonald* 99), they live on boats near one another in Ft. Lauderdale, and their relationship develops into a stable balance sound enough to withstand fierce assaults from the human predators they encounter. McGee thinks, acts, and records while Meyer begins with a cerebral contribution (something like Mycroft to Sherlock Holmes) and much later experiences a crisis of confidence and self-respect as he becomes increasingly involved in the dangers of McGee's cases. A brief contrast with two earlier detective duos—Holmes-Watson and Wolfe-Goodwin—will help illuminate the McGee-Meyer relationship. MacDonald initially establishes Meyer as humane and intelligent and, as the series progresses, graphically portrays the painful distortions that both he and McGee undergo as they repeatedly confront violence and evil. Meyer's and McGee's struggles reveal a disturbing irony. They must contend not only with the external dangers but equally with the internal stresses these forces produce and strive to emerge from the damaging contact whole, compassionate, and sane.

Although Raymond Chandler's Philip Marlowe and Dashiell Hammett's Sam Spade work alone, other prominent fictional detectives have operated with at least one other person. A comparison of the McGee-Meyer relationship with Holmes-Watson and Wolfe-Goodwin clarifies McGee's and Meyer's shares in the thought and action of the series. First, neither Holmes, Wolfe, nor Meyer, the principal thinkers, narrates the tales. Watson, Goodwin, and McGee tell the stories, Watson, especially, acting as a conscious narrator who publishes Holmes's cases. John G. Cawelti explains why the hard-boiled detective can function as narrator without encountering too many problems of concealing his thought processes: ". . . he is not presented as a man of transcendent intelligence or intuition and does not solve the crime primarily by ratiocinative processes" (83). As argued below, this only partially describes McGee's intellectual contributions to his salvages. Second, Holmes, unlike Wolfe and Meyer, is the primary actor as well as the principal thinker in his series. McGee, as primary actor in his series, thinks out the cases also, and Goodwin functions the least as a thinker and is the least introspective. William Ecenbarger observes that ". . . McGee is a practical intellectual—a sort of hard-boiled egghead—Meyer's cerebral edges are more rounded and complete" (24). Finally, McGee is the principal focus in his novels as well as the narrator. In this, he differs from Watson and Goodwin whose narratives provide frameworks to bring out the genius of their respective partners. In two other respects, significant comparisons can illuminate these detective pairs. In the Holmes-Watson relationship, Holmes is the stronger physically and while frequently indolent becomes energized once a case begins unless, like Nero Wolfe, he must retreat into himself to think out possible solutions to the mystery. While Wolfe is naturally strong, he is the least active of all the detectives, usually refusing to leave his home for any reason. McGee and Meyer are better balanced in the degree of general physical activity than Wolfe and Goodwin although Meyer is frequently sedentary while McGee generally maintains his life-saving physical condition. In the final comparison, Holmes, Wolfe, and McGee have initiated their businesses to which Watson, Goodwin, and Meyer, respectively and in differing ways, have joined. Although McGee and Meyer do not resemble the other two pairs in every instance, it is clear that MacDonald is extending the partnership tradition briefly touched on here.

Meyer does not appear in the first two novels, *The Deep Blue Good-by* and *Nightmare in Pink* and is only mentioned briefly in the next two, *A Purple Place for Dying* and *The Quick Red Fox* (1964). In addition, MacDonald includes Meyer briefly at the beginning of two other novels, *Bright Orange for the Shroud* and *The Girl in the Plain Brown Wrapper*. However, Meyer plays a larger role in *A Deadly Shade of Gold* (1965), and it is clear that MacDonald had Meyer in mind as a necessary part of the series at an early stage in its development. Meyer acts in a special way in *Gold* and in seven other novels spread throughout the series, e.g., *One Fearful Yellow Eye* (1966), *The Long Lavender Look*, *A Tan and Sandy Silence*, *The Turquoise Lament*, *The Green Ripper*, *Free Fall in Crimson*, and *The Lonely Silver Rain*. In these novels, Meyer functions as a framing device, appearing early and late to share McGee's adventures and help him either to understand what has happened or to recover emotionally or physically from the often traumatic salvages in which he engages to retrieve something for someone, keeping half the value of whatever he regains. In *Gold*, *Yellow*, *Lavender*, and *Silver*, Meyer functions as a weak frame. Meyer is the supportive friend in *Gold*, the symbol of sanity mentioned in *Red* (6) and elaborated on at the beginning of *Gold* (6). At the end of the latter novel, Meyer and McGee play backgammon. This peaceful culmination of the events, which included McGee being shot, a wound that David Geherin calls "a symbol perhaps of the inner anguish he is suffering" (65), distances Meyer; he is not called on to involve himself emotionally, to share the pain that McGee has undergone. In *Yellow*, Meyer plays his weakest role among the frame novels though he is present at the start and at the end. Of the weak frame novels, Meyer has the strongest involvement in the beginning of *Lavender*. However, Meyer quickly leaves the novel after being beaten by Deputy Lew Arnstead and reappears at the end when he brings the convalescent McGee home from the hospital. No discussions and analyses between McGee and Meyer occur at the conclusion of the novel. Instead, Heidi Trumbill from *Yellow* supplies Meyer's place and plans to return the favor that McGee did when he helped her back to health at the end of the earlier novel (*Lavender* 253-55). Finally, in *Silver* Meyer helps McGee identify Billy Ingraham's boat as they examine hundreds of aerial photos of the southeast Florida coast. After occasional help through the first third of the novel, Meyer plays a smaller role until he returns at the end as McGee's restored friend and uncle-designate to Jean Killian, McGee's newly discovered daughter by way of Puss Killian in *Gray*.

The four strong frame novels divide into two types, e.g., Meyer at the end discussing the events in which McGee has been engaged and Meyer participating in bringing the action to a close. *Turquoise* and *Green* represent the first type of strong frame novel. Meyer becomes ill in *Turquoise* a little more than a third of the way into the novel and gradually reappears past the midpoint as McGee consults with him on the best method of dealing with Howie Brindle, the cheerful, psychotic killer who they discover is planning to murder Pidge Brindle, Howie's wife and their mutual friend. On a cruise to the Bahamas at the very end of the novel, McGee talks with Meyer about the dramatic climax in Pago Pago and his awkward relationship with Pidge, now back in Florida. McGee describes Meyer's initial attempts to get him to talk about what happened as "[t]herapy sessions delicately spaced" (253). MacDonald removes Meyer from *Green* at approximately the same point as in *Turquoise* and brings him back at the end to help McGee recover from the shattering events in northern California during which McGee killed twelve members of a terrorist organization linked to the Church of the Apocrypha (*Green* 271). In addition, as Joseph Marotta notes (107-08), Meyer's comments at the end of *Green* serve to emphasize the potential for violence and chaos in the world (283-84).

Tan and *Crimson* also include Meyer at the end but with a greater degree of involvement in McGee's salvage operations. Meyer, in *Tan*, uses his skills and contacts as an economist and financial consultant to expose Paul Dissat, the carefully controlled but mentally unbalanced French Canadian businessman. However, at the end of *Tan*, after Dissat nearly traps them, Meyer shows little sympathy for McGee's lachrymose attempt to share his self-disgust, telling him, "'Don't suffer all over me, McGee'" (251). This is in sharp contrast to his support at the end of *Green* when Meyer knows that McGee has a real need for help (*Green* 282). At the end of *Crimson*, Meyer functions only as McGee's friend and confidant until Desmin Grizzel, the terror at the end of everyone's worst dreams, forces Meyer to trick McGee into allowing Grizzel to board McGee's boat, the *Busted Flush* (276). McGee states that Meyer remains devastated by what he sees as his failure of "his image of himself" (*Crimson* 283); he only recovers when he joins McGee in *Cinnamon Skin* in eliminating Cody Pittler, his niece's killer. In *Tan*, Meyer leaves the novel at approximately the same point as in *Turquoise* and *Green* and in *Crimson* only a few pages later, but in *Tan* and *Crimson*, Meyer returns much earlier than in the other strong frame novels. In addition, *Tan* and *Crimson* approximate much more closely than any of the works previously discussed to those novels in which Meyer operates throughout as a primary participant in McGee's dangerous work.

The seven novels in which Meyer completely participates overlap with the eight frame novels, even providing a rough alternation between the two groups. In addition, it is important to note that early in the series Meyer quickly becomes a full partner in their activities, sharing dangers and rewards and taking an equal share in starting their cases though McGee remains known as the salvage consultant and Meyer the economist. As Geherin describes their relationship, "Meyer is companion, critic, confidant, and confessor to McGee" (82). And George S. Peek, although he confuses Meyer with the Alabama Tiger, characterizes Meyer's qualities well as "kind, gentle, compassionate, and sexy" ("Beast Imagery" 93). In *Amber* and *Gray*, McGee draws a willing Meyer into the cases. MacDonald begins *Amber* in such a way that there is no awkwardness over why this sedentary individual would move from his safe academic world to one in which danger and death are real possibilities. McGee and Meyer are fishing from a boat under a bridge south of Ft. Lauderdale when a car stops overhead and a woman comes hurtling down into the tidal stream. McGee rescues her and the case begins though it is only later that Meyer joins McGee in tracking down Vangie's killers. On board the *Flush*, Meyer initiates a comparison of their relationship to the Holmes-Watson partnership with Meyer playing Holmes and McGee Dr. Watson. To Meyer's "'What we have, Doctor Watson,'" McGee responds with "'Age, Mr. Holmes?'" and other questions (*Amber* 18, 19). This role-playing leads to a sharper awareness of Vangie's acceptance of pain and the possibility of violence (19). As has been shown, this comparison is accurate insofar as Meyer is the principal thinker and McGee the narrator. Meyer's involvement in *Gray* comes somewhat later than in *Amber*, but it occurs also at McGee's request. This is the only novel of those in which Meyer is involved throughout that requires Meyer's professional help as an economist and financial consultant though he briefly poses as a business consultant in *The Empty Copper Sea* (1978). Meyer, in a complicated stock manipulation (to be discussed in more detail in Chapter Three) helps McGee fleece Preston LaFrance and Gary Santo in order to recoup some of the money that the two men had "stolen" from Tush Bannon, McGee's friend, and return it to Bannon's widow, Janine. Although Meyer ultimately is in no danger in *Amber* or *Gray*, thus requiring no rescue by McGee, McGee has some close moments, especially in *Amber* when he manages to kill Griff on an Atlantic beach at dawn before Griff can kill him (107). Mutually profiting one another in these two novels, McGee gets Meyer to take $10,000 for his part in breaking up the murder for profit ring in *Amber* (187), and Meyer returns the favor by handing McGee a substantial check at the end of *Gray* which comes from a side investment of Meyer's in the process of accomplishing their con (*Gray* 214). It is clear in these two novels that Meyer works on a nearly equal basis; only in the area of danger does Meyer play a lesser role. The next two novels discussed rectify this omission.

Meyer initiates the action in *Indigo*, thus becoming even more responsible for the growth of their partnership. Meyer asks McGee to listen to an old friend whose daughter is presumed dead, but McGee is reluctant until he realizes Meyer's emotional involvement, "a sort of unofficial godfather to the girl when she was smaller" (13), and agrees before Meyer can "say please" (13). T. Harlan Bowie, troubled over his early neglect of his daughter, wants them to go to Mexico and find out how Beatrice (Bix) Bowie spent the last months of her life. Meyer is nearly killed by Wally McLeen, a mentally unbalanced father searching for his daughter, Minda, who traveled to Mexico with Bix and three men. McGee finds Bix alive and rescues her and eventually brings her and Meyer back to Florida where the latter recovers from his injuries and Bowie attempts to reestablish a relationship with his daughter. Except for the payment from Bowie, neither man profits the other. In *The Scarlet Ruse*, Meyer also asks McGee to help a friend, Hirsh Fedderman, a stamp dealer whose business involvement with Frank Sprenger, an organized crime figure, threatens to break him. Although at the end of the novel McGee initially saves Meyer's life, McGee is injured, and it is Meyer who brings him ashore on Candle Key south of Miami. Meyer also returns to salvage McGee's boat, an action similar to one he will later perform in *The Dreadful Lemon Sky* (1975). However, the need to dispose of the three bodies (Mary Alice McDermit, Frank Sprenger, and Davis) powerfully affects Meyer:

He tried to laugh, but his face twisted and broke, and he put his head down into his hands and sobbed. It is the gentle people who get torn up. They can cope. They can keep handling the horrors long after the rest of us fade out. But it marks them more deeply, more lastingly. This was role reversal at its most bitter. (*Scarlet* 312)

Although neither profits the other in *Scarlet*, except as Meyer again sets up the operation for McGee, Meyer's role at the end strongly centers him as someone crucial to McGee's continued survival and repays the favor that McGee did him at the end of *Indigo*.

The next two novels with Meyer's extensive participation, *Lemon* and *Copper*, reveal a fully developed partnership. Although McGee initially receives the contacts that start the cases, he decides to help only after he consults with Meyer. Carrie Milligan approaches McGee in *Lemon* and asks him to hold some money for her for $10,000 (11). When she subsequently dies, McGee and Meyer choose to investigate before turning the money over to Carrie's sister, Susan Dobrovsky (29-31). They plan a typically indirect approach, posing as "a pair of real-estate gunslingers trying to cheat the little dead lady's estate" (31). Although Meyer later is slightly injured by the bomb blast that more seriously hurts McGee, he experiences no other danger and, along with Jason Breen, a young man who works at the marina where the *Flush* is moored, helps repair McGee's boat. In addition to this practical aid, Meyer does some separate investigation which helps solve the case; the economist, though not the thinker, thus recedes into the background as Meyer assumes some of the patterns of McGee's professional behavior. *Copper* repeats the same pattern of Meyer's involvement. After Captain Van Harder approaches McGee to restore his reputation, McGee first talks with Meyer, and together they decide to help him (11-19). Meyer, also, contacts a respectable businessman, and they go to Timber Bay on the West coast of Florida with a semi-legitimate cover to investigate the possibility of buying properties owned or controlled by the missing and presumed dead Hubbard Lawless, the man who "stole" Van Harder's reputation (26-27, 54). Meyer's involvement in *Copper* poses no danger for him although, as in *Lemon*, he investigates on his own and adds to the development of the case against Lawless. One point is important here; as the partnership has developed, money ceases to change hands between Meyer and McGee. Consequently, in *Lemon* and *Copper*, neither man profits monetarily from the other.

Cinnamon, the twentieth novel in the series and the last in which Meyer plays a major role, has its beginnings in *Crimson*, one of the frame novels discussed above. When Desmin Grizzel, at the end of *Crimson*, reduces Meyer to sitting "'on the floor like a dumb pudding, peeing in my trousers, while I watched a maniac start to kill the best friend I ever had'" (*Cinnamon* 16-17), Meyer loses both his sense of himself and his self-respect. At the start of *Cinnamon*,

Meyer is still recovering from that traumatic experience. McGee, through Meyer's friend Aggie Sloane, arranges for him to give some lectures in Toronto. McGee tells Anne Renzetti, his current girlfriend, that "[Sloane] talked one of Meyer's friends, a man named Pricewater, into backing out of a speaking engagement up there in Canada and asking Meyer as a special favor to fill in for him" (*Cinnamon* 4). Thus, Meyer, having failed in his own eyes in McGee's line of work, recovers through returning to his special life and recognizing that he is "'an academic'" and not "'some sort of squatty superman'" (17). When he learns that his niece, Norma, and, presumably, her husband, Evan Lawrence, have been blown up on Meyer's boat, the *John Maynard Keynes*, by Chilean terrorists, Meyer returns to Ft. Lauderdale (15). After determining that Lawrence was very likely not on the boat, the two men begin to track him down from hints that he had dropped on the one occasion that Meyer had met him (19-24). They subsequently learn, after several aliases, that his real name is Cody T.W. Pittler and that he specializes in marrying and murdering moderately wealthy young women (155, 160-61). Meyer's involvement and danger are hardly ever greater in the series. At all levels, as thinker, investigator, and man of action, Meyer, along with McGee, pursues Pittler, desiring to avenge his niece's murder and restore his sense of manhood so ruthlessly invaded by Grizzel. At the end, Meyer fittingly causes Pittler's death, committing himself fully to the action by jumping up and down on a ledge above Pittler's hiding place. Meyer rides down the rock, earth, and trees that bury Pittler and thus frees himself (268). Money is even further removed in *Cinnamon* as a motive for action than in the other novels.

From Meyer's gradual introduction to the Travis McGee series to his appearance in the frame novels that overlap and roughly alternate with the novels in which Meyer is continuously involved, MacDonald has developed the relationship between McGee and Meyer in unexpected and creative directions. A real involvement logically would lead to Meyer's acting as more than an intellectual resource and sharing some of McGee's dangers. To these factors, MacDonald adds the additional quality of the unforeseen and open-ended with Meyer's traumatic crisis in *Crimson* leading to his actions in *Cinnamon* to restore a fuller sense of his own humanity. Patterns thus formed and reformed create possibilities for development that cannot be predicted and thus deepen the quality of the fiction as Meyer and McGee struggle with their own flawed and limited selves.

Chapter 3

Masks and Diversions

The partnership concept developed in Chapter Two should not obscure MacDonald's primary focus on Travis McGee. In "How to Live with a Hero," MacDonald recalls his wide swings in initially characterizing McGee. From McGee's being "somber, full of dark areas, subject to a moody violence" (15) to being "a jolly, smirking jackass . . . a silly fellow" (16), MacDonald struggled to find the proper balance to enable him to develop McGee further. Logically, MacDonald could draw from McGee's past or possible future actions, and he makes use of both. Of course, McGee narrates the events in the past tense but with little sense of reflecting back on events that have already occurred; rather, the events seem to unfold for McGee and the other participants. This chronological device is probably one of the most essential acts of masking in the series. In "Introduction and Comment," MacDonald also notes how carefully he reveals McGee's family history (68). Over the twenty-one novels, he doles out scant information on what has formed McGee, purposely leaving him, and consequently the motivations for many actions, feelings, and ideas, somewhat enigmatic. References to people and cases not part of the series reveal another unexplored area of McGee's characterization. Thus structured, the theme of concealment underlies many others in the series and alerts one to MacDonald's careful craftsmanship.

In classical Greek drama, the principal actors wore large masks that indicated their roles and helped to project their voices to the audience. Given this static surface, any alteration in character was effected through gesture or language. MacDonald's Travis McGee, deprived of any similar outward cover, wears a modern equivalent in his smiling, affable manner concealing an inner watchfulness. And yet, this attitude, potentially limiting, is only one of his complex masks. When on a case, McGee becomes whatever the situation demands. In A Deadly Shade of Gold, he is at one time a tourist in Mexico with Nora Gardino and at another time Connie Melgar's newest lover in California. This functional role-playing is not necessarily damaging unless he can no longer detect the real person. However, McGee's sense that he is only fully alive when he is in mortal danger (*The Empty Copper Sea* 236) makes his watchfulness also a mask, a caretaker for the sometimes violent, though controlled, personality that lurks within. As David Benjamin states, McGee is a "bundle of contradictions, brutal yet likable, fairly honest, with a Marlovian sense of humor and honor" (30). In addition, the ability to assume the masks, whether spontaneously or through careful planning, is an integral part of his personality. From the con man in *Bright Orange for the Shroud* who wants to break into Calvin Stebber's organization to the good old boy in *Dress Her in Indigo* who purposefully humiliates Backspin to the television consultant for Lysa Dean's Take Five Productions in *Free Fall in Crimson*, McGee's masks range in power and diversity barely controlled by a man seeking himself while concealing his nature from a generally hostile world.

Any examination of the role of masks in the personality of Travis McGee should begin with his lifestyle. McGee lives aboard the *Busted Flush* at Slip F-18 in Bahia Mar, Ft. Lauderdale, Florida. He owns a blue Rolls Royce, named Miss Agnes, converted by a former owner into a pickup. McGee has no visible means of support and generally identifies himself as a salvage consultant (*Darker than Amber* 62). Along with his 6'4" physique kept in good to excellent condition (*The Scarlet Ruse* 10, *Nightmare in Pink* 137), the above aspects show that McGee has obviously not sunk completely into his background, but paradoxically, they conceal rather than reveal. He blends into the boating population, and compared to the Alabama Tiger's floating house party, the *Flush* is eminently quiet and respectable. McGee's quiet/loud manifestations reflect the doubleness at the core of his personality, an aspect to be explored below. However, while his material possessions are apparent, they symbolize a conflict in his life. MacDonald comments:

There has been over the series an existing tension between the two facets of McGee's life—the salvage function whereby he makes his living, and the retirement he takes in installments wherein he succumbs to the environment rather than trying to direct it. ("Introduction" 69)

The real McGee, admittedly problematic even to himself, remains open but hidden to those who observe his lifestyle. In an article-interview, William Ecenbarger quotes MacDonald on McGee: "'He's . . . believable because he feels out of place with the modern world'" (25), thus revealing another part of McGee's complex nature.

McGee assumes roles as a natural reflex to his environment. The subsequent masks accompanying the roles are not necessarily part of any case he is on. Possibly, they are responses to what prompts John Wiley Nelson's observation that "McGee's world is booby-trapped—things are never what they seem. Deception abounds" (174). In *The Deep Blue Good-by*, McGee describes himself as he looks for a sexual partner: "I nursed a drink, made myself excruciatingly amiable, suitably mysterious and witty in the proper key, and carefully observed the group relationships until I was able to identify two possibles" (27). This is a man living among friends and acquaintances; a role is more natural than his real self. In *Pink*, McGee attends a party in Greenwich Village with Nina Gibson where he passes himself off as in "marine hardware" in contrast to the pseudo-cultural types he meets (59). Obviously, this masking of himself has a large degree of irony, irony in this instance directed at those who pretend but who cannot face their pretension. Although McGee appears relaxed in his role of marine hardware devotee, ironic role-playing at the expense of the pretentious must produce echoes in someone who essentially masks his life from others, calling into question Anthony Moore's statement that McGee "can be considered to be fully matured and integrated" (45). And increasingly, these echoes will become loud and insistent, demanding an awareness that pretensions in his life be acknowledged and experienced if not overcome.

From *Blue* to *The Lonely Silver Rain*, McGee has used guile and deception to force a situation to its ultimate end. In *Blue*, McGee poses as someone who has no other interest than sex with Corry and a free cruise to the Bahamas provided by Junior Allen, McGee's real prey. Once he gains access to Allen's boat, he finds some of the gems Allen stole from Cathy and attacks Allen in order to recover them, doing so, as Edgar W. Hirshberg says of McGee's rescues in general, "as a preserver of a moral code that distinguishes civilized from uncivilized man" (*MacDonald* 74). Although he does not finally recover all of the gems, McGee's disguise is probably the only way to defeat Allen, a man who uses deception and violence on others and thus remains difficult to trick. Similarly, McGee becomes the loud talking, sincere, efficient TV delivery man in *Silver* whose real aim is to gain entrance to Irina Casak's home and subdue Ruffino Marino, Jr. McGee's brilliance at deception is always grounded in reality and in an intuitive grasp of what motivates others, what they will believe or want to believe. As David Geherin says in analyzing McGee's skills in deception in *The*

Quick Red Fox, "McGee is as subtle or as blatant as the situation requires" (58). Part of his keen intuition lies in his self-examination, an ability to probe his own motivations and even acknowledge greater levels of self-deception than he suspects. As with his own pretensions, McGee recognizes at times that he is as big a fool as he fears. Near the end of *Indigo,* McGee and Meyer confidently confront the seemingly inept and harmless Wally McLeen and accuse him of the murder of Walter Rockland and several others (199). Although Geherin thinks McLeen an "unlikely" suspect (103), MacDonald convincingly demonstrates McLeen's dangerousness when the deranged man employs an effective Indian weapon (200-01). McGee's startled reaction and subsequent caution accelerate his education in not underestimating anyone (200-02). Of course, McGee has experienced other instances when he has had to reexamine his assumptions. When he acquiesces to Lysa Dean's cheating him at the end of *Red,* McGee acknowledges the greater deceiver (159).

Although one way to analyze McGee's use of deception involves the types of ruses employed, the person for whom he initiates a search reveals significant aspects of deception or its lack in his business. Two basic categories emerge; McGee begins a job because of friendship or for himself. In the latter category, strictly business propositions (sometimes involving people he knows), a hint of loose money, curiosity, or personal revenge lure him into an adventure. Larry Grimes, in an article portraying a McGee split between involvement in cases strictly for business and involvement for more heroic motives, provides a similar list (104-05). Whatever category in which one places the jobs, McGee has a range of romantic involvements, from intense love relationships to friendly sexual encounters, sometimes, as in *Gold* with Nora Gardino and Junebug, in the same novel. And, these relationships add an edge to cases in which it is necessary to mask his intentions.

McGee takes on cases because of friendship in *Pink, Gold, One Fearful Yellow Eye, Pale Gray for Guilt, The Girl in the Plain Brown Wrapper, Indigo, The Scarlet Ruse, The Turquoise Lament,* and *Cinnamon Skin.* In *Pink, Gray, Turquoise,* and *Cinnamon,* McGee has a strong emotional involvement. Mike Gibson, in *Pink,* with whom McGee served in Korea, asks McGee to find out who killed his sister Nina's fiancé. Tush Bannon, McGee's former football teammate in *Gray,* dies and McGee investigates, both for the sake of his friend and for Janine, Tush's wife, and their children. In *Turquoise,* McGee falls in love with Pidge Brindle and must find out if Howie, her husband with whom she is sailing their boat to Pago Pago to sell and then split up, is as psychopathic as McGee and Meyer begin to fear. McGee was a good friend of Pidge's father and initially responded to her as a friend. His close relationship with Meyer is the foundation for their intensive search for Cody T.W. Pittler in *Cinnamon*. In the other five novels in this category, McGee, although called on through ties of friendship, is not at first as deeply committed. Whatever the degree of emotional involvement, McGee does not begin these cases by deceiving the person for whom he works or whom he helps nor does he act against their interests during the cases.

McGee's abilities, even more than his degree of personal involvement, determine his success at guile. For example, McGee helps Nora Gardino in *Gold* find the killers of Sam Taggart, a man with whom she was in love and a former friend of McGee's. They go to Puerto Altamura, Mexico, from which Taggart had fled. There, McGee initiates a complex series of cons and deceptions that include what could be classified as the open deception. McGee establishes an identity in the village as an easygoing, noisy American, a typical tourist. Under this guise, McGee hopes to find information about Taggart's activities and if possible locate the gold statues previously "owned" by Carlos Menterez that were taken from Taggart. At the bottom of many of McGee's efforts lies an eye for the money. However, Taggart was his friend, and Nora becomes his lover before she is killed. The memory of his friendship for the former erodes as he discovers the circumstances under which he left Puerto Altamura; in fact, once he meets Ramon Talavera, Sam's killer, he decides not to pursue the idea of revenge any further: "'[Sam] tried a bad gamble and it went wrong. There's been too much blood since then. It happened a long time ago, Talavera, and I have lost interest in it'" (*Gold* 273).

Of course, friendship does not preclude guile; he can operate even when his emotions are strongly involved. In *Gray*, McGee, with Meyer's essential help, organizes two complex scams, one against Preston LaFrance and the other against Gary Santo, because of the harm they did to Tush Bannon and his family. With LaFrance, McGee and Meyer work a version of the pigeon drop but one which nets $100,000 (181). The con used against Santo is more complex and involves the collusion of a reputable New York brokerage house. Meyer needs to find a company that looks good but which is less healthy than it appears. With his expertise and contacts, he provides McGee with seemingly authentic documents showing

McGee's previous successful financial speculations. With these as lure, McGee entices Santo to invest in Fletcher Industries, a company which Meyer's investigations show has secretly inflated its earnings. The result is that Santo loses money, and Meyer and McGee earn money for Janine Bannon and her children and, unknown to McGee, for themselves. The callousness with which Santo and LaFrance operated, in addition to his friendship with the Bannons, arouses McGee's anger and launches him into the case, supporting Grimes's view that McGee's "knightly self . . . is his true self" (104).

McGee's salvages that begin as business propositions or the more personal motives of curiosity, revenge, and the desire to snatch questionably held money also reveal his extraordinary talents for trickery. *Blue, Red, Orange, Copper, Crimson,* and *Silver* start with McGee generally accepting his work on his usual basis of half the value of the recovery. *Indigo* and *Scarlet* might fall into the strictly business category except that, as noted in Chapter Two, Meyer asks McGee to consider the cases. Even in *Blue,* Chookie McCall asks him to help a friend of hers, but McGee makes a thorough business arrangement with Cathy Kerr. And although Peggy Moran refers to Captain Van Harder as one of McGee's "old friends" (82), he is more of a friendly acquaintance. McGee takes his case, but there's no sense of an ongoing relationship, and Harder insists on paying him for salvaging his reputation (*Copper* 11). One of the most bizarre of these business propositions occurs in *Orange* and involves McGee with the dangerous Boone Waxwell and Calvin Stebber, whom McGee realizes he cannot con but whose temporary help McGee acquires by being vouched for by The Moaner, another con man with whom McGee once tangled (122-23). Arthur Wilkinson, a former acquaintance, turns up at Bahia Mar thoroughly bedraggled and asks McGee to help him recover the more than $200,000 which Stebber's organization stole from him in a quasi-legal land deal (33-36). McGee creatively decides to recover Wilkinson's money by seeking to work out a deal with the same organization on an even bigger target. While McGee fools Crane Watts, the weak lawyer who helped fleece Wilkinson, he has little success with Stebber and nearly gets killed trying to trick Waxwell.

The whole range of novels (e.g., *A Purple Place for Dying, Amber, The Long Lavender Look, A Tan and Sandy Silence, The Dreadful Lemon Sky,* and *The Green Ripper*) in which McGee gets involved for largely personal (but not friendship) motives reveals him at his most devious. While Mary Broll in *Tan* and Carrie Milligan in *Lemon* are old friends, they have not been a part of his life for years. Curiosity/revenge and money/curiosity, respectively, motivate his present actions. However, *Amber* probably best brings out his uninhibited desire to use tricks and guile whenever possible. *Green* dramatizes the most serious example of revenge, and *Purple* and *Lavender* show a McGee both curious and resentful over his treatment with the hint of money in the background, but *Amber* most effectively combines these motivations. After McGee rescues Vangie at some danger to himself, he and Meyer learn something of her precarious lifestyle, and when she is later murdered, McGee decides to learn more. Both curiosity as to what she actually did and a desire for some of the money along with a functioning social conscience lead him and Meyer deeper into the murder for profit scheme of Griff, Ans, and Del. It is even arguable that McGee seeks revenge for Vangie's murder because the murder ring killed someone whom he felt "proud of" (40) and whose "toughness of spirit" he "could respect" (40). In order to stop the operation, McGee tricks Del into betraying Ans, her lover, and writing out a complete confession of her and the others' activities. At the end, McGee employs a model, Merrimay Lane, to impersonate the, to Ans, presumably dead Vangie and to force the now mentally unstable Ans into a violent explosion which betrays him to the police. Though the novel involves some dangerous moments for McGee from both Ans and Griff, it largely revolves around the well-timed series of deceptions.

While McGee's general life-style and manner are a mask for his work and abilities and while he shows intelligence and adaptability in employing deception, McGee's personality and emotional life offer an even greater source of insight into his motivations for duplicity. After his first confrontation with Boone Waxwell in *Orange*, McGee analyzes his opponent to Chookie McCall and Arthur Wilkinson:

The essence of him is feline, and not house-kitty. A bigger predator. I wonder how many people he's conned with that swampy folk-talk which isn't even very consistent. It's a good cover. (102)

After he finishes his description of Boone, Chookie responds: "'Maybe . . . maybe he is *you*, gone bad. Maybe that's what he smelled. Maybe that's why you can handle him'" (103). Repressing an outward response, McGee's internal reaction helps discover and link his mental and emotional layers: "My immediate instinct was to get blazing mad, tell her it was a rotten analogy. It was a response the head-feelers would call significant" (103). What is important about his response is his sense of more than usually suppressed mental layers, layers that McGee is hesitant to explore and which reveal, at the very least, an essential doubleness at the core of his personality, a doubleness linked to his outward manner and use of trickery and which acts as a driving force in his life of deception.

From *Blue*, MacDonald has developed this sense of doubleness as a crucial part of McGee's makeup. After resisting the clumsy advances of Chookie McCall, who he knew was not the type for casual sex, McGee ponders "[t]he new culture" (*Blue* 26) in which sex is freely offered and contrasts those women with a different type:

Only a woman of pride, complexity and emotional tension is genuinely worth the act of love, and there are only two ways to get yourself one of them. Either you lie, and stain the relationship with your own sense of guile, or you accept the involvement, the emotional responsibility, the permanence she must by nature crave. (26-27)

However, realizing that "tension is also a fact of life . . ." (27), McGee goes hunting for one of the new women on board the Alabama Tiger's boat and later makes love to her on the *Flush*. After she leaves, McGee contrasts her with the more real Cathy Kerr and wonders if the point of his mood was that he "was despising that part of myself that was labeled Junior Allen" (28). But McGee quickly and ironically distances himself from this perception:

What an astonishment these night thoughts would induce in the carefree companions of blithe Travis McGee, that big brown loose-jointed boat bum, that pale-eyed, wire-haired girl-seeker, that slayer of small savage fish, that beach-walker, gin-drinker, quip-maker, peace-seeker, iconoclast, disbeliever, argufier, that knuckly, scar-tissued reject from a structured society.

But pity, indignation and guilt are the things best left hidden from all the gay companions. (28-29)

Although Peggy Moran states that "Always his Calvinist morality and sense of decency work against diminishing another" (86), this self-portrait never essentially changes. Even though McGee experiences moments of happiness and even times when he wants the permanence with a woman described above, as with Gretel

Howard in *Copper* and *Green*, he grows gradually more bitter, never resolving the conflict between what lives on the surface and what prowls in the depths of his mind. As Geherin notes, McGee is "a man struggling to reconcile his human frailties and self-doubts with his idealistic self-image" (159). This parallels MacDonald's observations about McGee in a 1965 article: "My man had to be just as troubled and uncertain as you and I. He had to win a little, lose a little, have good luck and bad, feel remorse, joy, self-contempt, greed, indignation, awe. . . . in short, he had to be a man" ("Report" 4-A).

Frequently, in novels such as *Pink, Purple, Gold, Amber, Yellow, Gray, Brown, Indigo, Lavender, Turquoise,* and *Crimson,* McGee can, either through a powerful emotional commitment or through his absorption in the hunt, suppress his ever present sense of apartness, of difference, a state in which Benjamin, in surveying the novels up to *Lemon,* describes McGee as "more remote with his friends, his women, even his enemies" (31). But, MacDonald probably needed the new situation described in *Silver* in which, almost in answer to a nostalgic desire for children, but grown-up ones, in *Cinnamon* (60), McGee is presented with Jean Killian, a daughter via Puss Killian (*Gray*). At the end of *Silver,* one sees a partially rejuvenated McGee proud of the daughter who plans for her future and whose life-affirming example encourages him to reconnect with his friends.

Chapter 4

Travis McGee and the Amoral Character

Living the dangerous life he does, McGee needs screens between himself and the outside world. While his essential nature projects deceptive images of his intentions and true self, sometimes real violence lurks beyond his safe haven in Bahia Mar. Normal precautions will occasionally neither allow him to achieve his ends nor adequately protect him and his friends. In *Pale Gray for Guilt*, McGee cannot prevent Deputy Freddy Hazzard from breaking through his boat's defenses and endangering him and Janine Bannon. Even his dislike for Harry Broll in *A Tan and Sandy Silence* does not forewarn him against the latter's presumably serious attack on his life. Of course, the psychologically disturbed Paul Dissat forces Broll to act for him, and when Dissat attacks McGee on Grenada, the latter is lucky to escape alive. Amoral characters such as Dissat, who assumes a woman's voice to trick both McGee and Meyer near the end of the novel (232), push the art of deception into a realm in which McGee cannot follow. Compared with the amoral types, McGee's acts of deception seem trivial and transparent.

Discussing what she calls these "genuinely sadistic characters," Carol Cleveland states, "On the thematic level, they typify the group of qualities MacDonald finds most distasteful, not to say frightening, in this civilization: power, expertise, nerve, surface charm and facility divorced from any sort of imaginative or moral connection with the rest of society" (407). From his moral and imaginative level, McGee must struggle to counter whatever edge their amorality gives them.

Beneath the calm surface epitomized by the genial McGee, McDonald paints a bleak picture not only of Florida but of twentieth-century American society. The land is overdeveloped, overused, and consequently endangered in more serious ways than the always steady erosion through misuse. Nature, in effect, warns that it may rebel against the arrogance and stupidity of some human beings. MacDonald parallels this natural danger to the social structure with the amoral character. Even more than Dissat, Howie Brindle, in *The Turquoise Lament*, is the archetype of the cheerful killer who has no remorse and even no real desire to kill. He will murder nearly anyone who bothers or irritates him. Thus, MacDonald's powerfully ironic construction of Brindle's character separates him from normal human experience. In contrast, McGee, a "salvage expert," represents something fundamental to American society, a conscience. Though he is graphically and concretely portrayed, combining physical presence with a certain type of intelligence and daring (balanced by his friend Meyer's more abstract intellect), McGee is also a representative, however halting, of a desire and need to counter the wasteful destruction of the amoral Brindles of the world. In a complex exploration of this latter type, MacDonald focuses on the amoral character whose absolute evil confronts the reluctant good symbolized by McGee.

In his essay "How to Live with a Hero," MacDonald's description of the evolution of the character of Travis McGee, quoted above in Chapter One, at first makes him seem no match for what David A. Benjamin has described as "the MacDonald villain . . . greedy, sexually twisted and amoral; in short, a sociopath, total madness only a flicker away" (31). Etta C. Abrahams has described Boone Waxwell (*Bright Orange for the Shroud*) as "a sociopath. He transcends all ethical judgment. To him, there is no right or wrong" ("Visions" 121). Yet McGee's size, strength, quickness, and ability to use violence when necessary enable him generally to defeat the evil he faces. This violence in Travis is usually under control, and when it appears, he employs it to help someone or save himself. As Benjamin says, ". . . McGee strives to preserve traditional values which he honors as an act of social good" (31).

Not all of MacDonald's Travis McGee novels oppose McGee and a sociopathic killer. In three (*Nightmare in Pink, A Purple Place for Dying,* and *The Empty Copper Sea*), no character or set of characters plays this role. In each, death and violence figure prominently in unraveling the plot, but the sense of evil is dispersed. The drug and medical experiments in *Pink* impersonally exploit the vulnerability of certain characters, but with the possible exception of Dr. Varn, no one character dominates and controls the, admittedly, terrible reactions to the drugs. Dolores Estobar, in *Purple*, is responsible for the deaths of John Webb and Mona and Jasper Yeoman. However, Jasper, her father, raped her and this traumatizes her:

"Yessss," she said in a dreadful half whisper. "When *she* was away. That filthy old man. That father I adored. He was drinking. He made me drink too. I tried to help him to bed. He forced me, that filthy old man. He didn't know who I was. Drunk! A woman to grab. I had loved him, like a daughter." She straightened, raising her voice. "*He destroyed me!* He dirtied me!" (152)

The direct cause and effect relationship, even though the deaths take place over several days, removes Dolores from the ranks of Junior Allen (*The Deep Blue Good-by*), Boone Waxwell, Lilo Perris (*The Long Lavender Look*), and Howie Brindle. Similarly, John Tuckerman (*Copper*) kills Kristin Petersen in grief and rage over the death of his friend, Hubbard Lawless, and her callous disregard of the event (239). Tuckerman's macabre burial of Lawless and Petersen sitting in a jeep on a lonely stretch of beach south of Timber Bay on Florida's Gulf Coast is a direct result of the derangement caused by his friend's death.

Seventeen of MacDonald's remaining eighteen Travis McGee novels have characters who resemble the amoral type, what will also be termed the Brindle type. These novels can be divided into two groups as they contain significant characters who more or less approximate Brindle's behavior. The first group of novels, with characters who less strongly match the amoral type, includes *The Quick Red Fox, A Deadly Shade of Gold, Darker than Amber, One Fearful Yellow Eye, Gray, Dress Her in Indigo, The Scarlet Ruse, The Dreadful Lemon Sky, The Green Ripper*, and *The Lonely Silver Rain*. Of this collection, only three were published after *Turquoise*. The second group of novels contains characters who strongly resemble the Brindle type. It consists of *Blue, Orange, The Girl in the Plain Brown Wrapper, Lavender, Tan, Free Fall in Crimson*, and *Cinnamon Skin*. This group includes only two novels published after *Turquoise*.

A composite picture of the amoral type reveals the depths of MacDonald's insight into the nature of the sociopathic personality. Frequently, the character is smiling and affable, though these traits bear little resemblance to his real self. The type is violent if necessary, but only if necessary since he usually has a sly cunning. MacDonald regularly employs animal imagery, especially predators, to describe these characters. Etta C. Abrahams describes one of MacDonald's types of villains as a "goon" with an "animal-like physique" ("Travis McGee" 241). These characters are generally well built, powerful and physically resilient, expressing no fear. They seldom have any feelings for others, and this lack of feeling is accompanied by a nearly complete absence of insight into their own natures even though they are completely focused on their desires and needs. A description MacDonald has applied to certain nonobservant friends would partially describe this type:

Their inputs are all turned inward, the receptors concerned only with Self. Self is to them the only reality, the only uniqueness. Jung defines these people in terms of the "I" and the "Not I." The "I" person conceives of the world as being a stage setting for Self, to the point where he cannot believe other people are truly alive and active when they are not sharing that stage with Self. Thus nothing is real unless it has a direct and specific bearing on Self. ("Creative Trust" 15)

Although some of the amoral characters have regular jobs and careers, they function well in nonstructured environments. Some have family ties, some act in groups, and some are isolated, alone. In contrast to David K. Jeffrey's belief that "the villain is uncomfortable with his isolation and will pair with a complementary 'other' . . ." (77), the most dangerous characters in the Travis McGee novels prefer to act alone. Finally, the amoral type is often sexually violent or powerful.

In *Red*, Ulka M'Gruder kills Patty, her husband Vance's first wife, when the latter tries to blackmail Vance and then kills Vance when it appears he is revolted by her. At the end of the novel, she focuses her powerful sexual allure on Travis and attempts unsuccessfully to get him to conceal knowledge of her guilt. Calvin Tomberlin, in *Gold*, plans the deaths of others with no compunction though he employs people to do the actual killings. Griff and Ans, in *Amber*, could have been developed into even more thorough Brindle types than they are, but their focus is on gaining money from unwary middle-aged men and then murdering them. They are businessmen with a twisted sense of the profitable. Anna Ottlo (Fredrika Gronwald) and Perry Hennigan (Wilhelm Vogel), in *Yellow*, are stock Nazis from the past though Wilhelm shows an impressively sadistic touch for violence and torture. In *Gray*, Hero and Freddy Hazzard psychologically complement each other. Hero has only a cameo role, but McGee's speculation about Hero's powerful sexual drive, a focus that renders Hero unbalanced, is more thoroughly developed in other characters. Hazzard, close to impotence, reveals a pleasure that is clearly morbid in striking people with a sap. His actions resemble those of Deputy Donnie Capp in MacDonald's *Deadly Welcome* (62). Wally McNeel, in *Indigo*, unbalanced by his daughter Minda's disappearance and rumored misuse at the hands of Carl Sessions, Jerry Nesta, and especially Walter Rockland, becomes violent and attempts to kill anyone who prevents him from avenging his daughter. Frank Sprenger's violent nature in *Scarlet*, while clearly under no moral constraints, generally serves organized crime. Mary Alice McDermit shows no compunction in murdering Jane Lawson. She and Frank are strong and healthy, and their affair and thefts represent a perfect combination. Frederick Van Harn, in *Lemon*, appears to be the classic amoral type, especially from his predatory sexual behavior, but he only kills Jason Breen and attempts to kill McGee when he feels he has no alternative. His powerful charm, however, seems correlated only with his ambition to succeed politically. Harry Hascomb, in the same novel, kills Carrie Milligan and Joanna Freeler for money, but he is too much in the background and only appears at the end as a serious figure of evil opposed to McGee. In *Green*, MacDonald disperses the sense of evil and destruction among the members of a terrorist group. However, their concept of violence has no personal quality. They plan to kill as easily as Brindle does in *Turquoise*. In fact, someone in the Church of the Apocrypha kills Gretel Howard and Herman Ladwigg on the off chance that they may cause trouble to the organization. Finally, Ruffino Marino, Jr., in *Silver* resembles Brindle but plays a relatively minor role until the end of the novel. Marino has acting ambitions and only kills, but that in horrifying violence, when Howard Cannon fails to follow orders during a Mexican drug buy (46-47, 140, 144-45).

MacDonald's first and twentieth Travis McGee novels have amoral types as the principal antagonists to McGee though what causes their amoral states is different for each one. In *Blue*, Cathy Kerr theorizes that Junior Allen went bad after five years in prison, and this has led to his predatory behavior (173). In *Cinnamon*, Travis argues that Cody Pittler is an example of real evil while Meyer thinks that an early traumatic experience is responsible for his actions (149-50); Meyer is possibly proved right when they learn that Cody's father shot his wife while she and Cody were making love and then was found shot after Cody ran away (157-58). David Black observes that

Most of MacDonald's books are moral fables. Two outsiders—one a hero who has learned how to play the game and participate in society, the other a sociopathic villain—are pitted against each other. Both share a strain of anarchism; each has renegotiated the social contract. The mystery is not who done it or how it was done, but why one outsider turns good and the other bad. Is evil innate or is it learned? . . . McGee believes in original sin; Meyer believes in conditioning. (12)

R. Gordon Kelly, after comparing Junior Allen to Max Cady in *The Executioners*, states that MacDonald is basically against an environmental explanation for Cady's behavior (153-54). Whatever the source of their amorality, both Allen and Pittler are powerful, smiling, isolated and alone, sexually dominant, and described in striking animal imagery. They seem well adapted, almost at peace, in their abnormalities, and MacDonald places both men in clear opposition to McGee. Similarly, Boone Waxwell, in *Orange*, although not McGee's primary focus, is sexually powerful, violent, and alone. He is one of the best examples in the series of the naturally evil figure. However, he is part of Calvin Stebber's organization and must share dubious honors with Wilma Ferner as the most dangerous member. Tom Pike in *Brown* and Paul Dissat in *Tan* are similar amoral types who function somewhat unlike the others. Their closest counterpart may be Frank Sprenger in *Scarlet*. Both Pike and Dissat fit the physically powerful mold and are emotionally isolated and dead. They brutalize and kill mainly for money. In addition, they are businessmen and do not have the outlaw flavor seen in Allen and Pittler to whom the world is a hunting ground. It is only when Dissat discovers the pleasure he receives from torturing others that he begins to resemble the latter two. Lilo Perris in *Lavender* is probably the most clearly developed amoral woman in the series. She is strong, sexually demanding, and happy when brutalizing someone as Doris Severiss, one of Deputy Lew Arnstead's part-time prostitutes, attests (165). Arnstead fits many of the characteristics of the amoral type with his strong body and sadistic streak, but like Fred Hazzard in *Gray* (199, 209), he has sexual problems, in his case impotence (103), and his death relatively early in the novel removes him as a focus of the battle between good and evil. In *Crimson*, the nineteenth novel of the series, Desmin Grizzel, aka Dirty Bob, emerges as an impressive figure of evil, a source of nightmare. McGee's search in the novel focuses gradually on Grizzel, but he does not purposely confront Grizzel at the end. Grizzel is large, powerful, and sexually violent. Meyer thinks that his participation in the pornographic films is an outlet for "his sadistic appetites" (256). However, Grizzel does not become the center of opposition, the primary figure of evil, since he shares this with the more ambiguous Kesner.

In *Sartor Resartus*, Thomas Carlyle's Teufelsdrockh ridicules dueling man. However, if seen from the protagonists' viewpoint and not as "Two little visual Spectra of men" (176), the duel is momentous indeed. Not only in the final confrontation with Howie Brindle but through much of *The Turquoise Lament*, McGee locks himself in a duel with Brindle. The tension which accompanies this unfolding drama of the two men, one the amoral killer and the other the upholder of a private and social good, dispels the charge of near boredom leveled against the novel by Thomas Doulis (43). John Wiley Nelson includes Brindle (182) among the "smiling villains" (180), "like spiders, whose smiles are shimmering webs, and who devour their snared prey bit by bit, at their own leisure" (181). Inclusion of so many villains under this type, from Junior Allen, Ulka M'Gruder, Lilo Perris, Boone Waxwell to Brindle, supports Nelson's idea that "The series is not progressive. . . . A system of beliefs consistent in its values operates throughout the sixteen books" (170). From the beginning, MacDonald develops the amoral type as an oppositional figure to McGee, and Brindle appears to be its ultimate exemplar.

First, Brindle is the preeminent amoral type because his evil is not environmentally caused; he is naturally evil. MacDonald has stated that "there exists in the world a kind of evil which defies the Freudian explanations of the psychologists, and the environmental explanations of the sociologists. It is an evil existing for the sake of itself, for the sake of the satisfactions of its own exercise" ("Introduction and Comment" 69). Brindle murders when someone irritates him, when someone gets in his way. In speaking with Gabe Marchman, his photographer friend, of possible motives for Brindle's murders, McGee says, "'I don't think there has to be very much reason. Mostly it would be a case of opportunity, plus some kind of minor annoyance. He's quick and powerful and sly. I don't think he's clever'" (*Turquoise* 151). Meyer describes Brindle as "'an amiable maniac. . . . An almost casual impulse. Irritation plus opportunity plus slyness, plus a total absence of human warmth and feeling'" (180). George S. Peek overstates his case when he says, "Howie destroys life on a whim and is generally indescriminate [sic] about whom he kills or why" ("Beast Imagery" 94). Brindle, as far as Travis discovers, has killed only people connected with him in some way, especially family members (174-76). The casualness of Brindle's violence makes him more frightening than the other amoral types. He exemplifies Jeffrey's statement that "words cannot describe the experience of violence: it is irrational, it is random; it is unspeakable" (81). In both *Blue* and *Cinnamon*, the question of natural evil versus environmentally produced evil is raised, but as noted, both Junior Allen and Cody Pittler are given plausible environmental explanations for their actions. Second, Brindle's size, power, and quickness are greater than any of the others'. At 270 pounds, he is as heavy as Grizzel (*Turquoise* 19, *Crimson* 261); his height matches McGee's 6'4" (*Turquoise* 19); and his great agility and quickness are demonstrated throughout the novel. At the end when McGee confronts Brindle on Mount Alava on Pago Pago, McGee hits Howie beside the head with a lug wrench, and Brindle recovers quickly enough to duck the next swing. To McGee's surprise, he even has enough agility shortly afterward to jump on the cable of the outgoing car to avoid falling from the cliff (249-50).

In one area Brindle differs from the most exotic of the amoral types. He is not sexually sadistic. Early in the novel, Pidge, Howie's wife and the woman who calls Travis for help, describes to Travis her sexual relations with Howie on their honeymoon voyage:

[T]he picture of the sensuality of Howie Brindle emerged. Beef and sweat, quickly stimulated, quickly satisfied. Some days early in the voyage, an almost insatiable gluttony, a dozen episodes a day, in a dozen places on the boat. Apparently very little tenderness, emotion, romance. (63)

She adds, "'Like those damned chocolate bars'" (63). Howie evidently eats them whenever he feels the impulse. Later, when Meyer and Travis begin to suspect that Howie Brindle is a multiple killer, Travis, discussing Brindle's possible murder of Susan Fahrhowser, speculates on Howie's sexual relationship with her: "'She is an added convenience. He doesn't have to go out and find a girl if he wants one. Maybe he never wants one badly enough to go to any great lengths to find one. But if one is right there, within reach, he'll reach when he feels any mild urge'" (161). This is not to say that Brindle would not be violent. The need for sexual violence never arises, and he feels no internal pressure to act out any violent sexual fantasies. This aspect of Howie is similar to another observation made frequently about him in the novel; he never makes any extra effort in any situation (143, 161, 171).

Tom Collier, the lawyer who has stolen Professor Lewellen's notes for his research projects and who points Howie toward Pidge, calls Brindle a "bug" (211). But, McGee makes a more chilling analogy after he has confronted Howie next to the hotel pool on Pago Pago. Howie looks at McGee and for an instant McGee gets a "quick glimpse of what he was" (240). When he was eleven, McGee surprised an old black bear with two cubs taking an early morning drink:

I couldn't tell anyone how it was. They would think it was just a bear. It could kill you, but it was just a bear. It was more than a bear. It was something out of the blackness. It was night. It was evil. It colored that whole year of my life with a taste of despair.

The blackness was there in Howie Brindle, and then it was gone. (240)

Howie Brindle, possible killer of ten people, former of "few lasting attachments" (162), inhabited by "a very cold and strange entity" (163), has become the ultimate amoral type; he is almost nonhuman, a man who feels little (152) and has no fear (251). Humanity could tolerate very few of his type and still maintain civilized values.

Chapter 5

Learning and Knowing:
Education and Its Uses

In *Reading for Survival* (1987), a work David Streitfeld terms "passionately angry, entirely convincing and a bittersweet coda to the McGee series" (15), MacDonald constructs a dialogue between Travis McGee and Meyer on the value of reading for both individuals and the larger culture. With McGee functioning somewhat as an interpreter and summarizer, Meyer's ruminations focus on the irreducible role of reading as a means by which one connects with important ideas and deals with the multiple experiences of life. Those who do not read have a meager sense of the past, a weak grasp on the present, and a tenuous ability to shape the future. This monograph contains the essence of MacDonald's ideas on learning and knowing in the Travis McGee series. In these twenty-one novels, MacDonald presents both positive and negative comments and examples on education in its broadest sense, with some characters who profit from experience, but, more significantly, others who either cannot or do not learn from it. And, McGee, in all his ambiguity as a richly developed series character, shifts, changes, retrogresses, and fades in and out of focus as he responds to the many dilemmas in which MacDonald places him. Finally, from Prof. Warner B. Gifford's passion for archaeology in *A Deadly Shade of Gold* to those many uneducated and thereby endangered young throughout the series to Jean Killian, pursuing an education with McGee's assistance in *The Lonely Silver Rain* and consequently enriching her life and his, MacDonald explores the impact of the formal educational process. And while knowledge may be used to distort or harm, witness Dr. Girdon Face in *Gold* and Dr. Varn in *Nightmare in Pink*, MacDonald presents the process of learning as an essential part of the individual's and the culture's survival in a complex and changing world.

Learning and knowing are not restricted to the academy. Although MacDonald makes important comments about the value of formal education and employs several professors as characters, examples of people learning from personal, practical, or social problems occur across class, ethnic, and cultural barriers. Some characters in the series benefit from their experiences and thus lead healthier or at least socially and personally more acceptable lives. Arthur Wilkinson and Chookie McCall in *Bright Orange for the Shroud*, Cindy Birdsong in *The Dreadful Lemon Sky*, and Gretel Howard in *The Empty Copper Sea* are some who survive and learn from their difficulties. However, MacDonald presents many others who do not and/or cannot profit from any experience and learn how to live communally. One category contains those who think they are too clever to be found out. They are not violently predatory, but they see most situations as opportunities to project themselves and their personalities onto an unsuspecting and unready world. When McGee first meets Lysa Dean in *The Quick Red Fox*, he realizes that she has become her profession, acting, and is probably always on. He recalls what a stunt man named Fedder once told him of the successful actress:

So suppose you get a chance at one who's a pretty good little actress. Let it go. The thing there, they sublimate. . . . They take all that steam and they shove it into their work and there isn't enough left over for bed. (14-15)

Although Fedder has couched the above advice in sexual terms, McGee sees immediate confirmation of Lysa's self-absorption in the way she walks, talks, and regards him (15). When Dana Holtzer, Lysa's assistant, lies seriously injured in the hospital after Ulka M'Gruder assaults her, McGee has to remind Lysa to ask about her (156); Lysa's only interest is in the successful recovery of the pornographic pictures that she hired McGee to find. At the end of the novel, Lysa attempts to trade sex for the $40,000 she has shorted McGee; he rejects the offer (25, 158-59). Ultimately, Lysa is not a bad person, but like an actress eternally condemned to play the same role, she cannot learn from her experiences. Flexible as he is with most people, McGee contacts her again in *Free Fall in Crimson* seeking her help and even offers advice at the end of the novel on how to protect herself against Desmin Grizzel (113, 252-53).

MacDonald does not exempt males from this fatal cleverness leading to an inability to comprehend their limitations in performing their proper roles in the world. In *Pink*, Baynard Mulligan sets up a scheme to embezzle millions of dollars from the fortune of Charles Armister for whom he acts as a lawyer. It would seem obvious that once the money was discovered missing the police would closely scrutinize those who handled it for Armister. Mulligan's answer is that it will be so complicated that he will have time to disappear (103). After the police find him, Mulligan marries Bonita Hersch, his assistant and partner in crime, to keep her from testifying against him (140). Nina Gibson, the woman whom McGee had gone to New York to help, remarks that Mulligan will regret this seemingly clever move and probably wish instead "'he'd settled for twenty years'" (140). Gary Santo in *Pale Gray for Guilt* has a peculiar quality of the terminally clever, an indignation when some scheme fails in its intentions to enrich him at the expense of others. After Preston LaFrance and Gary Santo discover their losses, Santo appears at McGee's boat in Bahia Mar with D.C. Spartan, his lawyer, and Mary Smith, his private secretary (214). Aside from the attempt at intimidation, Santo seems genuinely outraged that someone did to him what he had done to Tush Bannon. Santo has learned the processes of business and finance but does not understand that the structure is neutral and not created or maintained for his exclusive pleasure and advancement. David Geherin observes of LaFrance and Santo that "Relentless in their single-minded pursuit of monetary gain, both have lost sight of what it means to be human" (95). Meyer, applying his knowledge of the stock market and using his contacts, hurts Santo's organization though, as McGee acknowledges but which Santo denies, not seriously (217).

While the Deans, Mulligans, and Santos disrupt people's lives, they are not essentially dangerous. But, MacDonald portrays another group which cannot learn from their experiences as violent and unfit to live in society. None of them have a past which precludes some contact with morally or socially beneficial ideas, yet they all have one quality in common which, on the surface, is not completely harmful. They clearly perceive their own interests and needs and show an unmediated desire to fulfill them. Only caution appears to limit their conduct. Deputy King Sturnevan in *The Long Lavender Look* is probably one of the most affable examples of this type. Sturnevan, an ex-prizefighter, seems resigned to his lost chances of glory when McGee first encounters him in the Cypress City jail. When McGee tells him that he once saw him fight, Sturnevan appears pleased (33). However, Sturnevan states at the end of the novel that he deserves the money acquired through murder but which he could not make in the ring (249). Although Lilo Perris, one of Sturnevan's victims, resembles him in her willingness to use violence, she reveals other characteristics that show her as someone unable to see where her experiences lead her in any but the most immediate sense. Lilo is one of MacDonald's most physical villains and displays little ability to reflect on events or analyze future possibilities; she focuses almost entirely on her present life and sensations though she is able to calculate the possible effects of prompt, direct action, especially when she kills Frank Baither, one of her partners in the original robbery (214).

One common trait of the violent type is that past behavior is frequently confirmatory of future conduct. This trait may not be exceptionable with them, but it is more compelling than with others, especially if they have freed themselves from most social constraints. In *The Deep Blue Good-by*, Junior Allen, once released from Leavenworth, has few brakes on his conduct. His treatment of Lois Atkinson is clearly illegal, but since she is too helpless to complain, a weakness Allen seizes on and manipulates, he preys on her and others until, when McGee finds him, he is after the eighteen-year old Patty Devlan. Allen functions as a paradigm for later violent types, most going in a morally downward spiral. In *Gold*, Calvin Tomberlin is limited only by his imagination and desires. Dru, one of his accomplices, tells McGee that Tomberlin has pictures of people committing sexual acts with which he coerces them into helping him (253). Only his murder by a group of Cuban exiles stops him from manipulating others (275, 279). For Tomberlin, one anti-social act leads to another until his death. Those who might be labeled criminally insane, like Paul Dissat (*A Tan and Sandy Silence*), Howie Brindle (*The Turquoise Lament*), and Cody T.W. Pittler (*Cinnamon Skin*), must be discussed on another plane altogether since the idea of learning from their experiences seems singularly out of place. Referring to Allen and Pittler, Frank L. Vatai maintains that they "do not even know that they are spiritually and emotionally dead" (13). Others, like Tom Pike in *The Girl in the Plain Brown Wrapper*, and Ruffino Marino in *Silver* have more understandable motivations for their actions, and yet like Allen and Tomberlin, past conduct eases them into and confirms them in even more vicious future depredations such as Pike's murder of his wife Maureen (212-13), and Marino's murder of three young people and the debauchement of the eleven-year old Angie Casak (46-47, 55; 245). Although the above analysis argues that not all the villains can be understood in the same way, MacDonald does realize that characters like Allen, Waxwell, and Dissat represent "a villainy . . . that grows strong through its own pursuit of evil" ("Introduction and Comment" 69).

As the central figure in the series, Travis McGee's ability or inability to use the knowledge he acquires to learn and thus grow, with all the ambiguities the latter word implies, reveals the direction of MacDonald's thinking about education in the broadest sense. To the implied question, MacDonald dramatizes an answer which shows an ambivalent McGee who changes (discussed in Chapter Six), adapts, gropes for ways to control his sometimes bleak moods, but leaves the impression of one generally incapable of learning from experience in any meaningful way. Given the above permutations of his character, it might seem difficult to say he does not learn. Are not those component elements of any learning experience? However, because of the demands of a series character, MacDonald cannot bring McGee to completion. At best, he can, figuratively, raise and lower McGee's consciousness of his essential self and the direction in which his life tends. If Erling B. Holtsmark is correct and McGee is "Recognizable as a traditional hero . . . who has existed in our collective consciousness for millenia [sic]" (101), then one cannot rightfully expect realistic change. And Larry E. Grimes's portrait of McGee pulled between "retirement" and "the quest" (103) suggests that the very structure of the series prevents one from evaluating his activities in terms of one responding to and learning from his experience, even though one may agree with Jack Matthews's statement that MacDonald's novels "like all detective stories . . . are allegories of knowledge" (109). However, in *Blue*, Lois Atkinson breaks the flow of narrative and allows one to see McGee from the perspective of personal growth and change. After he has helped her from a "calculating" kindness, Lois asks why he is the way he is:

Isn't it a waste?
    Waste of what?
    Of *you!* It seems degrading. . . . You're so bright, Trav, and so intuitive about people. And you have . . . the gift of tenderness. And sympathy. You could be almost anything. (92)

Obviously, she sees his life as misdirected at best, but McGee repudiates her contention, first by rejecting the image of an ordered, settled routine where he could "'be pulling a big oar in the flagship of life'" (92) and second by stating that "'I'll never know you well enough . . .'" (93) to try to explain who influenced him. Thus, at the heart of McGee's characterization lies a mystery on which MacDonald never sufficiently elaborates. Karen Vander Ven speculates that his brother's suicide may have been the *"something"* that "occurred to give McGee's personality its greatest flaw: being stuck in the same pattern of activities" and not "using one experience to go onto another in a more expanded, complex, or goal oriented way" (53).

Given the above as a starting point in understanding McGee's ability or inability to learn, one might fruitfully examine those moments of crisis in which McGee hovers on the brink of some important self-discovery. At the end of *The Scarlet Ruse*, McGee senses that "I am apart. Always I have seen around me all the games and parades of life and have always envied the players and the marchers" (264). He says that "Once . . . I tried to tell Meyer all this. I shall never forget the strange expression on his face. 'But we are *all* like that! . . . That's the way it *is*. For everyone in the world. Didn't you know?' " (265). One might term McGee's lament a clear cry from the heart, a vulnerability that marks this as a moment of openness to illumination. However, Meyer's response, while not inappropriate and bearing an existential truth, does not materially alter McGee. Meyer reveals something apparently hitherto unknown by McGee but which does not leave any room for closeness; it is an almost pointless bit of knowledge. If McGee had been in despair, a complete acceptance of Meyer's statement would only have deepened it and thus hardly have educated McGee in any positive sense. If McGee ultimately rejects what he knows to be a truth and he does say that "belief is a very difficult feat . . ." (265), then he blinds himself in a way diametrically opposed to any real learning. Keats's negative capability will not work here, for life demands some choices for people to reaffirm themselves in moments of true crises.

McGee's decision after the loss of Gretel in *The Green Ripper* at the hands of the Church of the Apocrypha is also instructive. MacDonald portrays him as someone whose life collapses inwardly so that he changes his name and puts on hold his Bahia Mar existence. Vengeance is his only idea (189-90). In one sense, McGee has little pliability under moments of extreme emotional stress, and thus it is difficult to imagine him often reflecting on his experiences and especially so when he suffers such a loss. The images of his physically conditioning and reconditioning himself become prominent here. In his desire for vengeance against those who have killed Gretel, his body takes over and directs him. After the violent episode in Ukiah, California, he gradually regains a feel for the pleasures of life but with little sense of a greater understanding of the human condition or himself (284-85). Grieving before his trip to Ukiah, McGee cannot recover in any socially acceptable way through sharing with friends or working through his anger with a therapist. One would be hard-pressed to know what he has learned from Ukiah other than that suffering is the lot of humanity. Richard Pearson notes that "As the number of books increased, so did the scars on the McGee back, the lines on the boyish face, and an ache in the aging heart. For victory is not without price. Time and fortune often took from him women he loved, persons who could not be replaced." McGee basically is one who endures.

In *The Pursuit of Signs* (1981), Jonathan Culler discusses two different sources of power in constructing fictional plots. One source arises from the time relationships between a story's events. Although an author might structure a narrative in any one of many time sequences, the reader can disentangle the events, unless the author has deliberately written the work to prevent it, and put them into chronological order (171-72). The other power source lies in the demands of narrative discourse. Thematically, a particular outcome might be required for which there is no clear cause and effect relationship in the text (175, 178). Culler states that these two forces or "logics" cannot be reconciled and function in many novels "by excluding the other" (177). In *Gray*, Puss Killian abruptly leaves McGee but writes a letter partially explaining her reasons for departing which McGee later shares with Jean in *Silver* (*Gray* 219-22, *Silver* 267). At one level, Jean is a product of the sexual relationship between McGee and Puss. However, her appearance in *Silver* is a requirement of the narrative discourse. As Anne K. Kaler states in discussing mythic aspects of the series, Jean is the "insertion of a long-lost daughter" (149). MacDonald needs some force to shift the direction of McGee's life, and the unsuspected daughter does this thoroughly and shows a McGee who learns something important from his experience in contrast to the McGee in *Gray* (*Silver* 274). In *Gray*, McGee is moved by Puss's letter but quickly finds himself admiring the physical charms of Mary Smith whose fixation on the passing Hero prevents a sexual encounter with McGee (223). McGee then goes to Meyer's boat and says that he "is sick unto death of miniwomen, miniclothes, miniloves, minideaths and my own damn minilife" (223-24). *Silver* reveals a McGee who reacts in a profounder way to the letter because of Jean. Deriving her being from the logic of the narrative rather than events, Jean, as variously discussed in Chapters Three, Six, and

Seventeen, leads McGee into a new, sustained recovery of himself. He also experiences a more positive relationship with Meyer (see Chapter Fifteen) and has a better sense of his own future after knowing Jean (276-77).

MacDonald states his most important ideas about formal education in four of the first five novels in the series. Thereafter, he makes few statements about this area of education although he refers to schools and universities in several other works. While he is certainly not against science and technology, MacDonald focuses on the complexity of the technician's world. In *Red*, he favorably speaks of those kids in the suburban towns such as Santa Rosita who will not accept what he calls the world of "The Sleep-Lovers," those kids "with IQ's that are soaring toward a level too high to measure. . . . They are the ones who, one day, will stop playing with transistors, diodes and microcircuitry and look at Barrentown and start asking the rude questions" (97). In *Cinnamon*, he favorably contrasts the kids exploring the new world of computers with those playing games in a nearby video arcade (67-68). The above two examples contrast the active and passive youths, those engaged in the complexities of their world and those manipulated and controlled by the complexities and who "come smiling and confident and unskilled into a technician's world, and in a few years they learn that it is all going to be grinding and brutal and hateful and precarious" (*Blue* 179). However, MacDonald also sees the technician in a more negative light as someone who is limited and unable to look beyond the specific skill that he or she possesses. Naturally, these are technicians of a certain type, those who have become their skill: "A devoted technician is seldom an educated man. . . . [H]e has no more sense of the mystery and wonder and paradox of existence than does one of those chickens fattening itself for the mechanical plucking, freezing and packaging" (*A Purple Place for Dying* 40). Obviously a generalization that does not apply to everyone technically qualified, the word "devoted" implies an exclusive focus and preoccupation on technical matters and mastery. George S. Peek comments that in education "there must be a sense of curiosity, a sense of adventure, and a sense of confidence as well. The combination of education and individuality is what frees a person . . ." ("Conquering" 92). A statement in *Gold* about a building on the campus of Florida Southwestern clarifies his intent in *Purple*: "It was a building to house the men who could turn out fabulous technicians with that contempt for every other field of human knowledge which only the truly ignorant can achieve" (*Gold* 44). MacDonald speaks of "fabulous," not everyday technicians.

Although the overly technically focused are not the truly educated, MacDonald describes a precarious educational atmosphere even for those best able to profit by the learning available. In *Red*, he says of the suburban schools in towns like Santa Rosita that they "are group-adjustment centers, fashioned to shame the rebellious" (97). MacDonald elaborates elsewhere on this idea in two statements about college conditions. After an elaborate description of the overly structured environment at State Western University in *Purple*, he raises the problem of those who do not fit: "Today the good ones, the ones who want to ask why, find no one around with any interest in answering the question, so they drop out, because theirs is the type of mind which becomes monstrously bored at the trade-school concept" (40). The good ones in *Purple* become "the thinking young ones, the mavericks, the ones we need the most" in *Gold* (46) who "ask the wrong questions. Such as— What is the meaning of all this" (47). These people resemble what MacDonald in a commencement address to the Ringling School of Art described as "an image breaker" ("Creative Person" 96). The anti-hero of the educational world is the unprepossessing Professor Warner B. Gifford, whom MacDonald defines by his passion for archaeological knowledge (*Gold* 44) and who remains cutoff from "the young heroes" who aim at the "second class goal of reasonable competence" (46) and the questioners whom the university "weed[s] . . . out" as "cultural mistakes" (47).

In *Reading for Survival*, the "twenty-second novel" of the Travis McGee series, Meyer states:

The man who can read and remember and ponder the big realities is a man keyed to the survival of the species. These big realities are the history of nations, cultures, religions, politics, and the total history of man—from biology to technology. (12)

These lines echo the well-known Matthew Arnold–T.H. Huxley dialogue over the respective roles of science and the liberal arts in modern education. MacDonald's position is an amalgam of both men's contention, especially Arnold's, that education contains science and the liberal arts or as Arnold phrases it, *"to know the best which has been thought and said in the world"* (409). MacDonald takes an absolutist position that reading is essential to survival. Having argued for the role of memory in human survival

(7), Meyer, MacDonald's surrogate, ties further development in with reading: "'Reading! Complex ideas and complex relationships are not transmitted by body language, by brain-storming sessions, by the boob tube or the boom box'" (13). Those who do not or cannot read "'are disenfranchised, completely cut off from any knowledge of history, literature, and science'" (13-14). For Meyer, the nonreaders are open to most superstitions, e.g., the "literal truth" of the Bible (18), creationism (19), and "'the marvelously crackpot rantings of a Jesse Helms, a Botha, a Meese, a Khomeni, a Falwell, a Qaddafi, a Gorbachev, an Ortega, a Noriega'" (20); into the "'empty places in their heads . . . great mischief has crept'" (20). When McGee asks what the cure is for all of this, Meyer responds by saying: "'Education, literacy, reading, thinking, remembering. Using the brain which was developed by a million years of stress'" (21). As Meyer earlier states, "'The life unexamined is the life unlived'" (14). This Socratic echo sums up his humanist position that people learn through this-world capabilities and not through reliance on supernatural forces. For MacDonald, "Reading is indispensible [sic]" ("Public Lecture" 9).

The nonlearners in the series, while temporarily successful, frequently disintegrate and fail. Like the character in *Reading for Survival* who reaches for the delectable fruit placed in a most unusual environment (16), they overreach themselves. The narrowness of their visions prevents their survival in a world that can be unforgiving even to the unforgivable. Unlike the relatively sophisticated and cautious Calvin Stebber in *Orange* who resembles the skeptical Mog of *Reading*, most nonlearners repeat their pleasures until either time or energy runs out. The struggling McGee and those mavericks reading and possibly someday having the chance to ask the difficult questions of Professor Gifford in *Gold* establish a potentially expanding hope for survival. At the end of *Reading*, McGee has started Barbara Tuchman's *A Distant Mirror* and comments: "the world has a different look, a slightly altered reality. That fourteenth century was the pits!" (22).

Chapter 6

Tradition and Change

Any opposition between the ideas of tradition and change in the series appears paradoxical since they blend so well in McGee's personality, and yet a limited volatility does oppose the traditional images and symbols he manifests. McGee generates an enormous amount of energy, if not change, in his general behavior, his sexual attitudes and practices, his moral outlook, and his social awareness, the latter involving more than the word "conscience." An example of this energy occurs in *The Turquoise Lament* when McGee returns from Hawaii after involving himself in Pidge and Howie Brindle's marital problems. McGee sleeps with one woman after another, including one of the hospital nurses attending the seriously ill Meyer. However, McGee is not the only, if an important, focal point for these two crucial themes. MacDonald has embedded their tensions in the series to such an extent that, far from being empty abstractions, an analysis of their interactions pulls into consideration other important ideas needed for an understanding of his work. For tradition and change represent dual forces, values, ideas, and motivators that give meaning to the disparate actions in the series and a greater understanding of his ideas on American culture. Thus, MacDonald's multi-layered treatment of these two themes suggests an opening into the texts which offers the critic a deeper understanding of their significances.

Since MacDonald begins the series in *The Deep Blue Good-by* with McGee's life-style clearly delineated, two basic ideas on change are possible: either repetition of certain character traits within each plot structure with no basic changes or some progression, evolutionary or revolutionary in nature, approximating changes in real human beings. MacDonald's statement that ". . . I am trying to age him gracefully at about one third of the rate the rest of us must endure" ("Introduction and Comment" 65) implies the latter, but the question remains how much the former situation obtains in the series. At first, repetition with no basic changes seems to preclude discussing this under the concept of change. However, repetition or exchange of traits is change without the concomitant idea of aging. But even if one accepts this state as change, it appears to rule out growth, maturity, or any positive transformation over time. MacDonald states that "Chronological age is no great problem. The problem is . . . an emotional and psychological one" ("'Aging' of Travis McGee" 4). An examination of McGee's character over the twenty-one novels of the series calls for a fusing of the two poles of change, thus creating a realistic synthesis in which McGee exists as a fully developed personality who reacts to experience.

On a physical level, this pattern of both repetition and progression is most evident. McGee occasionally loses his physical sharpness and runs, swims, and stretches to regain a former endurance and quickness. As he states in *The Green Ripper*:

Except for a few dreadful lapses which have not really gone on too long, I have stayed in shape all my life. Being in shape means knowing your body, how it feels, how it responds to this and to that, and when to stop. You develop a sixth sense about when to stop. It is not mysticism. It is brute labor, boring and demanding. (31)

It is not that he ever becomes unhealthy but that he must, especially when "salvaging," be ready for an immediate response to any danger. Even when not engaged in an operation, McGee's excellent physical condition preserves his life. While on a treasure-hunting expedition in *Turquoise*, McGee initially saves himself by kicking his chair over backwards and rolling clear when Bunny Mills, an enraged fisherman-tourist, tries to cave in his head with a fish billy (32-33). Professor Ted Lewellen, the leader of the expedition, disables the man in a peculiarly effective manner, but McGee is only alive because of his quick response. In *Bright Orange for the Shroud*, McGee demonstrates his ability to recover a necessary physical conditioning. At the beginning of the novel, McGee states that he is planning a "slob summer" (5), but Arthur Wilkinson appears and disrupts this vision of disengagement. Although he tries to foist Wilkinson onto Chookie McCall, with whom Arthur had had a brief affair before marrying Wilma Ferner, Chookie appeals to McGee's good instincts, and they proceed to the west coast of Florida to recover Arthur's money. On the way, Chookie, a professional dancer, puts McGee through some of her exercises, and before long he recovers a needed conditioning. While swimming against Chookie, he remarks: "Suddenly the reserves were there—missing so long it was like welcoming an old friend. It was as if a third lung had suddenly opened up" (*Orange* 47). His first encounter with Boone Waxwell reveals the value of this recovery, and McGee saves himself from serious injury by his speed and strength. McGee will go through this cycle again in *The Dreadful Lemon Sky* (18), realizing once more the difficulty in reaching the performance level for his special work.

Neither McGee's physical fitness nor condition is immune to drastic changes, life-threatening experiences that MacDonald uses in a classical way to remind one of McGee's humanity, his relation to more vulnerable people. The image of Odysseus washing up on shore on the island of Skheria, land of the Phaiakians, in *The Odyssey* realigns the reader's sympathies with this otherwise more than mortal adventurer who has survived the Cyclops, Circe, the Sirens, and a trip to Hades. Cathy Kerr, one of MacDonald's more tentative heroines, restores McGee at the end of two novels. Beaten by Junior Allen in *Blue* and even worse by Frank Sprenger in *The Scarlet Ruse*, McGee receives physical and spiritual comfort from Cathy at the end of both works. After the episode with Cathy in *Blue*, he says, ". . . I was mended as much as I could ever expect" (252). For McGee, this is a mending, physically at least, to what he was and what is necessary to function independently as a salvage consultant. In *Scarlet*, the recovery takes longer and is chancier than in any previous novel with the possible exception of *The Long Lavender Look*, near the end of which McGee is beaten by Deputy King Sturnevan, an ex-prize fighter (249). And similarly to Cathy Kerr in *Scarlet*, Heidi Trumbill from *One Fearful Yellow Eye*, as discussed in Chapter Two, arrives to care for him at the end of *Lavender* and restores him emotionally and physically. MacDonald uses these previously introduced characters, both McGee's former lovers, to underline the seriousness of his physical danger and the extent to which such bodily insults require more than just medicine and rest to heal them. In stressing the severe physical changes McGee undergoes throughout the series, MacDonald portrays the precariousness of the world, the vulnerability of all traditions, private and public.

Being in good shape has the quality of a valued tradition; one can celebrate a tradition, but it is difficult to improve on it. Similarly, when one is in good shape one feels good, the body responds well, and all parts work satisfactorily. Any improvement is in the area of specific adjustments in strength or endurance, but beyond a certain point the sense of well-being is not measurably enhanced. McGee's quickness, mentioned above, partakes of this quality of being. In *Cinnamon Skin* when Jesse, the piano player, kicks at his head, McGee avoids his boot:

I have a lot of quick. It's nothing I've earned or worked for, it's just that the hookup between senses, nerves, and muscles works faster than most. And adrenaline makes it work even faster. (180)

Although one might think that good physical conditioning would help one's speed, McGee does not stress the link here. Rather, he implies that an inherent condition gives him the ability to avoid harm. While one may refrain from the temptation to see this quickness on a moral level, nevertheless the symbolic nature of his repeatedly rescuing himself is evident. When McGee dodges Wally McLeen's deadly Indian club in *Dress Her in Indigo* or successfully removes the terrorists in *Green*, his quickness allows him to evade or destroy forces worse than himself. This instinctive or subconscious ability, what John Wiley Nelson terms "an animal preparedness necessary to survival" (187), compounded of the physical (rest to movement) and the traditional reveals a natural integration of all his abilities.

One of the most intense aspects of the ideas of tradition and change occurs when McGee speaks of them together, balanced as elements of the general life-style he encounters in Florida and other parts of America. At any particular time, Florida is both worse than it was and better than it will be. This "worse" and "better" refer to the environment, manners, crime, numbers of people, and general quality of life. Water and air pollution, destruction of the wetlands, and the drying up of the Everglades are changes that present a negative picture of man's relationship to his environment. Opposed to these events is a world where man is seemingly in better balance with nature. Interference with this equilibrium only harms the quality of life. MacDonald's image is of a fragile structure that cannot easily absorb outside elements and either maintain itself or recover from any intrusions. Thus, rather than an ongoing balance between the forces of tradition and change, the latter takes a dominant position, absorbing tradition and making all situations somewhat worse, robbing people of the ability clearly to evaluate social and natural processes and know what they should reasonably expect. In *The Empty Copper Sea*, Meyer complains that he "had spent a whole day doing errands without running into a single person he knew" (17). Later, he analyzes the problem of change:

Florida can never really come to grips with saving the environment because a very large percentage of the population at any given time just got here. So why should they fight to turn the clock back? It looks great to them the way it is. Two years later, as they are beginning to feel uneasy, a few thousand more people are just discovering it all for the first time and wouldn't change a thing. And meanwhile the people who knew what it was like twenty years ago are an ever-dwindling minority, a voice too faint to be heard. (20)

The image Meyer presents is of an inexorable slide, a succession of new conditions with no dominant center of perception from which to evaluate and assess change. The backdrop against which change occurs continues to alter as well as the perceivers, and thus there is no time to stop and find agreement on what kind of world they want.

Occasionally, MacDonald speaks of tradition directing and managing change and thus creating a more serene environment. In *The Girl in the Plain Brown Wrapper*, referring to a West Coast Florida community, he notes, "Solid, cautious growth, based on third- and fourth-generation money and control—which in Florida is akin to a heritage going back to the fourteenth century" (41). However, here MacDonald implies that any sense of a real tradition is illusory, that their world cannot maintain traditions effectively with the pressures of people and events. Judge Jeff Ellandon in *Deadly Welcome* describes an anomalous situation in which the Janson family heirs control most of Ramona Key opposite the West Coast Florida town of Ramona as well as land north and south of it and refuse to sell, thus blocking any development (25-26). In contrast, McGee notes in *Copper*, "the plastic aromas of the new Florida" (32). This is "superimposed on all the old enduring things, known when only Caloosas made their shell mounds and slipped through the sawgrass in their dugouts" (32). Progress thus becomes suspect, destroying not so much human traditions but rather the natural base on which those traditions can build.

The lack of perspective is thus the greatest threat to the ability to evaluate either what to keep or what and how to change. In *The Quick Red Fox*, MacDonald describes Santa Rosita in California "full of plastic people, in plastic houses" (96) with "no one left to tell them what they are and what they really should be doing" (97). Their wire services, radio, television, schools, churches, politicians, goods, and popular literature do not "ask them a single troublesome question. Such as: Where have you been and where are you going and is it worth it" (97). Although MacDonald speculates that bright kids will develop different responses (97), the inhabitants of Santa Rosita live "as if some cynical genius had designed a huge complex penal colony in the sunshine" (97). This negative picture, foreshadowing Meyer's bleak image of a Florida with no sense of the past (*Copper* 20), encapsulates MacDonald's view of the balance between tradition and change in which change dominates and erases memory and value. This is not a view of a culture in which visions compete for attention and resources but rather a view in which no vision operates. The city council in *Scarlet* falsely claims that the permanent boating residents pollute the water (12). Rather, the city cannot tax the boat owners as they do property owners and thus carelessly move to wipe out a traditional community. To the claim that they "have added to the population density" (11), Meyer enumerates the many highrises and other units that have been built in the area contrasted with the relatively small growth among the boat owners. The council's moment of focus is too narrow to value what the boat community represents; the council operates in the too bright sunshine whose glare erodes even a clear view of the present.

Contrasted with this image of tradition and change in which the latter gradually commands attention, McGee and Meyer throughout the series intersperse more radical visions of change. Both men speculate on apocalyptic changes that could erupt in the midst of ongoing social processes. In *Blue*, McGee muses on Junior Allen's discovery of where David Berry had concealed the gems he had smuggled back from Asia after World War II. According to George Brell, Berry had put the gems in a canteen with wax to keep them from rattling (133), and his daughter Cathy reports that he apparently had hidden them under the markers at the entrance to his driveway on Candle Key (16-17). After the canteen had corroded, McGee imagines that bugs had eaten the wax:

Bugs would eat the wax. Chaw the old canvas. And one day there would a mutation, and we will have new ones that can digest concrete, dissolve steel and suck up the acid puddles, fatten on magic plastics, lick their slow way through glass. Then the cities will tumble and man will be chased back into the sea from which he came. (146)

McGee's nightmare image of man's destiny is an isolated pondering on a flight from Houston to Miami, but it highlights, if in an exaggerated form, the inadvertent possibilities of change, the directions natural processes can take.

In another version of apocalyptic change in *A Deadly Shade of Gold*, McGee analyzes "the virus theory of mankind. The pretentious virus, never knowing that it is a disease" (37). Superior beings from another galaxy draw near earth and destroy life on the planet before it can spread its contagion. McGee describes mankind and its works from the viewpoint of these visitors: "A little cave-dwelling virus mutated, slew the things which balanced the ecology, and turned the fair planet sick. An overnight disease, racing and explosive compared with geological time" (37). MacDonald's focus is clearly the comparative speed with which change occurs. And, with no traditions against which mankind could assess change from within, some force from without, almost with theological overtones, will assume the responsibility of stopping the danger (37). Conversely, in *Nightmare in Pink*, MacDonald presents a picture of a final change coming from within. He states that "New York is where it is going to begin" (21). Comparing human beings and their multiple effects to locusts, MacDonald asserts that "We're nearing a critical point" (21). He says that the ultimate violence will start with two strangers bumping into one another and from this an uncontrollable escalation will lead to widespread death with at last "the most powerful ones, ragged and bloody, slowly tracking each other down" (21). In both cases, MacDonald presents an inevitable scenario in which mankind, merely through existing, heads toward disaster. And although in *Copper* Meyer implies that McGee can through openness offset a sense of stasis, of winding down in his own life, which the second law of thermodynamics predicts for the universe (107-08), both in *Lemon* in which McGee says that the kids on a passing boat shot at them "'For kicks. For nothing. For self-expression'" (34) and in *Green* in which Meyer tells McGee he has met

man's primal urge to decimate himself down to numbers which can exist on the wornout planet. It is man's self-hatred. The god of the lemmings, and of the poisonous creatures which can die of their own venom. (283-84)

MacDonald describes a world that hangs on, at best accomplishing personal, short-lived victories.

MacDonald uses Meyer as a complement to McGee. As observed in Chapter Three, MacDonald notes the difficulties in finding the right balance for McGee. In "Introduction and

Comment," MacDonald indicates that the first person point of view traps McGee in his own "internal monologues" and that Meyer, a close friend and later partner in most of his cases, adds "atmosphere and physical detail through dialogue" (67). Of course, Meyer also opens up McGee's character and imparts a further dimension of awareness to his thinking and motivations. Thus, MacDonald gradually brings Meyer into the series until he is more than a referent and background figure; he extensively participates in the action beginning with *Darker than Amber* (see Chapter Two). However, in developing Meyer's character, MacDonald creates an individual with a life and personality of his own who occupies a permanent position, if still secondary to McGee's. In essence, Meyer symbolizes traditional values while still functioning as a character of some depth and complexity, able to maintain his identity in relation to McGee with a sense of humor and an awareness of his own individuality.

Respecting and maintaining traditions do not occur automatically in people or societies; one must work to preserve what is valuable in a culture. To do that, one must be able to value, to evaluate. Although not alone in his ability to choose what is central and worth keeping and nurturing, Meyer plays a pivotal role in knowing and expressing what is of value. Meyer's knowing does not simply function as a rational process of assessing cultural artifacts and traditions and deciding what to keep and what to discard. It involves as well a sensing of the good around him. This intuitive basis for his evaluations does not diminish either his learning or intellectual gifts. Rather, it ties these latter qualities into his experiences as a man. McGee's spoken and unspoken admiration for Meyer rests on his awareness of Meyer's wholeness, his trueness to his deepest nature and reflects McGee's own ability, though from a different slant, to know the good.

Compassion and tolerance are central aspects of Meyer's nature and are demonstrated in a variety of ways and situations. From his ability to tolerate bores (*Copper* 17) to his requests of McGee to help friends, Meyer exhibits his concern for others and underlines the sense that for the human community to survive one must reach out and respond to others' needs. As noted in Chapter Two, in both *Indigo* and *Scarlet*, Meyer enlists McGee's somewhat reluctant help for Harlan Bowie and Hirsh Fedderman, respectively. Neither man is an appealing object for aid, but Meyer's concern reaches past their character flaws to their real needs. While he may recognize their limitations, he does not let these interfere with his desire to help. The status of old friend seems enough for him gently to prod McGee, and in responsible fashion Meyer puts himself in equal danger with him in both novels.

In contrast to McGee, MacDonald does not stress Meyer's sexual life. However, on at least two occasions with some sexual overtones, Meyer, while admittedly enjoying their company, succors tired but accomplished women. In *Amber*, McGee refers to Meyer as someone who acts as a refuge for "that breed which he calls, with warmth rather than irony, the iron maidens. These are stern, mature, aggressive, handsome women who have made their mark in the world . . ." (22). As Meyer sees it, "'They want a ribbon in their hair . . . and someone who does not want to make any use of what they've achieved . . .'" (23). McGee remarks in *Free Fall in Crimson* that

Though Meyer loves to look upon the lively young beach girls and is often surrounded by little chittering platoons of them . . . [he] feels most at ease with—and is usually attracted to—mature capable independent women. . . . (40)

Although MacDonald's portrait teeters on the edge of a foolish and somewhat suspect altruism, his consistent presentation of Meyer as someone who cares and puts himself out for others allays this suspicion. If the measure of one's compassion reveals itself in the response shown to those nearest to one, then Meyer's emotional support for McGee reveals the depth of his humanity. In at least two instances when McGee has lost someone he has loved, Meyer responds to McGee in ways that help him recover a sense of life. At the end of *Pale Gray for Guilt*, McGee brings to Meyer's boat a letter that he has received from Puss Killian. In the long letter, Puss explains why she left so suddenly. She reveals that she is dying and tells McGee how important he was to her during the time she spent with him. After Meyer reads the letter, McGee says that he wants to take Meyer and the latter's more useful boat and sail "'as far down the Exuma Cays as the range of his boat would allow, and then we were going a lot further down in the Little Doll'" (223-24). Meyer's response is an immediate and unconditional agreement, having sensed his friend's need for a new affirmation in life. After returning from the California violence in *Green*, McGee says that "Meyer had been patient and understanding . . ." (282). At one point Meyer asks, "'Are you sure you're all right?'" McGee says, "'I don't know how I am. Or exactly who I am'" (283). Meyer then reminds him of their conversation before he went to California about "'the new barbarism'" in the world and that "'You met it, Travis'" (283). He says, "'It takes time to back away from that, Travis. Time'" (284). McGee credits Meyer with helping him cross "a black, deep, dreadful ravine separating me from all my previous days" (284). Meyer's support for McGee exemplifies his deeply held belief that help and compassion for others make man truly human and give meaning to his actions. Amid modern life's powerful currents, this remains a constant.

Any series character must possess certain identifiable habits and traits while allowing for change that occurs under the pressure of experience. In Rex Stout's *In the Best Families*, Nero Wolfe loses "'a hundred and seventeen pounds'" (430) while eluding Arnold Zeck, and Archie Goodwin does not recognize him; of course, it is not long before Wolfe says in a letter to Goodwin that "I am beginning to feel more like myself" (502). One of the most permanent traditions in McGee's life involves his work. While he does not always follow through with his stated requirements, McGee will recover something for someone at half the value while paying his own expenses. This operational structure is the most consistent element in the series, and yet it is in the variations from it that MacDonald is most creative and says the most about the nature of tradition and change. For, McGee establishes his "business" requirement only to break it under the pressure of circumstances and his own character. After he turns down Debra Brown's offer of herself in *Orange*, he reflects on people "perfecting themselves in their own image" (190). Thus, MacDonald shifts the value from some traditional, though mundane, observance to changes that arise from moral and other pressures in McGee's life. He never knows when he will cross his own line, obeying some sense of what is right in a particular instance. At the end of *The Lonely Silver Rain*, McGee astonishes Meyer by putting all but $400 in a trust fund for Meyer to invest for his new-found daughter (277). The traditional image of the pleasure-loving beach bum engaging himself in salvage work only for healthy profits cannot be accepted even by McGee.

One of the personal traditions in the series imposed on McGee by his own choices but reflective of a constant human experience involves the dual ideas of loss and recovery. The discussion in Chapter Five of McGee's complex relationship to learning from his own experiences helps reveal the significance of the above two ideas. McGee's life-style requires certain risks that lead to physical injuries which necessitate long periods for healing. This paradigm appears early in the series and continues throughout, establishing on a physical level McGee's vulnerability. In addition, McGee refers to himself in *Blue* as a "scar-tissued reject from a structured society" (29) and fixes the rhythm of loss and recovery as a permanent part of his life. At a deeper level, MacDonald early on shows McGee as someone who cannot maintain an ongoing relationship with a woman, who cannot accept marriage and what it involves in the various levels of responsibility. In *Red*, McGee balances the costs of marriage and its obligations against his ability to give up everything:

I am not properly acquisitive. I like the *Busted Flush*, the records and paintings, the little accumulations of this and that which stir memories, but I could stand on the shore and watch the whole thing go glug and disappear and feel a mild sardonic regret. No Professional American Wife could stomach that kind of attitude. (46)

Later, McGee sees this not so much as a loss but rather a trade in which he maintains his ability to involve himself in the hunt by giving up the settled aspects of family life.

However, McGee's reaction to Dana Holtzer as "an impressive handful . . . the mature female of the species, vivid, handsome and strong, demanding that all the life and need within her be matched" (*Red* 129-30), while largely positive, has overtones that match his statement in *Orange* that "Maybe I could be stirred only by the wounded ducklings" (51). It is possible that McGee's assertion in *Lemon* that ". . . there are one hell of a lot more grown-up ladies than grown-up men" (26) comes too close to him. Before Gretel's death in *Green*, McGee is moving toward that settled life with a woman that he always thought was for others. As his relationship with Anne Renzetti winds down after she takes a job in Hawaii, McGee speaks with her by phone: "The conversation with Annie was soon over. It might be the last one, I thought as I hung up. There was a little edge of loss, but it had softened. It no longer bit" (*Cinnamon* 273). McGee appears to have shifted into earlier patterns, prior to Gretel's appearance, in which women pass out of his life, neither person to be blamed, reflecting a leveling of his emotions. From too much loss, McGee has subconsciously returned to a protective stance. Recovery is too difficult, and McGee never again experiences the emotional threats of a committed, unreserved love relationship.

Throughout the series, McGee has moments that could only be classified as loss of will. At times, these moments occur because of the death of someone he loves. Although McGee experiences real loss over Lois Atkinson's death in *Blue*, his sense of grief is even more powerful, as mentioned above, after the deaths of Puss Killian (*Gray*) and Gretel Howard (*Green*). However, a more problematic loss and recovery occurs in the novels in which McGee turns against himself. At the end of *Amber*, McGee sees a shooting star and suddenly pulls himself from the "sours" (188). This pattern of descent into moodiness and self-disgust repeats itself until McGee at times has difficulty coming all the way back. In *Yellow*, McGee speaks of being outside of life. After Heidi Trumbill confesses the possibility that if she stays with him "'then you would own me, every atom of heart and soul and body forever, and life would have no meaning except as it related to you'" (223), McGee agrees that it would be better if they parted. However, he later wonders if he made a mistake and senses that he is "outside the gates and there is no one to open them" (224). Heidi responds to his assertion in *Lavender* that "'Everything that happens takes away, and less flows back'" (254) with the belief that "'It's second adolescence'" (254), thus coaxing him to some comfort. When McGee speaks at the end of *Green* of a "rising joy" (285), one cannot help remembering what it has risen from or McGee's sense that ". . . I didn't have the faintest notion, either, of what I might do next, today, tomorrow, or ever" (276). McGee near the end of *Silver* once again experiences this recovery from some bleak mood that overcomes him:

In the last few years I had been ever more uncomfortably aware that one day, somewhere, I would take one last breath and a great iron door would slam shut, leaving me in darkness on the wrong side of life. But now there was a window in that door. A promise of light. A way to continue. (274)

In this instance, it has taken the previously unknown daughter referred to in Chapter Three to rescue him emotionally, rendering more doubtful the possibility of the cycle of loss and recovery functioning successfully in any possible future.

The manifold aspects of tradition and change in the series reveal MacDonald's subtle approach to his craft. While concerned with the narrative line in each novel and McGee's role in the unfolding series, MacDonald is also open to the many aspects of a changing American culture. Against its rich traditions, he measures, probes, and stretches his characters to find meanings in their lives and actions. He knows that one cannot fully live and remain the same. Through the tensions produced, something new frequently appears that must be assimilated, continuing a process that many, including MacDonald, would call life. In a 1967 letter to the editor of the *JDM Bibliophile*, MacDonald states that "I want to try to nail down in fiction at least a few hints to the fearsome randomness of all fate and fortune" (Letter 7). The traditional need for continuity provides the glue, however illusory, that the randomness can be limited for enough meaning and value to be created and sustained.

Chapter 7

Work and Professionalism

MacDonald approached his writing with a professional attitude. In addition to McGee's character discussed at the beginning of Chapter Three, "How to Live with a Hero" reveals the care MacDonald took with plot, setting, and theme. Thus, it is almost inevitable that work and professionalism loom large in McGee's life and appear regularly as strong concomitants to other elements in the novels. From the care which McGee takes for his boat and in working on his cases to Meyer's work as an economist to the various law enforcement officers and their attitudes toward their profession to Chookie McCall's concentration as a dancer, MacDonald evokes the possibility of a world in which work is done well, many times seemingly for the sake of doing it well. In *The Scarlet Ruse*, it appears General Lawson started a second career in construction from the disgust he felt in witnessing sloppy work on a paving project near his home (139-40). And, Heidi Geis Trumbill in *One Fearful Yellow Eye* feels better about herself when she plans to paint from a true sense of what she wants and can accomplish (192, 224). Attitudes toward work and professionalism, thus, frequently function as measures by which McGee, and MacDonald through him, judges the moral, emotional, and intellectual qualities of others and himself. To not care, to do work only half-attentively and without interest in its results and the effects on others and the world around one is to come perilously close to failing as a human being.

Among the many areas of human experience explored in MacDonald's fiction, what one does and how one does it help define one's personality. Accordingly, the varied types of work included in the novels are no surprise. From policemen to photographers to boat captains and workers to lawyers, shady or otherwise, to bankers, businessmen, art gallery workers, artists, and criminals, MacDonald saturates his fiction with workers and their experiences; portrays them before, during, and after work; and probably uses this social experience as the principal setting for human activity as often as any other. Two questions arise from this abundant portrayal of work in the series: Is work as crucial to the novels' plots as to those who perform it? And, is there any progression in the series as to the nature, quality, and attitudes toward work? Possibly only fortuitously, MacDonald sets in opposition in *The Deep Blue Good-by* and *Nightmare in Pink*, respectively, the lifestyles of Junior Allen for whom work has no meaningful role and Nina Gibson who not only values hard work but also recoils at the suspicion that her dead fiancé, Howard Plummer, might have stolen the $10,000 she discovered in her apartment closet after his death (*Pink* 9, 17). Though somewhat simplified, one might say that Allen needs people to provide goods and services that he can purchase (if not steal—though with regard to the gems he takes, could one steal what was illegally obtained in the first place?) while Nina needs work from which she earns life's necessities and a sense of self-worth (*Blue* 14-15, *Pink* 31-32). Allen resembles Terry Drummond, the wealthy heiress in *Pink*, in this regard while Nina reflects the qualities toward work that Chookie McCall has in *Blue*. What arises from plot analyses of these two novels is that MacDonald has made work central to *Pink* while keeping it peripheral in *Blue*. What is peculiar about *Pink* in relation to work is that it shades into criminal activity, e.g., the looting of Charles Armister's business, the call-girl ring, and Dr. Varn's illegal medical experiments, from a legal and moral core represented by Nina and Howard.

While *Bright Orange for the Shroud* and *Scarlet* are also important when considering the crucial relationship between work and plot, two other novels, for quite different reasons, center work even more strongly in the action. *The Empty Copper Sea* does not present the reader with many ongoing work situations, but the very reason for McGee's travels to Timber Bay on the west coast of Florida lies in Van Harder's loss of his captain's license. Van Harder's good name is nearly all that he has, and his compulsive desire to retrieve it and his license overcomes any resistance McGee may have to the operation. Furthermore, Van Harder's promise to pay $10,000, money he does not presently have, underscores his seriousness and his great need to face the world with a name that commands respect (11). Hubbard Lawless's business failures, which led him to "steal" Van Harder's good name and which McGee spends much of the novel attempting to unravel, fade in the remembered intensity of Van Harder's request. In one sense, Vangie Bellemeer in *Darker than Amber* is the opposite side of the coin, for she wishes to escape her reputation among her murderous companions. But, MacDonald makes Vangie's actual "work" central to the plot. Once Meyer and McGee reconstruct Vangie's story after her rescue and once McGee extracts from the dying Griff the name of the boat that the current victim has sailed on, they develop a plan to put the ring out of operation. Although they are too late to save the man, their actions cut across the illegal activities of Ans Terry and Del Whitney who operate in the work setting of a cruise ship. Against this background, McGee and Meyer, with the help of Merrimay Lane, restore a moral balance, as it were, in the sphere of work. In this instance, the criminals have been sucked out of an honest work environment much as Vangie's and Del's weighted victims were drawn down to the bottom of the Caribbean. Merrimay Lane's failure before the cameras at the end of the novel and her return to modeling emphasize a fairly objective world where success or failure occurs in the open (*Amber* 189).

The great discovery of Thomas Carlyle's Teufelsdrockh in *Sartor Resartus* is that one should do the work one is given as well and diligently as one can. Begin now in the situation in which one finds oneself. It is fruitless to search for some imagined task that will give one complete satisfaction for the effort expended; rather, one should put one's hand to the nearest work and do it well (187-88). Does MacDonald arrive at some comparable vision as to the positive nature of work? The answer is mixed since in MacDonald's fiction people fail more often than they succeed to invest work with the needed value. Willie Nucci in *Scarlet* and *The Lonely Silver Rain* represents the problematic nature of good work as its own reward. McGee reveals in *Scarlet* that while Nucci owns and attentively operates a Miami Beach hotel, he is at great pains to hide his ownership (39-41). Nucci realizes that if he were known to be the sole owner and not the representative of others, the unions and corrupt officials would drive him out of business. They would control him as thoroughly as organized crime figures control Frank Sprenger, one of their own (*Scarlet* 46), whose belated recognition that he likes his work as a bond salesman is like an infant crying in the wilderness (183-84).

However, other people are more successful achievers than Nucci and Sprenger but with interesting twists that blur MacDonald's concept of work. Gabe Marchman, the photographer in *The Quick Red Fox* to whom McGee brings Lysa Dean's sex photos; Prof. Warner B. Gifford, whom McGee consults in *A Deadly Shade of Gold* with regard to the source and nature of the statue Sam Taggart showed him; General Lawson, the construction supervisor in *Scarlet*; and the "Silver Tips" in *Free Fall in Crimson* that McGee threatens to involve in the business which Ted Blaylock leaves him and Mits if Preach does not let him give it to Mits are all good at what they do but insulated to a certain extent from any core model of American work trends (*Crimson* 268-69). Marchman, crippled from war wounds, works in a studio at home. Professor Gifford pursues studies that are valuable to his students and learning in general but remove him somewhat from the larger world's activities. General Lawson and his ex-servicemen with whom he began his construction company are retired soldiers, presumably with pensions, and the "Silver Tips" are retired business executives living in Florida who probably donate their time and talents to help small businessmen and -women. None of these people are in work situations which present clear models as to the direction of work in America. Even though McGee is professional enough to use Marchman's and Gifford's skills, the above characters are all somewhat set aside, cut-off, even above the mass of workers, businessmen, and executives.

Another group of novels presents a more vulnerable picture as to the efficacy of work to transform one's life. In *Red*, Stan Burley, a therapist who runs a clinic for alcoholics, functions more as someone who works to maintain the stability of his patients, especially Nancy Abbott, than to cure them. Arthur Wilkinson in *Orange* ultimately achieves some stability in his work ambitions after rejecting the role of a successful department store owner, losing most of his money to con operators in what he hoped would be a successful real estate venture, gaining some sense of value through manual labor and hard-won carpentry skills, and ultimately repairing and selling homes after he marries Chookie McCall (170-71, 189). Tush Bannon in *Pale Gray for Guilt* is destroyed by forces stronger than himself, never really understanding that he has no chance for success regardless of how hard he struggles. Sheriff Norman Hyzer's professional approach to his work in *The Long Lavender Look* does not withstand his guilt over his relationship to Lilo Perris (he is her father), and this guilt prevents him from admitting her essentially evil nature. In *A Tan and Sandy Silence*, Jeannie Dolan's diligent attempts to sell condominiums do not overcome a hopeless business situation, and for all her efforts she is out of work at the end of the novel. Gretel Howard's job at Bonnie Brae in *The Green Ripper*, a health resort, is an effort to sort out her life and recover some degree of independence, but it ironically leads to her death. And finally, Anne Renzetti in *Crimson* and *Cinnamon Skin* cannot match her personal happiness with job satisfaction. Her company offers her a larger hotel in Hawaii after her success in Florida, but taking the new job means losing McGee; she chooses the job (*Cinnamon* 106).

While the above two groups present ambivalent views on the value of work and do not clearly support the idea that MacDonald portrays the work ethic in a generally positive light, a final group corrupts the very idea that any progressive element is inherent in or contiguous with work performed well. Anna Ottlo's service to the Geises in *Yellow* seems an admirable model, but her Nazi past, discussed in Chapter Four, and her minor brutalities to the Geis children coupled with her recent violence towards Gretchen belie this image. Part of the surprise at such a revelation of her true nature lies in the positive image she presents as the loyal housekeeper. In *The Girl in the Plain Brown Wrapper*, Tom Pike is transformed after McGee's investigation from the hard-working, long-suffering husband into the callous murderer of his wife Maureen. Again, the shock lies not only in what he does but also in the extent of his betrayal of the community's and his wife's and sister-in-law Bridget's trust. As with Anna, Pike shows that work can be only a surface, a facade, however well performed. Of course, Howie Brindle in *The Turquoise Lament* emphasizes the potential deception in working hard. Wherever he is, Florida or Hawaii, Brindle cheerfully aids anyone with his boat chores. While McGee's reluctance to see Brindle as a murderer is partly because he seems so friendly, it also springs from Brindle's helpfulness. Finally, Cody T.W. Pittler's skills and enthusiasm as a salesman of almost anything in *Cinnamon* are the obverse of his need to kill and profit from anyone who loves or trusts him. Any sense in the series that work can rescue, build, or uphold man's achievements is seriously weakened by the examples of Ottlo, Pike, Brindle, and Pittler, and because potential must be followed by application and work, the presence of these characters in the series renders MacDonald's vision appreciably more negative.

It may seem ironic, given such a hero as Travis McGee, that work permeates the novels to such an extent since McGee's stance remains outside the world of work except when necessity requires him to take a salvage job. Frederic Svoboda states, "The ritual meanings of work are, perhaps, the most important to an understanding of the detective novel because such a novel is essentially a chronicle of the hero's work" (564). When applied to McGee, this statement highlights his ambiguous relationship to compensated labor beginning with his initial reluctance to respond to Chookie McCall's appeal for him to help Cathy Kerr (*Blue* 9). However, his observer/participant status does not prevent him from recognizing the conflicting nature of work. *Dress Her in Indigo* presents several examples that underscore this idea. Jerry Nesta does not initially offer a greatly more appealing picture than Walter Rockland, but when he discovers that Rockland is attempting to destroy him with drugs, he flees and, surprisingly, works at his craft as a sculptor. McGee and Meyer recognize his abilities, but when they question him about his relations with Bix Bowie and the other members of the group, he evinces no strength of character commensurate with his artistic gifts. Mike Barrington and Della Davis, the former "a painter" (39) according to Della, encourage Nesta but die at the hands of Wally McLeen along with Luz, Nesta's Mexican lover. Della's and Mike's good intentions and work and the latter's promise as an artist do not save them. Harlan Bowie, Bix's father, also presents a wide disparity between work achievements and success in life. As both McGee and Meyer observe, Bowie prospers in business but fails in raising his daughter (14, 15, 20, 251). When McGee returns to Florida with Bix, her hostility and indifference to Bowie ironically emphasize the inadequacy of his business triumphs.

While the examples from *Indigo* and those from other novels might make McGee wonder whether the effort required to do something well is worth it, he encounters people who function superbly in their various fields and whose competence he admires. Dana Holtzer in *Red* is a model of thoroughness and efficiency and initially overwhelms McGee with her abilities. When he learns her tragic family circumstances, his admiration only increases. Dana exemplifies that old adage that if a thing is worth doing, it is worth doing well. She is a "member" of that unacknowledged group who match efforts to tasks and whom McGee fully appreciates. Prof. Ted Lewellen in *Turquoise* is another. Like Dana, Lewellen immerses himself in the possibilities of the work he performs, instinctively creating the standards by which one judges his accomplishments. Lewellen fully researches his potential treasure projects and converts any participators in his efforts into supporters of his aims and goals. Methods and results become the measures of his success since the risk of failure is acknowledged by Lewellen, McGee, Meyer, and all who help them. Connie Alvarez in *Gray* resembles Lewellen in that while circumstances might limit their ultimate success they put few limits on their efforts to achieve their aims. At one level, McGee functions as a perspective through which MacDonald can recognize the dedication shown by Lewellen and Alvarez as well as people like Ben Gaffner, the state attorney in *Brown*, through whom the structures of society cohere. Once McGee contacts Gaffner, he finds it difficult to avoid being swept up in the state attorney's efficient pursuit of Pike and take any independent course of action.

As an echo, a recurring motif, Travis McGee's relationship to work develops MacDonald's ambivalent representation of the manifold efforts Americans make to hold their society together with some degree of belief that at least an incremental social progress is possible if not easily discernible. The thematic complexity of MacDonald's fiction is nowhere more evident than in McGee's often torturous efforts in energizing himself to endure honest labor. This honest labor, of course, includes his salvage work, but he is almost comical in his lugubrious reaction in *Crimson* to the more commonly experienced rigors of working for a living or what MacDonald elsewhere calls "the rude business of making a living" ("Creative Person" 59). Before committing himself to investigate the circumstances of Ron Esterland's father's death, McGee says to Meyer,

So. So I know now that I can't make it doing odd jobs here and there, and if I want to make it, I will have to seek honest work, like in Rob Brown's Boat Yard. Or with Acme Diving and Salvage. Or working for a yacht broker. Travis McGee, your friendly boat salesman. With a salary, bonuses, and a retirement plan. (*Crimson* 11-12)

Once he accepts society's rules and limitations, McGee realizes he must go all the way. MacDonald similarly remarks about himself that if he has to accept limitations on the direction of his work then ". . . I believe I would give it all up and go seek some honest way of making a living" ("Introduction and Comment" 64).

Aside from a "straight-arrow salvage" job in *Brown* (5) and the treasure hunt in *Turquoise*, McGee generally restricts himself to his career as an unofficial private detective, salvage consultant, or favor-doer for friends. This murkiness as to naming what he actually does is only the first level of ambiguity in defining his activities. If to name is partially to be, McGee is far better at stating what he is not than what he is. McGee's vehement rejoinder to Lois Atkinson's question in *Blue* as to how he got the way he is effectively separates him from nine to five jobs and the traditional ideas of family and community that appeal to most people (*Blue* 92-93). However, McGee does not and possibly cannot explain what does appeal to him as a life ambition. The very ambiguity in the phrase, "salvage consultant," supports the sense of suspension in which he lives. The word "salvage" implies an act of recovery, a picking up of the pieces of one's activities or those of others. The word "consultant" conveys a sense of limitation, of observation and evaluation of the efforts other people expend on the various tasks that hold a society together. As Larry Grimes observes,

After all, the term "consultant" suggests impersonal expertise, a hard-nosed business approach to any matter at hand. Further, the title suggests that its bearer is an expert who works for financial gain, an expert whose interest in the affairs of others is contractual and temporary. (104)

Combined, they pull in somewhat opposite directions. And, McGee appears most comfortable with this sense of duality whether in a state of danger or not.

A further ambiguity lies in the answer to the question as to whether McGee is a professional in what he does. Colonel Marquez in *Gold*, while admiring McGee's "'good intuitions'" (203), states that he is "'a talented amateur'" (203), a claim that McGee does not dispute. This sentiment appears also in *Silver* when McGee reacts to the future harsh treatment of Marino, and Captain Wesley Davenport remarks, "You always do fine up to a point, McGee, and then you get a little bit mushy at the edges" (247). Of course, no one can deny that throughout the series MacDonald presents McGee as quick, clever, and courageous. And, he gets jobs or they come to him, gets paid for his effort in some fashion most of the time, and completes his cases usually with a degree of success. Yet, McGee is far from professional in many instances; one example is in the way in which certain cases start. When McGee travels to Esmerelda in *A Purple Place for Dying* (1964) to discuss Mona Fox Yeoman's problem with her, someone kills her shortly after his arrival (15). For a professional, this would end the case; without a client no one will pay him, but McGee stays to investigate her death, and although he earns some money, it is accidental. One can argue that this is a successful pattern in which McGee stirs up trouble and hopes to profit from the confusion. The reward he earns in *Lavender* from recovering $920,000 stolen in a years earlier money-truck robbery comes in a similar fashion (251). However, McGee's actions are only tenuously related to those of a true professional who would have a closer relationship between talents and profit and who would exhibit less personal involvement than

McGee. The recovery of Ingraham's boat in *Silver*, the investigation into how Bix Bowie in *Indigo* presumably spent her last six months of life, and the attempt to find out how Ellis Esterland died in *Crimson* are far more professional than many other cases.

Broadly speaking, *Yellow*, *Turquoise*, and *Cinnamon*, as noted in Chapter Three, start as favors for past or present friends. The three "clients" know McGee's talents and need his help. Gloria Geis in *Yellow* is the most traditional client since her problem stems from the disappearance of Fortner Geis's estate, and although she initially calls on her old friend McGee to find out what happened to the money, she also pays him at the end from the recovered proceeds. In *Turquoise*, Pidge Lewellen Brindle, who had a teenage crush on McGee, wants his advice on whether her husband, Howie, is trying to kill her. McGee volunteers his services to Meyer in *Cinnamon* to track down Norma Greene Lawrence's husband and killer, and McGee's professional skills definitely lead to a successful resolution of the case. However, in all three cases McGee borders on the nonprofessional in regard to the cases' initiations and his compensation. In *Amber*, he operates in both areas even further away from a professional stance. True, the scent of money, noted in Chapter Three, quickly leads him to Vangie's apartment after her death, but what draws him and Meyer into the case is principally a desire to avenge her death even though, paradoxically, parts of her character repulse him (40, 61, 66).

Four other novels, i.e., *Orange*, *Gray*, *Tan*, and especially *Green*, reveal a McGee who employs professional skills but pursues largely nonprofessional aims. *Orange* might seem an unlikely candidate for this group; however, McGee knows that Arthur Wilkinson has been expertly conned, and his perfunctory attempt to recover the money from Cal Stebber supports the inference that he never believed it was possible in the first place. Yet, McGee learns enough to assume that Boone Waxwell has a large portion of the money, and so McGee is able to help Arthur after all by retrieving some of it. And, the pattern of benefiting from the confusion sown repeats itself after McGee implicates Waxwell in the deaths of Crane and Vivian Watts and has most of the law enforcement agencies in southwest Florida looking for Waxwell. In *Gray*, McGee's worries about Tush Bannon lead him to visit Shawana County and discover Bannon's death and the bankrupt boatel business. Although McGee employs both his and Meyer's considerable professional skills, he profits only because of Meyer's secret investment during their attempt to recoup Bannon's losses. Harry Broll's strange behavior in

Tan leads to McGee's investigations, but he involves himself more for the sake of Mary Broll, Harry's wife, than from any professional interest. Indeed, McGee never has a client and has trouble discovering who his adversary is. With Mary and Lisa Dissat dead, McGee has little satisfaction in either the money stumbled on or any sense of punishing, however inadvertently, the guilty Paul Dissat. His spirits only lift when Jeannie Dolan reenters the novel at the end.

Finally, *Green* merits a special focus since it deviates the most from any model of McGee's professional motivations. It is true that McGee calls on most of his long-acquired abilities, from his training as a soldier during the Korean War to his well-honed skills as a con artist, to defeat the Church's would-be killers. However, after Gretel Howard's death, McGee, as noted in Chapter Five, drops out of his normal life and devotes his energies to avenging her murder. McGee alters his appearance and manner of relating to people, involving more than just a disguise with which to con someone. Symbolic of this is his name change to Tom McGraw, a drifter looking for his daughter who he asserts has joined the cult. Thus, the portrait McGee presents in the novel is not that of an objective professional hired to employ his skills for someone else's ends. McGee has other love relationships in the last three novels of the series, but no one so deeply affects him as Gretel with the possible exception of his daughter's appearance in *Silver*, and it is the overwhelming personal involvement in *Green* that emphasizes his nonprofessional aims. In the lower forty-eight states, California is almost as far away as McGee can get from Florida and his life with Gretel, and this distance, along with the above changes, represents the extent that McGee, absorbed in personal revenge, is willing to go.

In *Reading for Survival*, Meyer discourses on the importance of curiosity, memory, thinking, and reading to the development and survival of humans. At one point in speaking of ancient man, Meyer says,

If you control your environment, control your food sources, then you do not have to depend on luck. You depend on hard work and on more learning and remembering and handing down to your children and the younger members of the tribe what you have learned and remembered. (MacDonald 9)

What applies to ancient man also applies to modern man: hard work and continuous effort across generations give man a chance to progress, to build. However, in his portrayal of work in the modern world, MacDonald has made it problematic as to whether man still has the instinct to continue improving his life through diligent application of his mental and physical abilities. Yet, McGee's ability to recover his mental and emotional balance signal some hope that one can make a difference.

Chapter 8

Law, Justice, and Violence

MacDonald's Travis McGee is both a figure off to the side who narrates the action and one through whom, paradoxically, the events come to a conclusion. Understanding this leads to a more systemic approach to the novels rather than an episodic one in which the reader is led from one occurrence to another in McGee's life. Consequently, in addition to well-crafted plots, MacDonald's fiction deals with a variety of concerns which add thematic depth to the mystery and suspense commonly found. Among these concerns, ones broadly defined as legal play an important role. From lawyers to policemen to criminals and their illegal actions to counteractions taken by McGee and others in the name of justice or fairness, MacDonald infuses his novels with ideas and actions that probe the balance of forces in society. Although policemen figure in most of the novels, sometimes prominently, lawyers also appear in roughly half of them. Shady lawyers such as Crane Watts in *Bright Orange for the Shroud* and Tom Collier in *The Turquoise Lament* balance against honest ones like Leonard Sibelius in *The Long Lavender Look* and Ben Gaffner in *The Girl in the Plain Brown Wrapper*. Judge Rufus Wellington in *Pale Gray for Guilt* probably exudes the most potent sense of power even though his particular context is small-town Florida. As for policemen, *Lavender* contains the range from honest to corrupt, reflecting MacDonald's observation that "[i]n respectable suspense fiction one finds good, average and bad cops . . ." ("Introduction and Comment" 64), with Sheriff Norman Hyzer representing the former and Deputies King Sturnevan and Lew Arnstead the latter, bad cops making infrequent appearances in the series. Deputy Sheriff Freddy Hazzard in *Gray* accidentally kills Tush Bannon (195), and McGee thinks of him as being emotionally and sexually unbalanced (209). Throughout, McGee, inspired with his own individual sense of justice, interacts with the various forces of law, revealing or concealing according to his own aims, and creates a pattern through which he resolves or at least brings to a close the difficult moral issues explored.

MacDonald portrays a remarkably stable criminal justice system. In some novels, it does not play a significant role although implied by the modern American setting. Of course, this can mean either the system's weakness or strength given the level of violence in the series: weakness in that it cannot prevent the violence from happening, thus becoming by implication merely reactive, or strength in that the violence appears so minor the police and courts are not extensively required to protect the community or resolve social difficulties. Naturally, this apparent strength could in reality be ignorance and reflect an imperfect system in which criminal elements operate undetected or at least undeterred. For instance, do the authorities know of Frank Sprenger's money operation in *The Scarlet Ruse*, and if so, how do they deal with this knowledge? Some police officials could be accepting money for their silence, a not unknown practice in large American cities. And in *One Fearful Yellow Eye*, what is Ragna's relation, or lack of it, to the Chicago police? It strains credulity that any large, profitable criminal organization could operate unknown to the authorities or at least without its effects percolating through the social system. Possibly by setting *Yellow* in Mayor Daley's Chicago, MacDonald begs the question and expects one to infer some level of corruption.

However, whether weakness or strength, no undue strains threaten to overwhelm the system. Given MacDonald's healthy skepticism about the efficacy of modern American social structures to adapt to changing conditions, this is a puzzling situation. One possible reason is the nature of some of the cases on which McGee agrees to work. In *Nightmare in Pink*, no one realizes there is a further case for the police; Howard Plummer's death appears as a tragic result of a mugging gone bad (19). After he discovers Nina Gibson has $10,000 which she wrongfully believes her fiancé Plummer stole (9), McGee talks with Robert Imber, who worked with Plummer at Armister's headquarters, and asks him if anyone could have siphoned off money from their operation. Imber is suitably shocked and says no (22-23). Subsequently, someone breaks into Nina's apartment (49), and McGee seriously begins to speculate that something is amiss and that Armister's is a good place to look (33-34, 51). When McGee talks with Sergeant T. Rassko, the policeman who investigated Plummer's death, he meets with resistance and an explanation of the process by which the detectives place priorities on their cases. Since new cases constantly arrive on their desks, only the most probable candidates for success receive their continued attention (20-21). In effect, by shifting their cases from active to inactive, they create a bureaucratic symmetry, and if a case does not receive outside pressure or extensive publicity or if the percentage of unsolved cases does not grow too large, the police maintain an image of a stable investigative system preserving an aura of control. Ironically, McGee appears to accept Dr. Varn's explanation that Plummer "'was actually mugged'" (104).

Since not all of McGee's cases come to the attention of the police, hidden crime thus symbolically flourishes, and this might be a proper inference MacDonald wishes one to draw. This is no indictment of the criminal justice system but rather an admission of the contextual forces of human experience versus what David Jeffrey terms "abstract and bloodless principles" (80). In The Quick Red Fox, Lysa Dean has important reasons for her decision to hire McGee to retrieve the photos of her in a California orgy. As a film star, growing older and somewhat temperamental, Lysa cannot afford the publicity. Also, she hopes to marry a wealthy man, one who would take a very dim view of such activity (23). Ultimately, the case involves not only the blackmail of Lysa but also several murders. The police naturally handle the latter but only deal at the end with the apprehension of Samuel Bogen, who initiated the second round of blackmail (105-06). When McGee talks with Sergeant Bill Starr, Santa Rosita police, he lies about his client's identity and generally misleads him (104-07). McGee suggests a way for Herm Louker, Lysa's security adviser, to obtain the photos of Lysa that Bogen possesses before the police can find them (152-53). Thus, private decisions circumvent the criminal justice system's ability to clarify Ulka M'Gruder's murders and link them to the blackmail scheme. The system has not so much failed as been rendered ineffective by the citizens' recourse to other means in resolving the conflict.

Pressure to solve all crimes might place great stress on the criminal justice system. In fact, the police might be singularly maladapted to find some perpetrators. If McGee and Meyer in Darker than Amber had gone to the police with Vangie's story after her death, the likely outcome would have been to alert Griff and his associates. Police arriving at Vangie's apartment instead of McGee, with Griff's living next door, would probably have cut off the connection to Griff and the latter's knowledge of the whereabouts of Ans and Del on the Monica D. It is unlikely that without Del's confession the murder ring would have been so thoroughly penetrated. Much as in the case of Bogen in Red, the police come in at selected points, their strengths and assets not unnecessarily challenged. But if one might argue that so many deaths and people involved as in *Amber* would ultimately lead the police to the ring or one of its members to the police, what police authority would have tracked down and served justice on Cody T.W. Pittler in *Cinnamon Skin*? McGee discovers the murder of Norma Greene Lawrence, Meyer's niece, discussed in Chapter Two, purely by accident when someone sends him photos of the *John Maynard Keynes* immediately before the explosion. As in the somewhat similar circumstances in *Pink*, no one knows a crime has been committed prior to McGee's reception of the photos, and like *Red*, powerful motives determine the course of the action. For, Meyer both deals with the grief over losing his "'very last blood relative'" (*Cinnamon* 16) and, as noted in Chapter Two, his deep sense of betraying his friend Travis in *Free Fall in Crimson* when he let Grizzel use him to gain access to the *Busted Flush* and McGee. Local criminal investigations do expand with sufficient warranty, but a brief consideration of McGee and Meyer's investigation raises a doubt as to whether this would have happened in Norma's case. After reviewing Pittler-Lawrence's remarks some days before the explosion, McGee and Meyer contact Pittler's previous employers. Even though he used different names, they feel their description of him matches the man who left a murder trail through Texas (and elsewhere as they learn at the end of the novel [*Cinnamon* 265]). Even more precarious is their tracing him, through a picture in a college yearbook, to his Texas hometown. From there, they contact his sister in New York State and learn of a woman with whom Pittler corresponds. Using this information and statements Pittler made to them about his career as a condominium salesman in Cancun, they finally locate and kill him in Mexico. Local, national, and international authorities would have had to combine in an effort which strains credulity. Thus, MacDonald once again presumes the image of a stable criminal justice system by not asking it to do the impossible. The answer to Pittler's violence is an extra-legal violence which serves the ends of justice and produces no false regret in those who resort to it.

No criminal justice system exists in the abstract. The interaction between its officials, e.g., lawyers, judges, and police, and powerful outside influences produces a reciprocity of uses none of which are necessarily for the good of the community as a whole. In *A Purple Place for Dying*, Jass Yeoman's accompanying Sheriff Fred Buckelberry to McGee's motel the night of Mona's murder underscores MacDonald's understanding of these symbiotic relationships. After Buckelberry initially questions McGee, Yeoman dismisses the sheriff so that he and McGee can talk. The novel clearly demonstrates Yeoman's dominant position, along with several other powerful men, in the city of Esmerelda and consequently Buckelberry's seeming subservience to them. Although Buckelberry's future ambitions somewhat control his actions, his position relative to Yeoman is not only personal. MacDonald seems to pose the following question: Within unnamed limits, how could Buckelberry not do what he is asked? The sheriff is part of the system and does not have a place to stand outside the system. Walter Ruppert's cooperation in *Purple* with the IRS is, of course, the reverse of the local system's functioning. Rather than the powerful controlling the system, the system controls the powerful, albeit a local man in Ruppert's case. Buckelberry's reaction to outside pressure is to attempt to restrict McGee's movements and investigations. Only the latter's assertion that a murder has occurred provokes the police to assume the responsibility for the direction of the case.

In addition to McGee and Meyer's con operation discussed in Chapter Three, *Gray* presents a split-screen image of powerful forces, national and local, manipulating the official system, though one group is so bound up with the system that disentangling it proves impossible. To begin with, Gary Santo, through his interest in acquiring a large parcel of land in Shawana County, Florida, to sell to Calitron (92), sets local lawyer Preston LaFrance in motion. Although based in Florida also, Santo's type of influence could operate from anywhere. His impersonal relationship to the dynamics of the Calitron land purchase resembles Brother Titus's actions against Gretel Howard in *The Green Ripper*, and while not as deadly or destructive, it demonstrates MacDonald's awareness of business currents that recognize few restrictions. In analyzing the local situation, it might be most useful to begin with the effects on Tush and Janine Bannon's boat business. Tech-Tex Applications gets the county to close the bridge and road near Bannon's business (19). After Bannon meets with County Commissioner P.K. "Monk" Hazzard, the county suspends the Bannons' license to do business. In addition, the local bank will not extend a loan and thus, the intended result, the Bannons' business folds (24-27). LaFrance will profit if the scheme continues to develop in the expected way and so will Whitt Sanders through his bank's relationship to the power structure, both official and unofficial. Commissioner Hazzard is the final link in the plan to sell the entire parcel of land to Calitron. He expects to win both privately (through his family connection to LaFrance [24]) and publicly since the tax revenue and new jobs will benefit the county and his image as one of its leaders. After McGee discovers that Tush Bannon has died under suspicious circumstances, he investigates and runs into the Sunnydale power structure. The Byzantine convolutions of this small Florida town undergoing the stresses of development, a theme used in *Brown* and *The Empty Copper Sea*, offer themselves as a paradigm for the phrase "local corruption." Judge Rufus Wellington, Janine Bannon's lawyer in *Gray*, explains:

These little counties all got what you could call a shadow government. These folks have known each other for generations. They got to putting this land deal together, and there is a little business right in the way and doing pretty good. Expanding. So they use the county government to stunt that business and knock it down to where the price is right. It doesn't take all five county commissioners. Just a couple, plus the other three needing favors themselves sometime, with no need of anybody asking too many questions. (59)

Judge Wellington's analysis echoes Elmo Bliss's similar statements in *A Flash of Green* in which Jimmy Wing prevents Bliss's successful development of a bay fill project. Without McGee's and Meyer's aid to Janine, Tush's death and the local power structure's machinations would have gone unchallenged.

Carlos Menterez in *A Deadly Shade of Gold* and Calvin Stebber in *Orange* represent a different attitude toward the system as prey than does Yeoman in *Purple*. Both of the former men attempt to manipulate the system in question for their benefit rather than dominate its representatives. Of course, Menterez openly profited in Batista's Cuba from his position of wealth and power. However, the revolution forced him into exile in Mexico, and there his money buys silence and tolerance. Menterez might be seen merely as a refugee, and probably few countries would wish to send anyone back to the Castroite dictatorship, but he needs protection for his notorious behavior during Batista's rule. Sam Taggart's murder results from his part in preventing an assassination attempt on Menterez. After his stroke, Menterez's assets fall to Cuban associates in Mexico City according to Almah Hichin, and the last thread to Menterez's shadowy protectors is followed by Colonel Marquez when McGee alerts him to other Menterez assets vulnerable to the looters (201). Although MacDonald does not produce the Mexican government officials involved with Menterez, he implies a realm of influence open to penetration by the Menterezes of the world who thus internationalize the privatization of social systems.

Calvin Stebber functions more subtly than others in the series, as one might expect since he is a con operator. The executor for the Kippler tract and Crane Watts, a Florida lawyer, serve Stebber's ends (*Orange* 75). Both men play official roles, one through his estate responsibilities and the other through his position as an officer of the court. Stebber has pulled at the outlying threads of the system where there is little oversight and much dependence on the trustworthiness of those involved. Added to the weakness is the profitability if successful. Since Stebber relies very little on violence (Waxwell acts largely on his own), MacDonald posits a system that has deeply buried flaws which do not necessarily react to counterbalancing forces. Yeoman and even Menterez live overt lives in contrast to Stebber's more covert life, and though police may know a crime has been committed by someone at some time, they may never trace the illegal actions to their sources. Of course, con operators are not the only ones who succeed in this way, and even overt corrupters of public order may escape punishment. Stebber's threat, however, lies in its cleverness and the potential for an even greater diversion of public funds and trust than more public predators.

While MacDonald's fiction offers many examples of the powerful using the established order for their own ends, fewer examples occur of the reverse process. Seen in a positive light, this could be the result of a democratically structured government within which officials have relatively little room to operate. However, as S.H. Jackson observes about *Lavender*, this does not restrict the larger society: ". . . MacDonald places the detective hero in a social atmosphere riddled with an unsettling, confusing brutality" (8). Notwithstanding the skillfulness with which some officials do operate, MacDonald appears to imply that they are, at most, a constrained threat. *Lavender* reveals one reason for this: a corrupt official opposed by an honest one. Aside from Deputy King Sturnevan's attempt to kill McGee at the end of the novel, Sheriff Norm Hyzer also has to deal with Deputy Lew Arnstead's beating of Meyer soon after the latter's incarceration. Hyzer does not shut down Arnstead's prostitution ring, but he does fire Arnstead after the violence done to Meyer (56). Initially outraged, McGee reluctantly admits Hyzer's "thoroughness" (27, 30-31, 64). While recognizing his flaws, Etta C. Abrahams sees Hyzer as a policeman "who tries to carry out his job in a clean and honest way" ("Cops" 98).

A far more insidious instance of official corruption and intimidation occurs in *Brown*. Through his duties, Deputy Dave Broon collects information on private citizens and uses it to blackmail them. However, Broon's success expands because he works with Tom Pike, a man with neither conscience nor government authority. Pike's contacts in the business and professional community and his allure for investors give Broon a much wider scope than his petty blackmail schemes offer. In contrast to the implied systemic weaknesses, MacDonald hems Broon in with two honest officials. McGee works with Detective Al Stanger who has observed Broon's suspicious activity but has found no way to attack him. And, Detective Stanger leads McGee to state attorney Ben Gaffner, a man who radiates honesty. Officials may fail to act or uncover crimes, but when they turn corrupt, systemic forces can limit their depredations. MacDonald does not suffer from a foolish optimism nor does he ignore government corruption, witness Elmo Bliss in *A Flash of Green*, Justin Denniver in *Condominium*, and Wilbur Barley in *Barrier Island*, the latter two novels written near the end of the Travis McGee series, but he does appear to think that in America those outside government have a wider scope for their illegal talents than those within.

Aside from inadequate investigation of some crimes (at least in hindsight) and ignorance that crimes have been committed, MacDonald also dramatizes the system's inability to control violence even when the authorities know who commits it. *Crimson* presents two instances of this bizarre situation, one more controllable than the other. Attempting to find out who killed Ellis Esterland, McGee goes to an army friend from the Korean war. Paralyzed from his war injuries, Ted Blaylock now runs a combination motorcycle repair shop, cafe, and tattoo parlor. Blaylock is knowledgeable about motorcycle gangs and is even under the "protection" of the Fantasies (129). McGee asks Blaylock to enquire about any unusual exploits concerning motorcycle gang members. Through this contact, McGee learns that Dirty Bob and the Senator rode across the country in fifty hours over a year ago. McGee ties this in with what he knows of Peter Kesner's motorcycle movies and this leads to Esterland's killer, Grizzel. While the police in Citrus City do not know who killed Esterland and have stopped actively investigating, Lieutenant Goodbread, a Miami policeman, informs McGee that Preach and Magoo, another set of motorcycle gang members, are under suspicion for drug dealing and other illegal activities but remain free (151-53). Similarly to Jornalero and his associates in *The Lonely Silver Rain* and Frank Sprenger and his mafia bosses in *Scarlet*, Preach and his partner stay out of jail, but MacDonald does not state or imply that they pay someone for protection or are in imminent danger of arrest. In contrast, the police in Iowa, after the apparent suicides of Karen Hatcher and James Revere, allow the town to invade Kesner's movie set where Grizzel and Linda Harrigan have established a pornographic film sideline which uses force on the reluctant or unwilling (195). Several people die from the riot although Grizzel escapes. Apparently sympathetic, the police stand and watch while the townspeople chase down and kill some of the outsiders (226-28). The Iowan incident reveals a culture, however temporary, in which there is no appeal since the authorities have acknowledged the mob's legitimate right to decide guilt or innocence without recourse to the law.

When McGee informs Jornalero in *Silver* that Marino killed the Peruvian girl (181-82), thus starting an internecine crime war, the police play no significant role aside from their nominal investigations. MacDonald does not dwell on the police effort or lack of it to stop the murders, but the impression is that they could not stop them if they wanted to. The carnage continues until it runs its course. The image MacDonald creates is of at least two societies existing side by side—the larger society and the organized-crime society. For the most part, the latter obeys the laws of the larger society, possibly even better than some elements of that admittedly unwieldy construct that includes everything outside the crime organizations. However, when the latter, for some internal reason, go on a rampage of self-extermination, no state power exists to stop it even though the police may know most of the participants if not exactly who does what. Of course, a concomitant image is the relative stability of the larger society while this happens. MacDonald implies neither moral nor social fragmentation from the gory elimination of so many people but rather the outer limits of state power and control. Certainly, no official can announce a lack of concern over the killings (although DEA Agent Browder privately says something to that effect to McGee [*Silver* 208]), but the murders can continue with some degree of toleration. Contrast this with the reaction to Dr. Varn's experiments in *Pink* once McGee escapes from Toll Valley Hospital. If they had known of Dr. Varn's activities before McGee's disruption and exposure of them, no government official would have tolerated what Varn did unless somehow corrupted. The examples from *Silver* and *Pink* stress the gaps in the criminal justice system which belie any model that claims personal rather than systemic reasons for the continued existence of violence. People fail ethically, but they also fail in an ability to construct rational systems of order that can contain human diversity.

Orange presents an example of these gaps, although on a much smaller scale than in novels like *Crimson, Silver,* and *Pink.* Aside from his role in Calvin Stebber's organization, Boone Waxwell has another life that has existed for years. When McGee arrives in Goodland and asks the way to Waxwell's shack, an old man warns him of Waxwell's reputation, especially how he fights. The old man's picture of Waxwell is of a large predator roaming his hunting area in near-perfect freedom from any outside control (88). After the predicted fight, McGee goes into Boone's house:

I looked in the door of the tiny bedroom. The double bed was a rumpled tangle of soiled sheets marked in a leopard pattern. They looked like silk. The pattern seemed apt. The bedroom had the pungent odors of a predator's cage, a cell for the cat carnivore. (95)

McGee learns of Waxwell's powerful attraction to and for women and the inability of some of them to stay away from him regardless of the consequences. Waxwell has an affair with one woman and severely beats her husband when he has the temerity to object. Boone tells McGee, "'He got such a strong memory of it, I even say hello to him, his chin gets all spitty'" (93). In addition, Boone has moved from the wife to her daughter, Cindy, who is equally attracted to him; she is still in high school, and when McGee wonders about her youth, Boone replies, "'The man says they big enough, they old enough'" (93). Cindy even tells McGee that Waxwell is quite capable of killing someone and throwing them into the nearby swamp for the alligators to feed on (136-37). On this first visit Waxwell claims that he has done that before and threatens to do the same to McGee (94). Waxwell later states that he put Wilma Ferner, Arthur Wilkinson's ex-wife, "'up the Chatham River, boy, down in the deep end of Chevelier Bay, her and her pretties sunk down with cement block, wired real good'" (180). Although the police intermittently involve themselves in Waxwell's affairs, he lives in the gaps in the criminal justice system where there is no meaningful law enforcement. Only when McGee frames Waxwell for the murders of Vivian and Crane Watts, a fairly prominent couple in Naples, do the police focus on him as a social threat. David A. Benjamin uses Vivian Watts to illustrate the following probable reaction to those innocents caught in the gap:

Often we meet them first after they have already been victimized, and are fully aware of how much they have suffered, and how cruel and destructive any further suffering would be. We are therefore almost as psychologically vulnerable as they are themselves to the idea of further pain, and we cringe when such violence recurs. (31)

For Vivian, Waxwell inflicts the penultimate violence in her life, and she prevents any future victimization from him by killing herself and her husband.

Whether or not McGee in general acts as a just man or even as a law-abiding citizen is a problematic issue in the series. Thomas Doulis calls him "an articulate, witty strong man who operates in the morally gray area of the law" (41). From *The Deep Blue Good-by* to *Silver*, McGee consults with or calls on the police for help, and they generally view him as on their side, admittedly sometimes with reluctance. After McGee and Patty Devlan burst into the party at the Bearpath Motel in *Blue*, the people present and later the authorities accept McGee's version of Allen's actions (226, 244). However, a Rhadamanthine weighing of the motives and actions of all the participants might hesitate fully to clear McGee. After all, McGee steals from a stealer who stole from Sergeant Berry's family, and Berry illegally acquired the gems in question. Aside from the question as to whether or not Berry's actions should have been illegal, McGee appears to ground his position in the idea that the end justifies the means. Initially, McGee, whom John Cawelti terms a "master of violence" (70), intends to rob Allen with a minimal level of violence. Later, knowing that Allen still has Lois Atkinson on board, McGee pursues him with no limits on the violence he might employ. Even with the gruesome image of his impalement on the anchor McGee throws at him, few people would have sympathy for Allen the predator, and possibly McGee's actions are the inevitable result of those gaps in the legal system that allow Allen to operate. However, the necessity for McGee rather than the police to stop Allen calls into question the ability of the system to create an environment in which the law upholds the ends of justice. John Wiley Nelson notes the limitations of McGee's role:

Although these activities may in fact restore the *social* balance, McGee does not believe that society itself can be redeemed. There is no "answer," no final resolution for the whole, for the social world. McGee's destruction of evil may benefit society, but he intends to bring justice or satisfaction only to some particular individual. (186)

Only society's assumption of this responsibility will ensure a general benefit from the removal of particular evils.

The vigilante methods employed by McGee are especially clear in *Turquoise*. Pidge Brindle commits a foolish act in going to Pago Pago with Howie, but sooner or later McGee must confront him. Howie, the amoral killer, has slipped through the chinks in the legal justice system without even being suspected of committing a crime. McGee's investigations, stemming initially from the altered photographs and Pidge's fears about Howie, lead him to examine Howie's past and thus uncover a gruesome trail of probable murders. However, it is highly unlikely that any of this could be proved, and McGee goes to Pago Pago as a private citizen. One might argue that a higher justice accompanies him, but the criminal justice system is generally loath to accept such an argument. The scene by the pool, discussed in Chapter Four, when McGee surprises Howie with his sudden appearance and the revelation that he knows about the latter's past is especially important for what is absent (239-40). McGee has brought neither local police nor American consular officials; he is alone. In addition, he does not attempt to think out what he might do to stop Howie nor to think of him, as George S. Peek observes about man in contrast to nature, as "one who cannot be predicted or seen correctly" ("Beast Imagery" 94). This strongly implies that McGee's intentions are open-ended and without limits, including killing Howie. As Joseph Marotta notes concerning McGee's actions in *Green*, "McGee turns out to be as much a promoter of violence as he is a preserver of order" (108). Howie probably deserves to die even more than Allen, but should McGee be the one to cause his death? In the end, Howie dies accidentally by falling from the cables into the harbor (252). But, this merely suspends McGee's role as an ultimate avenger in the series. The questions MacDonald raises about the relationship between law, justice, and violence continue to appear.

In *Green*, according to Rick Lott "his darkest novel" (14), MacDonald poses the questions in their most extreme forms. McGee and Meyer learn that the federal government has the cult under investigation. Whatever his sense of loss over Gretel's death,

McGee could allow the system to continue to function and, possibly, succeed in stamping out the cult. However, McGee will not wait for this, and the authorities, bound by rules, appear too tentative to stop the organization. Consequently, private impatience and systemic process clash with no mediating forces apparent, an example of the "sense of dissolution" Marotta finds in the novel (106). McGee's choice of the Ukiah camp for his attack on the cult does not lie in any belief that its members actually killed Gretel. Rather, they are, paradoxically, the nearest face to strike since she went there years before, and the government's relationship to McGee's purposed violence shows the problematic nature of the criminal justice system's ability to stand between the citizens, diverting their wrath into legal processes that substitute for violence if they do not lead to complete healing. After the killing is over, government agents collect McGee and the dead bodies, concealing from the local authorities all traces as to what happened (269-70). The system thus is sucked into McGee's private desire for revenge, hierarchically subsumed under his dominant action. Cleaning up after the battle is the clearest image of the legal system's ineffectual ability to play its proper role. Max, one of the government agents, tells McGee that they did not previously shut down the camp because "'We're understaffed'" (269). Logically, McGee's career has prepared him to kill the cult members, suffer from Gretel's death and the killings, and recover at the end of the novel. In McGee's doing so, MacDonald emphasizes that neither the adjudication nor the definition of justice lies, in reality, within the sole purview of the state. Without the state at least satisfactorily performing the first function, private actions and decisions widen the system's gaps and allow such violent resolutions as also occur in *Silver* when McGee goes to Jornalero with his knowledge of Marino, Jr.'s actions.

MacDonald's dramatization of the inter-locked themes of law, justice, and violence leads, like all good art, to no simplistic answers. The Travis McGee series is both an imitation and intensification of the real world, and MacDonald's characterization of McGee brings recognition and uneasiness. The author's exploration of these gray areas of human conduct with the flawed Travis McGee as his protagonist, a McGee, as Larry Grimes observes, "pulled apart from the formula [as salvage consultant] and tossed more and more into the profane world [of adventure] outside it" (107), reminds one of the sustained fragility of human institutions and their continuing formations in the eyes of their beholders. G.K. Chesterton's observation that ". . . the whole noiseless and unnoticeable police management by which we are ruled and protected is only a successful knight-errantry" (6) is echoed in MacDonald's frequent depiction of McGee as a knight-errant, both authors raising the question of effectiveness in combating crime. McGee, beholder and actor along with the rest of the world, shares the sense of the unknown direction of his society and the responsibility, however paradoxical, to give it the needed direction, leaving one with an example of MacDonald's almost cosmic idea of irony.

Chapter 9

In Sickness and in Health:
The Role of Medicine

Medical images, ideas, and analogies abound in the series. Health and sickness thus intertwine in the characters' physical, mental, and emotional states, affecting the action to a significant degree in most novels. Referring to thirteen women in thirteen of the first seventeen novels, Peggy Moran comments that "Each of these women, to an extent evoking a greater or lesser degree of sympathy, is a victim" (82). Assessments by one character of another's health lead to choices, judgments, and warnings. Although still somewhat enamored of Junior Allen, Cathy Kerr in *The Deep Blue Good-by* judges him mentally ill (172-73). Cathy's decision grows from intimate, certain knowledge of his actions in personal situations in which she lost important areas of her self-esteem. As Mary K. Jackman writes, "The specter of Junior Allen, masculine oppression and sadism taken beyond the limits of being human, comes to the reader within the feminine narratives of Cathy and Lois" (45). However, Cathy's statements to McGee have no flavor of distortion prompted by revenge. McGee's immediate help of Lois Atkinson in the same novel receives the approval of Dr. Ramirez, the physician he quickly calls after meeting Lois and realizing her weakened condition (*Blue* 63-65). Though he makes numerous references to individuals and health, MacDonald's focus is not solely on them. Sometimes the sickness of an individual infects a larger segment of a society as is the case with Lilo Perris in *The Long Lavender Look*. Paralleling and interacting with her, Deputy Lew Arnstead's drug-induced psychic imbalance destroys additional lives. Furthermore, MacDonald's use of doctors, nurses, and hospitals in the series represents his view of a society both sick and coping. While he occasionally includes the likes of a Dr. Varn (*Nightmare in Pink*), he counters him with a Dr. Geis (*One Fearful Yellow Eye*) and the nurses who minister to Mike Gibson in *Pink*. Hospitals are places of death and recovery, corruption and ethics, but surprisingly, MacDonald leans, on balance, towards a positive view of the medical profession. Although McGee sometimes provokes a "health" crisis, witness his speculations in *A Deadly Shade of Gold* about the possible future emotional weakness of Almah Hichin after he has terrorized her (174-75), MacDonald strategically places McGee as an observer and critic of a society in need of healing but which unevenly moves toward that goal.

Travis McGee is central to understanding MacDonald's examples of individuals' judging the health of one another, mutually assessing each other's strengths and weaknesses, and not always disinterestedly. McGee thus lies at the heart of MacDonald's ambiguous characterizations of human nature. In *Blue*, McGee responds in the only possible way to Lois Atkinson's obvious state of debilitation, and he expends time and energy in caring for her. Dr. Ramirez even trusts him to nurse her back to health (65). McGee also consults him as to whether he should take her back to his boat, but given all of McGee's proper attitudes and self-designation as "'Mother McGee'" (66), Lois does wind up in McGee's bed aboard the *Flush*. MacDonald does not describe their sexual relationship as exploitation, but in this episode and in many others, McGee's reasons are open to question. In *A Purple Place for Dying*, Dr. Kuppler, the hotel doctor McGee calls in after Isobel Webb attempts suicide in his room, trusts McGee to look after her and not prey on her (115, 117). Again, McGee spends time and energy on a fellow human being, and they eventually become lovers. David Geherin states that "McGee . . . nurses her back to consciousness, then ministers to her psyche, gradually restoring her self-confidence and sense of self-worth" (56). While McGee is sometimes no more than an equal participant or even occasionally the pursued, the above two episodes are crucial since he presents himself as either an implied (*Blue*) or direct (*Purple*) conduit to greater physical and emotional health. One might well say to him, "Physician, heal thyself."

One question that arises is, Are there any instances in the series of sacrificial giving that either temporarily or permanently lead to a physical or emotional healing? After the death of Lois Atkinson in *Blue*, Cathy Kerr tentatively offers herself to McGee if it will comfort him (250-51). Carol Cleveland calls her "that sweet, rather dumb woman whose resources of dignity and courage are inexhaustible" (410). Attitudes toward sexuality in American society make this a much more plausibly disinterested offer than in the several instances in which McGee does the same. Any possible pleasure that Cathy will receive, and it is important to remember descriptions of her and

Junior Allen's lovemaking (44-45), is subsumed under the gift. A similar pose by McGee raises suspicions in a society that sees male sexuality from a pleasure-getting rather than pleasure-giving perspective. For a symbolic reversal of this, MacDonald goes outside this culture to Mexico in *Dress Her in Indigo* and uses Enelio Fuentes as an intermediary between Elana and Margarita del Vega and McGee and Meyer, respectively, to convince the men that they will give physical and psychological benefit by sleeping with them (149). Not surprisingly, McGee often helps women either before or after a sexual relationship. However, he does have moments when he has nothing to gain and sensing the hurt and vulnerability of a fellow human, reaches out to help with no expectation of reward. Karen Vander Ven notes that "he [is] extremely caring for various individuals" and that he "has an incredible ability to understand how others feel" (37). In *The Quick Red Fox*, McGee lies to Jocelyn Ives about her father's activities, activities which McGee claims led to an honorable death in service to his country but which McGee is not at liberty to discuss (101). From what he knows, the woman's life was closely bound up with her father's, and even though his statements continue to allow her to live in a state of illusion regarding her blackmailing father, McGee apparently sees no emotional benefit to her in the truth. Since he does not plan to stay and help her and given her obvious isolation, he rightly sees that her image of her father is all that remains.

McGee functions in the above instance as a therapist, albeit in a limited fashion, and continues in a similar vein in *Bright Orange for the Shroud* with both Arthur Wilkinson and Vivian Watts. Not a convinced altruist, McGee reluctantly agrees to Wilkinson's request for help; however, he shifts some of the responsibility onto Chookie McCall. Nevertheless, McGee recognizes the man's physical and emotional problems and cannot avoid a sense of obligation where none, for him above all others, exists. He crosses a similar boundary with Vivian for whom he provides emotional aid. From her, McGee expects only a phone call to Boone Waxwell to lure him away from his cabin; part of McGee's motivation in helping her springs from an admiration of her courage and loyalty (139-42). Admittedly, the help he gives to Jocelyn and Vivian requires little effort unless one reflects on the ways a predator or someone indifferent to the sufferings of others would view them. Then, it is clear that what matters almost as much as the practical aid is the willing heart, the orientation to succor rather than use another. MacDonald's use of the knight motif comes more clearly into focus in these examples of nonexploitative help. While McGee cannot completely trust himself to live out this pattern, he does occasionally, even with a sense of wonder, experience it. When in *The Empty Copper Sea* he does not awaken the injured Gretel Howard recovering in the hospital from her brother John Tuckerman's attack on her, McGee wonders, "I had thought of her . . . instead of my own dramas and concerns. Could I possibly be growing up? After so long?" (245). Not only does he thus contribute to Gretel's health but also to his own through an exercise of maturity and compassion from which he gains nothing but an increase in self-esteem.

In another instance, McGee recognizes a friend's psychological and emotional needs and does something to help. Near the end of *Pale Gray for Guilt*, McGee takes Janine Bannon on a cruise. Janine comments that McGee does not see her as sexual prey and attempt to comfort her physically (213). Tush, her husband, was one of McGee's close friends, and McGee's actions, even though he has formerly realized her reservations about him, reveal someone capable of making a gesture that eases another's hurt when she is in that gap between a generally healthy emotional balance and its opposite. As the many examples in the series show, professional medical care does not answer all exigencies. McGee does not plan to play an important role in her or her children's lives. His gesture merely eases her hurt and says more about his ability to offer kindness than the magnitude of the aid.

Those individuals who harm others and society are not always completely to blame for their condition or actions. Unmentioned in several of MacDonald's works is the effect of illegitimacy on some young women and their relationships with their fathers. Dolores Estobar in *Purple* encourages her half-brothers, Pablo and Carlos, to kill Mona Fox Yeoman; indirectly causes the death of those same young men; and poisons Jass Yeoman, her father (152-53). At one point while McGee attempts to discover any reason in Jass's past why someone would kill Mona, his young wife, Jass says that when he and Cube Fox, Mona's father, were young "'Cube was plain death on Mex gals'" (119) and that he was not reluctant either (119-20). After Jass's death, Sheriff Buckelberry tells McGee about a woman named Amparo in Burned Wells, a village near Esmerelda (130), who was one of Jass's lovers, and McGee learns that she is Dolores's mother (134). Jass hired his daughter as a household servant and, she later reveals, raped her while he was drunk (152). Other than her statement that she loved him as a father (152),

MacDonald does not explore her possible anger at her position in the house, as well as the rape, which results in Mona's death. Mona remarks early in the novel that she is close to Dolores (14). Admittedly, rape can destabilize one (see the discussion of this episode in Chapter Four), but the callous murder of Mona bespeaks a consuming desire for revenge, for an equalizing of the imbalances in Dolores's life. Critics must be cautious where the author does not elaborate, but the ingredients of race, class, and sex do explode and project her "illness" over everyone with whom she comes in contact. It takes very little for McGee to ignite the explosion, and Dolores's passionate rage as she confesses her conduct shows someone more in dialogue with her still unexorcized demons than with the outside world.

Lilo Perris in *Lavender* is a somewhat parallel character to Dolores Estobar. In question is the source of her exuberant sense of violence and the pleasure she takes in hurting others. Lilo appears to have an almost unlimited capacity for betrayal and displays little anxiety in even the most seemingly desperate situations. When McGee comes to her trailer near the end of the novel, he manages to subdue her, but even tied up, Lilo directs her mind and body to changing her situation. Her clearly directed will is as awesome as her physical strength. McGee, 6'4" and over 200 pounds, is glad of the strong tape that secures the muscular young woman. Of course, something about her sets up this implied unease in his ability otherwise to handle her. Henry Perris, her stepfather and lover, when he learns that McGee has tied her up, says, "'Tied and gagged, eh? . . . That would take some doing. That I would like to see. I really would'" (211). Lilo stirs almost primeval fears and caution. Is she someone with a deeply suppressed anger at Sheriff Norm Hyzer, the absent father who lives a respectable life that involves no public acknowledgment of her, or is she, as suggested in Chapter Seven, a figure of uncaused evil? Other possibilities than ones revolving around her parentage might account for her conduct. However, MacDonald is silent on the origins but not on the effects of her essential nature as he clearly portrays the devastation she causes.

Not to blame or hold responsible individuals who spread violence or evil through their societies is not to accept, tolerate, or forgive their actions. Determining their mental health or lack of it is difficult in the cases of Dolores and Lilo, absent any professional diagnosis. However, one can see their acts of terror and trace them back to their sources and realize that something unusual occurs in the psyches of those who perpetrate them. Occasionally, a character will make a statement at which even a layman will pause. Paul Dissat in *A Tan and Sandy Silence*, after killing Mary Broll, his cousin Lisa Dissat, Harry Broll, and attempting to kill McGee and Meyer, reveals the satisfaction these violent actions give him. Since he has acquired enough money to retire, he plans to venture out into the world as an unknown pleasurer at the expense of those too vulnerable to protect themselves from him (235). He speaks feelingly of those moments when he tortured Mary, Harry, and Lisa (189-90, 235, 237-38). Dissat's remote attitude toward obscene indignities, his amoral speculations about the proper technique to indulge his pleasure in another's pain would short-circuit prolonged discussions about what to do with him. A probable communal response would be, Lock him up; we'll figure out what to do with him later. As with Lilo, MacDonald does not trace out the formative influences that have shaped Dissat, and like her, one chooses either unrevealed past experiences that have produced this sickness or an uncaused evil, a possibility that MacDonald does not dismiss ("Introduction and Comment" 69).

MacDonald presents Desmin Grizzel in *Free Fall in Crimson* as both mentally (270, 273) and physically sick (277). When McGee first hears of him, Grizzel has killed Ellis Esterland, a man already dying from cancer (217, 277). When last seen on the *Flush*, Grizzel, also dying from cancer, attempts to kill McGee and Meyer (277). In the interim, he has killed, at the very least, Curley Hanner, aka the Senator; Joya Murphy-Wheeler; Jean Norman; and Lysa Dean and her servants (267, 277-78). One is tempted to see Grizzel's cancer as an outer manifestation of his inner illness. After Esterland, he murders those whom he perceives as responsible for Peter Kesner's death, the man who raised him from the obscurity of his outlaw biker days. Grizzel tells McGee that he has methodically tracked down those whom he has murdered and has taken great pleasure in killing them. He is especially proud of the rape-murder of Lysa Dean, the movie actress:

"Wish I had time to tell you about the snuff job on that movie-queen pal of yours. Would have made a great tape, Ace." He motioned toward his crotch with his free hand. "Old King Henry here hasn't lost an ounce, and he can go as good as he ever did." (278)

As in the case of Dolores, Lilo, and Paul Dissat, MacDonald does not use any professional medical diagnosis to decide Grizzel's mental illness and thus possibly separate him from the consequences of his actions but rather uses the enormity of his crimes and his attitude toward them to do this. And, through the healthy responses of McGee and Meyer, MacDonald contrasts the "normal" world's reactions to those of Grizzel who while he cannot be cured in any sense can be excised and thus protect society by his death. Donnie and Gavin, the criminal types sent by Preach to help McGee when Grizzel comes (271, 273), symbolize with Grizzel two pathological aspects of society warring against one another and leading to a minimally healthier social climate.

While one character assesses and cares for another and while other characters spread contagion and violence nearly unchecked, what role does the medical profession play in either healing people or containing and limiting the effects of illness? At best, it plays a marginal role in these novels. It is not that MacDonald substitutes other groups or other remedies to create images of health. Largely, the professionals can only contain where they do not harm. Exceptions do occur. Dr. Fortner Geis in *Yellow* and the physicians and nurses who worked for him, especially Janice Stanyard, relieved suffering. McGee relates that Geis had a highly successful career before he died (17). After Waxwell shoots McGee in *Orange* and leaves him for dead, McGee crawls back toward his car and the waiting Arthur Wilkinson who eventually comes seeking him (151). McGee has Wilkinson take him to a hospital for emergency aid. While there, several car accident victims are being worked on and require help even more urgently than McGee. The air of desperation as the doctors and nurses try to cope with the victims underscores MacDonald's use of them as little more than movable band-aids rushing from one emergency to another but never fully able to handle the people who need their care. The harried doctor who briefly tends to McGee reveals not only the specific conditions that night but also the tensions under which they operate (154). And, when McGee decides to leave, he merely walks out of that porous environment (157). In *Red*, Stan Burley, with no clear indication of medical training but some psychotherapeutic knowledge, runs an alcohol treatment facility (50-51). McGee visits Nancy Abbott there, and Burley quite candidly tells him that there is no hope for her, that she drank too much and had too many shock treatments ever to recover (51-52, 58). In effect, Nancy's family warehouses her, reflecting family and medical limits to aid since neither has a solution to her problems. Gretel Howard's deterioration in *The Green Ripper* also exemplifies medicine's inadequacy when faced with the unknown. When Brother Titus purportedly orders her killed and she lies dying in the hospital, neither Dr. Vance Tower nor McGee can offer a solution (36-39). They can only watch helplessly as she dies, and it is instructive that the dramatic developments later in the novel involve the killings McGee commits to avenge her, not a healing.

In addition to the medical profession's limits in both knowledge and time, MacDonald describes a system with numerous flaws from human and professional viewpoints. Some problems are merely reflective of the people who become doctors or nurses. In *Crimson*, Dr. Prescott Mullen is, at the least, somewhat removed from the emotional lives of Anne Renzetti and his wife. Anne awaits his coming at the hotel she manages, evidently expecting, with some reason, a response to her own desire for him (56-57). Instead, he arrives with a new young wife whom he has chosen partially because of her probable ability to bear children easily (72). In *The Turquoise Lament*, Pidge and her psychiatrist fall in love (256), which on the surface appears innocuous enough except that the profession discourages emotional involvement with one's patient. MacDonald does not make this point, but it needs addressing. In *Yellow*, Dr. Geis guiltily sleeps with the fourteen-year-old Gretchen Ottlo, an action which he regrets but which he continues until her pregnancy (35-36).

The foregoing might seem more like character flaws which do not in every case call into question the medical profession, but in other cases MacDonald shows doctors and the hospitals in which they practice as dangerous. The most notorious example occurs in *Pink*. Dr. Varn conducts illegal drug and surgical experiments in Toll Valley Hospital north of New York. Dr. Varn is a menacing figure who does not play a large role in the novel but stands as a warning to possible excesses when people are seen as means and not as ends. In *The Girl in the Plain Brown Wrapper*, Dr. Stewart Sherman is thought to have killed his wife (169, 226). However much his wife deserved some retribution for her unpleasant personality, Detective Stanger describes her as "'a horror'" (169), Dr. Sherman certainly exceeded his oath, if he indeed did kill her, and used his special knowledge to harm rather than heal. In *The Dreadful Lemon Sky*, MacDonald uses a hospital rather than the people who practice there as a source of danger when Jason Breen murders Cal Birdsong for brutalizing his own wife, Cindy (91, 246, 252). The irony lies, of course, in that Birdsong is killed in a place of healing invaded by outside forces. Characters in other MacDonald novels die in hospitals, but in this instance, MacDonald subverts the very purposes for which hospitals are set up, revealing their vulnerability to social pressures.

In *Cinnamon Skin*, MacDonald devotes an entire chapter to McGee's past, present, and possible future relationship with Dr. Laura Honneker. In many ways, she is symbolic of the medical profession's complexities in the series. Dr. Honneker is a Fort Lauderdale psychiatrist, and McGee first met her eleven years before the events in *Cinnamon* (195). He retrieved some patient files for her so that she did not have to go to the police. Later, McGee saved her from an unpleasant situation with one Ron Robinette, whom McGee said was afflicted with "'what you professional people call satyriasis'" (198), after she drank too much when one of her patients killed herself (197). She and McGee "drifted into an affair" and out again within a month (199). McGee calls her regarding Pittler and over dinner gives her a hypothetical case with Pittler's details and asks her advice. Dr. Honneker is obviously a caring person, but when McGee tells her that his hypothetical involves a real person who has killed three women, she responds with, "'My God, tell me about him! Tell me all about him!'" (204). While not one of what Meyer calls the "psychiatric mafia which believes that the way to process your average psychopath is to dump him or her out onto the city streets, clutching a lithium prescription he or she is unable to read and unable to get filled" (MacDonald, *Reading* 21), to Laura, Pittler apparently has become a source of symptoms, a construct of actions and motivations that interest her professionally. To a certain extent, the human dimension, the personal tragedies of his victims, have receded in importance. Of course, she can never treat Pittler or prevent his crimes, but she sees him as a series of functions, a way of looking at people that many professionals, medical or otherwise, fail to avoid. McGee felt a certain detachment during their affair as if "she was watching both of us with her professional eye . . ." (199). She also tells him that she avoided marriage because she essentially did not want to make the commitment much in the same way that McGee has held back from Anne Renzetti (*Cinnamon* 207-09). However, during their conversation, Dr. Honneker gives McGee sound advice on how to deal with Pittler, some of which he later uses. MacDonald's portrait of her stresses the difference between possibilities and capabilities, revealing the person in the professional that not so much demystifies the medical profession as shows the interwoven strands in the lives of those who assume that responsibility.

When she drives away that night, Laura and McGee agree on offering and receiving some comfort even if it is little more than physical (*Cinnamon* 209).

MacDonald's use of medicine in the series is another instance of an area that reveals both limitations and possibilities. Mental and physical sicknesses that prod characters into certain actions and the medical profession that plays victim, healer, and transgressor show several more layers of the social fabric employed by the novelist. And as in so many other instances, MacDonald integrates this theme in the unfolding stories so that there are no absolutes, thus indicating his central concept of a humanity struggling with a blurred vision but somehow coping. And, McGee, facing in a positive direction, acts as a paradigm for this coping. As Wister Cook suggests, "Back of McGee's skill at playing with violence, his phenomenal rate of success, his ability to get permanent results, we catch our own fears and our own helplessness; we catch our own sense of irony about ourselves" (61).

Chapter 10

Science and Technology

In any body of creative work reflective of its society, the most important aspects of the culture will figure prominently, either as objects, practices, or ideas. For a writer as aware of the importance of concrete detail as MacDonald, the products and practices of the modern age reflected in his work force themselves on the reader in the entire range of imagery. However, MacDonald carefully measures what he includes: "Give [the reader] some of the vivid and specific details which you see, and you can trust him to build all the rest of the environment" ("Creative Trust" 44). At times, MacDonald is acutely aware of what modern technology produces, and he explores the uses McGee and others make of it. Also, MacDonald interweaves fundamental human processes with the modern accretions that compete or combine with them in an age-old adjustment to change. However, scientific ideas, buried beneath the fast-paced stories, function as thematic support. Occasionally, as in *The Deep Blue Good-by*, he uses an idea from evolution to stress the balance between man and nature. Or, he emphasizes the negative ecological effects of modern industry as support for his belief in mankind's tenuous ability to know what is best for both the earth and itself. More abstractly, MacDonald integrates scientific approaches as part of the intellectual structures of his plots, especially in McGee's empirical testing of evidence to arrive at the truth or in Meyer's belief in reason and an orderly universe on which it operates. As a consequence, science and technology enrich MacDonald's Travis McGee series both as product and process and struggle with a teleology of limited choices, paradoxically enrolling and indicting it.

The Travis McGee series abounds with examples of modern technology. McGee without some technological product would be a different man in a different world. A list of what he uses and probably needs, even without conscious acknowledgment, clarifies this point: his boat and its runabout, the *Munequita*; his car; and his weapons. The *Busted Flush* also contains other items: music system, television, safes, fishing tackle, various tools to repair the boat, and security devices. The image MacDonald creates is someone operating from within a technological web, however improbable the idea. His occasional use of the spider-bug analogy might appropriately be employed to parallel McGee's activities: Spiders weave webs to capture prey and the male spider of some species brings a bug for the female so that he will not be eaten after they mate (*Nightmare in Pink* 76, *A Deadly Shade of Gold* 237-38, *Bright Orange for the Shroud* 102). McGee's boat becomes a lure at times (*The Scarlet Ruse, Free Fall in Crimson*), and he operates nearly always in a defensive mode. When Crane Watts in *Orange* says, after McGee takes him into his own bathroom and turns on the shower full force, "'You're more careful than you have to be, McGee[,]'" McGee responds, "'I always am'" (72). When McGee leaves his home environment, he relies on modern technology as much as he does in Bahia Mar, Ft. Lauderdale. He goes by boat, using the *Busted Flush*, car, or plane. He smooths his way with credit cards, telephones, and rented cars if Miss Agnes, his converted Rolls Royce, is unavailable. In *The Empty Copper Sea*, MacDonald states: "Man is the tool user" (235), and McGee is not without tools, either his own or those he acquires, and sometimes refers to prybars and wedges, either literally, or as an image of mechanical aid to human force (*Blue* 210, *Pink* 50, *A Purple Place for Dying* 22, *Gold* 48; *Darker than Amber* 135). It is almost as if the lever with which Archimedes would move the world hovers in MacDonald's mind as he writes. As McGee notes in *Blue*, the future belongs to the technicians (179); they have adapted but others in the same novel, like Dee and Corry and their incompetent boyfriends, past and present, will become sullen workers in a world they do not understand.

At a more fundamental level, MacDonald portrays a world saturated with technology rather than the more humanistic idea of people with technical expertise managing social processes. For instance, he presents Dr. Varn controlled by his drug experiments in *Pink* which McGee disrupts with some difficulty. At a less threatening level, McGee says of himself, "My mirror consistently reflects that folksy image of the young project engineer who flung the bridge across the river in spite of overwhelming odds, up to and including the poisoned arrow in his heroic shoulder" (*Blue* 57). He earnestly discusses boats at the end of *Blue* (244) in order to deflect interest from the press concerning his recovery efforts on behalf of Cathy Kerr. However, this folksy use of technology reverts in later novels to the more ominous image foreshadowed in *Pink* in which man desperately reacts to technology's dominance. Preparing his boat for the confrontation with Sprenger at the end of *Scarlet*, McGee encourages himself:

Think, damnit! [sic] Like the little signs IBM used to distribute before they suddenly realized that if it were ever obeyed, if men everywhere really began to Think, the first thing they would do would be take a sledge and open up the computers. (276)

This suspicion of technology out of control lies behind the fear expressed in the industrial conditions in which machines make machines (*The Girl in the Plain Brown Wrapper* 153), thus diluting man's input and even the decision whether or not to produce something.

MacDonald generally uses scientific theories as complements to the ongoing stories, and while they might closely reflect his own beliefs, he usually integrates them into the plots. In *Scarlet*, MacDonald moves from the imagined view by a helicopter pilot of Mary Alice McDermit's waterskiing behind the *Munequita*, representing the good life, to McGee's feeling an unexplained depression until he remembers something Meyer has said:

. . . so divide everything into two hundred million equal parts. Everything in this country that is fabricated. Steel mills, speedboats, cross-country power lines, scalpels, watch bands, fish rods, ski poles, plywood, storage batteries, everything. Break it down into basic raw materials and then compute the power requirements and the fossil fuels needed to make everybody's share in this country. Know what happens if you apply that formula to all the peoples of all the other nations of the world?

You come up against a bleak fact, Travis. There is not enough material on and in the planet to ever give them what we're used to. The emerging nations are not going to emerge—not into our pattern at least. Not ever. We've hogged it all. Technology won't come up with a way to crowd the Yangtze River with *Munequitas*. (114-15)

Here, MacDonald introduces the much-discussed idea of scarcity according to which developed nations use up irreplaceable resources that undeveloped nations will one day want to share in and from which they will be hindered because nothing remains. MacDonald couches Meyer's description in both moral terms ("'And they can all look over into our corner and see us gorging ourselves and playing with our bright pretty toys'" [*Scarlet* 115]) and technological terms ("'Sorry. You're a little too late. We used it all up, all except what we need to keep our toys in repair and running and to replace them when they wear out. Sorry, but that's the way it is'" [115]). Moral questions aside, are resources being used up or will scientific theories and technological inventions expand possibilities as they have dramatically done during the last two centuries? McGee ends his ruminations somewhat ambiguously, "What's your message, Meyer? Enjoy?" (116), but one can see their applications to him, one so dependent on technology who nonetheless consumes and will continue to consume however aware he might be of the effects of over-consumption. As Wister Cook observes, "Like McGee's, our consumer and ecological concerns are serious, and our efforts a drop in the bucket. We see in our own experience the same fearful discrepancy between what troubles us and what we do about it" (60).

Paralleling this concern with scarcity, MacDonald employs ideas and images of ecological damage from science and its technological applications. In *Reading for Survival*, Meyer reflects MacDonald's ambivalent attitude toward science:

The final critical reality is the reality of science, a geometric progression of discovery and implementation, space flight and toxic wastes, genetic engineering and acid rain, microchips and endangered species. To be aware of the world you live in you must be aware of the constant change wrought by science, and the price we pay for every advance. (13)

From his Malthusian "'geometric progression'" to his balance between positive and negative outcomes from the whole scientific project, one senses the power that science and technology have over modern man living within their structures and which McGee especially reflects. After his recollection in *Scarlet* of Meyer's lecture on scarcity, McGee realizes that the lecture's source lies in Meyer's

. . . happy, single-minded pursuit of truth. He is not to blame that the truth seems to have the smell of decay and an acrid taste these days. He points out that forty thousand particles per cubic centimeter of air over Miami is now called a clear day. He is not complaining about particulate matter. He is merely bemused by the change instandards. (116)

Mary Alice McDermit turns out to have the "smell of decay," and MacDonald thus thematically integrates an ecological comment into his story with this use of foreshadowing.

Travis McGee's life-style provides a way to connect the many other comments about the harmful effects of technology on the environment. As a salvage consultant, McGee functions in a world of wrecked hopes. And, rather than obtrusive comments, his statements about the strains, as well as the benefits, that science and technology produce usually fit quite well into the overall thematic structures. As Edgar W. Hirshberg notes,

Even in his longer dissertations about the eternal strife between man and his environment that is taking place in Florida, MacDonald manages somehow to blend what he has to say into the story, so that it doesn't distract the reader's attention from what Travis is trying to do. (*MacDonald* 83)

Beginning with his remarks about New York smog in *Blue* (100), MacDonald introduces the image of tension that in *Pink* (21) and *Gold* (37) spills over into the apocalyptic visions of destruction discussed in Chapter Six. In *Purple*, the catastrophe is more localized as Jass Yeoman remarks to McGee that the Southwest will self-destruct when it pumps the last bit of fossil water from underground (76). This parallels statements McGee makes to Anne Renzetti in *Cinnamon Skin* during a discussion on Florida's over-population:

And the rivers and the swamps are dying, the birds are dying, the fish are dying. They're paving the whole state. And the people who give a damn can't be heard. The developers make big campaign contributions. And there isn't enough public money to treat sewage. (101)

Extrapolating from the murder of his friend Sam Taggart in *Gold*, McGee sees in his death an inability for humans to balance their lives, and while he only subsequently learns that Sam had unbalanced his own life, McGee's instinct is to relate individual actions to larger consequences affecting the environment. McGee's observations in *Orange* on the destruction of the Everglades emphasize the single actions that combine into major effects. He notes that

In the questionable name of progress, the state in its vast wisdom lets every two-bit developer divert the flow into the draglined canals that give him "waterfront" lots to sell. . . . As the Glades dry, the big fires come with increasing frequency. The ecology is changing with egret colonies dwindling, mullet getting scarce, mangrove dying of new diseases born of dryness. (58-59)

Later in the same novel, McGee comments on the harmful effects of the automobile on America's cities, specifically Tampa (114), and the "industrial smog" (115) permeating Tampa's harbor. MacDonald's ecological comments focus on more than one issue, and he merges the details into the novel, adding a sense of danger to the city to which McGee has come in order to trace Calvin Stebber.

MacDonald uses the idea of evolution in interesting ways but with one firm principle underlying it: No signs appear of mankind moving toward a superior life form. In an essay on the painter Syd Solomon in a catalogue for a 1961 Sarasota art show, he says, "We are composed of a brittle scum of our recent tameness atop a few million years of fears and darkness and the panic of lives too short" ("JDM as an Art Critic" 11). He does note in *Blue* that Junior Allen seems a "less evolved" form than Lois Atkinson (165), thus giving one the impression that in addition to Darwin's idea of natural selection there is a moral evolution as well. However, when in *The Lonely Silver Rain* McGee speculates about the deaths of young people as part of an evolutionary pattern, he quickly shifts to the idea of chance as an equally possible cause:

I wondered if it could be some kind of Darwinian design, getting rid of the ones unsuited for the rest of the ride. But that would leave out the earthquakes, the floods, the little and big wars, the famines and the deadly diseases that knock off the millions without regard to age or merit. (52-53)

Although in *Reading for Survival* Meyer's "'survival of the species'" (12) is not Darwin's "survival of the fittest," Meyer's phrase connotes more than stasis. In the same work, speaking of the confusions of creationism, Meyer notes that

They say that it is as respectable a point of view as the *Theory* of Evolution. Out of their abysmal ignorance comes the idea that *theory* in this context means some kind of assumption open to dispute, not yet proven, whereas the word is used in the same way it is used in the *theory* of diminishing returns, or the *theory* of relativity. Those theories are not open to dispute because the proof of their correctness is available to anyone who can read. (19)

In this last statement on the subject, evolution appears to play a prominent part in MacDonald's thinking about human development even without some clear and positive direction of the process.

Several other works present evolution in a radically different light, at least one of them leading to the concept of entropy. The alien cancellation of the earth in *Gold*, discussed in Chapter Six, presents the idea of mutation as a negative evolutionary outcome with aliens representing supernatural forces that intercede in the natural cycle and destroy the "human" mistake (37) much as the Flood does in Genesis. McGee's vision in *The Turquoise Lament* adumbrates an evolved species that can live, as it were, by brain alone. Reacting to the ministrations of a stewardess on his flight to Hawaii to help Pidge Brindle, he imagines that

In A.D. 3174 the busy, jolly nosexicles on the planet Squanta III will sever our spinal cords, put us into our bright little eternity wombs, deftly attach the blood tube, feeding tube, waste tube and monitor circuitry, remove the eyelids quickly and painlessly, and, with little chirps of cheer, strokes and pats of friendship and farewell, they will lower the lid and seal it, leaving us surrounded by a bright dimensional vista of desert, a smell of heat and sage, a sound of the oncoming hoofs on full gallop as, to the sound of a cavalry bugle, John Wayne comes riding, riding, riding. . . (9)

Hardly an outcome more preferable than that in *Gold*, it still might be better than the one Meyer projects in *The Green Ripper* to help explain Gretel Howard's death. Meyer combines ecological dangers, "'Poisons abound. The sick birds fall out of the air,'" with evolutionary-like statements, "'The real world is out there in a slow dreadful process of change'" (112). Meyer calls this "'process of change. . . a *thing* . . . patient'" (113). This image of an evolution toward disintegration in an environment that appears to be wearing itself out resembles the idea of entropy in which natural processes cease to function. MacDonald's picture here is indeed a bleak one and might give some clarification to his statement in *Reading for Survival* about the truth of evolution.

A final aspect of MacDonald's use of concepts relating to science and technology involves basic processes that occur in many disciplines, from literary criticism to historical interpretation. Analogies to scientific approaches from these and other areas of study that do not concern themselves with the functioning of the natural world are also applicable to McGee and Meyer's use of scientific methods and reason to solve their cases. Even before Meyer figures largely in the series in beginning with *Amber*, McGee approaches his cases with an orderly mind. (See Chapter Two for McGee and Meyer's relative roles as thinkers and Chapter Thirteen for the value of reason to their political community.) Though he will benefit from Meyer's logical abilities, especially beginning with *Amber* (25), McGee's methods in all his cases, while admitting a large emotional component, befit a rigorous scientific approach. For example, in *Orange* McGee first collects all the information he can from his and Chookie McCall's discussions with Arthur Wilkinson. This is not an aimless collection of data but one controlled early on by the rather obvious hypothesis that a person or persons unknown illegally defrauded Wilkinson of his money. At every stage of Arthur's recital of the incidents that led up to his reappearance in Bahia Mar, McGee checks and re-checks names and the sequence of events. In addition, McGee tests his reasoning and the evidence like any good scientist. If McGee cannot recreate the same results, then his hypothesis must be rejected. Arthur knows that Cal Stebber's organization somehow stole money from him, but only McGee's careful analysis of all the information and meticulous testing of various scenarios lead to the successful recovery of some of Wilkinson's money.

When Meyer joins McGee in the series and their generally unstated partnership develops, McGee gains an enormous increase in brain power. References to examples of Meyer's logical approach to problems and his financial and economic expertise abound. What McGee chiefly gains by his aid is time and even greater possibilities of success. Mick, the pilot and aerial photographer in *Silver* whom McGee contacts to help find Billy Ingraham's boat, *The Sundowner*, responds with incredulity: "'McGee, am I hearing you? You are looking for a damn boat? In Florida?'" (23). Meyer's response is to think logically. He first constructs a method to recognize the boat from the air (16) and then organizes their handling of the enormous number of photos that flow in from Mick's flights (28). Without this "scientific" approach, something similar to what McGee has used alone but more sophisticated, success would not have been impossible but highly improbable.

MacDonald's most sustained view of Meyer's logical abilities does not occur in any of the Travis McGee novels but rather in *Reading for Survival*, a work with an obvious pedagogic intent. However, MacDonald's portrait in that work of Meyer's intellectual approach to problems is consistent with his portrayal in the series. In *Scarlet*, McGee feels a needless guilt in keeping Meyer waiting while he talks with Willy Nucci. However, he realizes his error:

He never paces up and down, checking the time. He has those places to go, inside his head. He looks as if he was sitting and dozing, fingers laced across his middle. Actually he has walked back into his head, where there are libraries, concert halls, work rooms, experimental laboratories, game rooms. He can listen to a fine string quartet, solve chess problems, write an essay on Chilean inflation under Allende, or compose haiku. He had a fine time back in there. (49)

Similarly, in *Reading for Survival* McGee describes Meyer's thinking processes in ways that separate him from people who have not developed their minds to the same extent:

When you and I think, it is a fairly simple process. A lot of fuzzy notions bump about in our skulls like play toys in a roiled swimming pool. . . . With Meyer it is quite a different process. He has a skull like a house. . . . He knows where the libraries are, and the little laboratories, the computer rooms, the print shop, the studios. When he thinks, he wanders from room to room, looking at a book here, a pamphlet there, a specimen across the hall. His ideas are compilations of the thought and wisdom he has accumulated up until now. (4)

Meyer's role in *Reading for Survival* is to stress the vital importance of reading to present human development. Meyer speaks of the "'process of logic'" (9) by which civilization developed and includes writing and reading in the process. In effect, Meyer's use of his own mind imitates mankind's creation of writing and asserts the absolute need to interact with this repository of knowledge and ideas through reading and thinking.

MacDonald's employment of metaphors that stress the mechanization of life do not mean that he abjures all science and technology. If nothing else, the stress in *Reading for Survival* on the need to know about them and control their use belies that. And, the many dangers that beset humanity and the planet from science and technology do not mean that his portrait of human activity counsels resignation. Rather, his dramatizations of the extensions of human knowledge advocate the need for enlightened engagement. Only then can one participate in whatever direction this knowledge takes.

Chapter 11

Money and Choice

Some helpful analogies when thinking about the power of money in the series are money as a driving force behind people's actions or money as a source of corruption and divisiveness. The analogies, mechanical and moral, respectively, acknowledge that while one may not exactly know what to make of money one recognizes its omnipresence, its detachment from the goods and services it buys, its function as an essence apart from its countability. McGee places his money in a safe on the *Busted Flush*, secreting it in such a way that no one has ever found it (*Bright Orange for the Shroud* 169-70, *Darker than Amber* 111-12). McGee has many reasons why he keeps his money so well hidden and so close by. Obviously, he does not want it stolen, but on display in his boat he keeps some of the valuable pictures he has bought (*The Quick Red Fox* 43-44). Another answer is that McGee generally avoids banks and the records they require, but he does pay his taxes, so apparently he is not out to cheat the government (*The Lonely Silver Rain* 74). He also uses credit cards, however reluctantly, for their convenience in renting cars and giving him a certain amount of surface respectability and camouflage (*The Deep Blue Good-by* 99-100, *A Purple Place for Dying* 38). Third, McGee enhances his sense of independence with his money immediately available and unmediated by anyone. These reasons reveal an animal-like secretiveness in storing his money, implying a certain neutrality toward it as object. However, as Jack Matthews states, MacDonald's position differs: "[He] is fascinated by money" as part of the "*processes*" of "how the intricate things work" (109). Of course, McGee's presumed neutrality toward money as object does not preclude Martin Green's observation that "He is extremely knowledgeable about money, particularly about land-development corporations but also about trusts and tax-dodges and investment dossiers" (123). Yet, money's effects, not only in McGee's life but in that of others', reveal a far from neutral force that evinces itself in unsuspecting ways, drawing its possessors into acts that they cannot predict or control.

On many occasions McGee transfers large sums of money to others. These actions bring joy to some and a measure of compensation to those who have suffered the loss of a loved one. An example of the first instance occurs in *A Deadly Shade of Gold* when McGee gives Shaja Dobrak $125,000 with which to ransom her husband from a Hungarian prison (286). Robert K. Phillips states that "In the course of the 21 novels the quest for money seems to fade while McGee's tendencies to value life are emphasized" (30). In the second type of situation, he sends $26,000 recovered from Ans Terry in *Amber* to the divorced wife of Powell Daniels, the man Terry had dropped overboard on his last murder cruise with Del Whitney (185). Meyer gives a wrapped stack of hundreds in *A Tan and Sandy Silence* to Joshua and the "tribe," with McGee's later approval, for Joshua's help in disposing of Paul Dissat's limousine after the latter's death (245, 246). These exemplary actions reach their zenith in *Silver* when McGee transfers his money, as noted in Chapter Six, to his daughter, Jean (277). The question arises, why this compulsion to divest himself so thoroughly of his hard, even dangerously earned money, especially as he poses as one out to take his retirement in segments while he is young enough to enjoy it?

One reason may be that McGee seldom takes a case just for the money. Frequently, money is merely an exchange point, a neutral area which McGee and his client temporarily occupy in order to make a connection that will draw him in or not. When Helena Pearson Trescott wills him $25,000 in *The Girl in the Plain Brown Wrapper* to help her daughter, Maureen, if he can, McGee has the money with no legal strings (34, 36-38). The sole connections are their former friendship and his sense of honor. Although he gives back only his time and effort, any action he takes, from a financial standpoint, subtracts from the capital with which he starts. However, McGee tries desperately to save Maureen and after her death, to prevent Pike from using her sister, Bridget. A similar situation occurs in *The Dreadful Lemon Sky* when Carrie Milligan leaves $94,200 with McGee to give to her sister in the event of her death, a case discussed in Chapter Two in relation to Meyer's role (11). With no discernible profit in view, McGee investigates the circumstances of Carrie's subsequent death, and after an attempt on his life, he continues his activities until he and Meyer stumble onto Harry Hascomb as the murderer (258-60). From being little more than a well-paid messenger, McGee, who could easily have kept the money, not only surrenders it but uses it as a lever for his and

Meyer's involvement. The circumstances of his profession put him into dangerous situations regardless of their financial potential. But, they must be situations of his own choosing, which is why he refuses Colonel Marquez's offer in *Gold* to use him as a catalyst in an unending series of investigations with little pay (203).

Brown and *Lemon* portray money as an activating convention which allows people to connect with McGee and thus engage him. In neither case does McGee seek money; he already has it, and the possession leads him to solve problems the money reveals. However, in both cases money is a structural feature which usually stays hidden though powerful. Conversely, *Purple* presents the objectification of money as physical presence in a way that Carrie Milligan's box of money in *Lemon* never does. After Carrie shows McGee the money and tells him her requests, McGee hides it away in his safe. From object, it transforms itself again into an abstract agent powerful enough to lead to murder. In *Purple*, Jass Yeoman, thinking to hire McGee, tosses a wrapped bundle of $5,000 at his face. McGee knocks it on the floor near the fireplace and then tries to kick it in; both men watch as the thick block of money begins to burn around the edges (79). Yeoman has used the bundle as a contemptuous weapon; McGee's deflection has begun the transformation from block of material into its idea of wealth which Yeoman completes by dragging the money from the fire. Through this action, McGee and Yeoman establish a sense of contact which Yeoman believes would be even more firmly established if they could go outside and knock one another around for forty minutes (79-80). Striking McGee with the money is like striking him with his hand; the connection is thus made when McGee acknowledges the mutual respect and activates the contract by accepting the symbolically personalized and purified money.

Although MacDonald does not completely equate money with friendship and trust, he does create an intriguing relationship between money and betrayal in *Purple*. In order to protect himself and his family from the IRS, Wally Ruppert systematically reveals every business transaction that he formerly had with Yeoman although at the present time they only have a few business deals to complete with one another (83). When Yeoman and McGee visit Ruppert at his ranch outside of Esmerelda, the latter freely admits his complete revelations to the government (105). With Ruppert, once money connections cease between him and those outside his family, all contacts and responsibilities end (105). Ruppert, whom Jass previously referred to as "'one feudal son of a bitch'" (85), strikes McGee as "'an unusual man'" (107) when he and Jass visit him. Jass replies, "'Unusual! One of those is all the world can stand'" (107).

But if money is an exchange point through which McGee involves himself in dangerous situations and in the lives of others, it plays a far more negative role in instances in which it functions as a reason for aggression toward others or a means to manipulate them. In *Dress Her in Indigo*, Bix Bowie goes to Mexico with $8,000 and four people near her age (21-22). Walter Rockland, fired from his job as a swimming pool attendant, ultimately dominates the group, and with Bix's money temporarily relieving any necessity to work for his survival, he abuses his male and female companions. For example, Carl Sessions dies from Rockland's none too polite ministrations, including sex and drugs. And, like Jerry Nesta, Bix and Minda McLeen, Wally McLeen's daughter, escape from Rockland though Minda dies in mysterious circumstances and Bix remains drug addicted. From Nesta's portrait, Rockland appears to have more than just a careless attitude toward others' lives and property. He is indifferent to the use to which he puts their bodies, minds, and emotions. With no sense of self-reflection, he gratifies his momentary desires by abusing the members of the group. The change from Florida to Mexico and the isolation from anyone's family and friends contribute to his ability to expand his field of behavior, but the money, however limited, is the necessary ingredient in his liberation. Rockland's renting Bix as a prostitute to a group of anonymous Mexicans is the ultimate act of her degradation and his freedom to do whatever appeals to him (175). After the money begins to run low, Rockland's planned drug deal fails (171), along with a subsequent robbery attempt on Bruce Bundy (71). Eva Vitrier, a wealthy and reclusive citizen of Oaxaca, informs McGee how she managed to subdue Rockland and transfer him to the deranged Wally McNeel (242-43), who later kills him (115-16, 199-200). As Rockland's case shows, aggressors can become victims to money's power, and unintended consequences occur when money obscures their sense of humanity.

MacDonald initiates the aggressive function of money with Junior Allen in *Blue*. A paradigm for the series in many areas, *Blue* especially explores the possibilities of money as an aggressive force. Money organizes Allen's life. First, he sets up illegal scams while in the Army Quartermaster Corps (43). Convicted and sent to Leavenworth, Allen obtains information from ex-Sergeant David Berry which leads him to suspect the latter has secreted something valuable in or near his home in Florida. While this turns out to be true, there is no necessary connection between Berry's statements and Allen's belief in them. In fact, it is almost a cliche that prisons spawn exaggerations, from one's knowledge to one's abilities, influence, and accomplishments in sex and crime. Why does Allen believe Berry's claims? Possibly the manner by which Allen elicits the information from him during their prison conversations convinces him of its accuracy (146, 173). Berry reveals enough information to point Allen at his family. Once pointed and released from prison, Allen homes in on them, especially Cathy Kerr.

Allen's return to Candle Key after converting the stolen gems into money reveals another aspect of money's ability to organize or release aggressive forces. Although Allen is psychologically disturbed, the strand of money's influence can be clearly detected. Lois Atkinson's weak rejection of Allen's advances while he works at a local gas station and conducts an affair with Cathy as he searches for Berry's wealth later draws him to sail his newly purchased boat to a dock opposite Lois's home (*Blue* 17, 75). Stolen, secreted money helps to free him from any social inhibitions in his attack on her (35, 72). As a predator instinctively selects the weakest member of a herd, Allen only seemingly takes enormous chances, as McGee later observes, in raping her, in confining her to his boat for several days, and in then moving into her house (75-76). He leaves after reducing Lois to a shell of her former self. Allen's possession of money has even blunted his desire for more money. When McGee goes to Lois's home and helps her, he discovers months of her uncashed checks (68). Later, he speculates that Allen would have progressed to females even younger than the eighteen-year-old Patty Devlan:

And Patty Devlan was next. As if each satisfaction required that the next victim be more vulnerable, more open to terror. Taste is quickly jaded. Make a projection of his trend and his needs, and it might well end up with the jump-rope set, and then become murderous because smaller mouths would not stay closed. (204)

Money sets Allen up in a style to which he is not accustomed, but it also makes him careless of the world's structures and social forms, leading McGee, ultimately, to find him.

It might be argued that Boone Waxwell in *Orange* is not such an extreme case of social pathology as Cody T.W. Pittler in *Cinnamon Skin*, but money helps both men expand their personalities into the world, preventing them from distinguishing the limits of their desires and needs. Both men have isolated home bases from which they roam into the world. Boone's reach is limited to several counties around his swamp retreat. Pittler, more severely disturbed, has a wider area for his depredations. From a fancy home in Cancun, Mexico, where he is known as Roberto Hoffman, he usually operates in the United States. Oppressing women is another area in which they overlap. Although Boone pursues women, widely, it is only after he kills Wilma Ferner and takes her money that any mention is made of rape. Vivian Watts represents a higher social class than the other women he has in the novel. With Wilma's money he buys "at least twenty-five thousand dollars' worth of toys" (89) and buries the remainder behind his shack. Later, he goes to the Wattses' home and repeatedly rapes Vivian. Pittler's actions with women are as violent, usually, from the beginning as they are at the point at which he kills Norma, but money has changed his methods. With money, Pittler has not only purchased his Mexican home but has also acquired the time to go after wealthier women whose pursuit requires careful thought. Waxwell's and Pittler's experiences reveal a growing confidence in their abilities to match actions with desires. In simple terms, disregard for the consequences of their actions and an inability to sense a threat from the police or someone like McGee are symptomatic of the expansion of these desires, partially liberated and released by money.

As an economist, Meyer adds an additional level to understanding the function of money in the series. Of course, Meyer makes a living from his profession either directly in consultant fees or from investments based on knowledge of economic and financial conditions. However, he also studies the very conditions which support him and occasionally forecasts economic trends. A sports analogy would be a player-coach who while actively participating also prepares and directs his team. While his dual career is not as brief as a player-coach's, he does relate to money on two levels, only one of which, the academic, MacDonald stresses. Meyer does not dispossess himself of money like McGee, but he has the same sense of distance from it as the latter. When McGee persuades him to take $10,000 in *Amber*, Meyer invests the money and says that each year he will withdraw the interest and give a party, his "Meyer Festival" (187). Thus, Meyer hands it on, unsentimentally, and with no hesitation or sense of sacrifice; money flows outward from Meyer into contact with others, which seems to suit his personality.

It is obvious that if he wished Meyer could become wealthy. Aside from the specifics discussed in Chapter Three of the con against Gary Santo in *Pale Gray for Guilt*, Meyer's actions reveal his wide knowledge of financial and economic trends. However, instead of using this knowledge to enrich himself, he appears far more interested in understanding the many forces that propel markets to move in one direction rather than another. Meyer's expertise in finding a company in *Gray* that only seems successful could clearly be used to locate one that really is. However, he does not appear to see his many contacts in the business world in *Gray, Tan, The Empty Copper Sea,* and *Cinnamon* as sources for exploitation. He appears to have relationships based on mutual respect with the important business people he knows. Never developing this aspect of Meyer's past, MacDonald gains depth for Meyer's character by the past skill one infers he must have demonstrated. This implication of past accomplishments with an occasional reference to his ongoing research and writing is a clever device MacDonald uses to create an interest in Meyer and counterbalance other approaches to money centered more on violence.

It does not occur to Meyer that his talents are wasted in his usual academic and professional pursuits. Aside from helping the widow of Travis's friend, Meyer approaches his activities in *Gray* with the air of someone solving a puzzle, as if they were an extension of his more important concerns. Thus, the concrete effects of money do not disappear for Meyer, but rather the problem of money in its manifold economic effects is an intellectual one, intriguing in its complexity and presenting a challenge to Meyer that the Santos of the world could never fathom. When McGee tells Meyer at the beginning of *Tan* as he repairs the latter's automatic bilge pump on the *John Maynard Keynes* that "'another half inch of rain'" the previous night would have seen it sink to the bottom of Bahia Mar (10), the image of concentrated knowledge in books and journals strongly suggests where Meyer places his values—not in the physical representations of wealth but rather in the physical manifestations of the intangible, in ideas and knowledge.

The focus of this chapter might well be money as danger. No novel in the series is without incidents which endanger one or more characters either because they possess money or are near it. In *Silver*, Billy Ingraham's death in Cannes (72) occurs not from any culpability on his part but merely as an indirect result of his wealth. Ingraham owns a boat worth nearly three-quarters of a million dollars (8). After it is stolen, he hires McGee who finds it with three bodies on it, one a daughter from an influential Peruvian family (84). Apparently believing that McGee killed the girl and that Ingraham is connected somehow with her death, the family more than likely hires someone, according to McGee's lawyer Frank Payne, to stick "'something thin and sharp and curved right into the inside corner of his left eye'" (76) and also tries to kill McGee (74). It might be argued that this is a long trail of happenstance back to Ingraham's money, but MacDonald's view of the world tightens the connection between money and danger. The latter lies not only in the method by which one acquires it. Ruffino Marino, Sr., as a member of organized crime in *Silver*, might expect that he would be a target and a target of his associates if no one else (187-88). Frank Sprenger in *The Scarlet Ruse* handles money from the mob from whom, McGee learns, Sprenger expects no appeal if he endangers their activities by any careless behavior (46). No, the danger also lies in the social currents that money sets in motion or disturbs. Money thus becomes a force that, paradoxically, operates separately from the substance and in Ingraham's case leads to his death.

Money's dual nature thus creates a movement that traps most people in its effects. Possibly this vortex-like quality is what influences McGee, as has been shown, to seek it and divorce himself from it; its power and danger are evident. Two characters in *Brown* exemplify this faculty of money—Tom Pike and Special Investigator Dave Broon. The tableau which Detective Al Stanger and McGee witness near the end of the novel in which Broon hangs Pike brings a temporary hiatus to the events (247-48). Stanger says that Broon has the simplest motives for his acquisition of money: "'penthouse apartment,'" "'[b]ig convertible,'" "'speedboat,'" clothes, and women (167); in other words, material possessions and sensuous experiences seemingly order and motivate his behavior. But, Stanger notes the increasing extremes to which Broon is driven (193). Pike's life is also out of balance. Although married to a beautiful, loving wife, Pike only sees the money he could inherit with her death. Admittedly, his reputation after a minor stockbroking scandal is somewhat shaky (200-02), and McGee learns that some people refuse to risk their money with him (186-87, 234). But, on the very night when he kills Maureen, a new office building of his has an open house, and he still has his considerable talents as an entrepreneur (202). When Broon and Pike fall out, the contradictions in their attitudes toward money surface, bearing them on to the fatal resolution (247-49). Maureen, the innocent and unknowing victim, dies because she has money, but the predators destroy their own lives as well.

The torturous trail of money as danger surfaces in both class relations and time. An instructive analogy to the following examples is an automobile accident in which one traces the lives of the people back to what caused them to be present at the fatal moment. In *Free Fall in Crimson*, Ellis Esterland and Desmin Grizzel appear at the opposite ends of almost any spectrum of social class. Grizzel kills Esterland for the following reasons. Romola, Esterland's daughter by Josephine Laurant, his third wife, lies in a coma from a bicycle accident. If Romola dies first, the greater part of his fortune goes to a research foundation (9). If Esterland dies first, Romola inherits, and if she then dies, Josie would inherit. In addition, Josie would probably continue to back her lover Peter Kesner's film career, especially if she remains his principal actress. Grizzel appeared in two biker movies directed by Kesner some years before (160) and still works for him (175). Thus, Esterland, who probably does not know Kesner or Grizzel, even by reputation, is the latter's necessary target and must die.

The forces in *One Fearful Yellow Eye* that lead to Anna Ottlo's successful blackmail of Dr. Fortner Geis begin some twenty years before the events of the novel in the last days of Hitler's Germany. Anna, a concentration camp guard along with her friend Perry Hennigan, murders a prisoner, switches identities with her, and escapes punishment after the war. Eventually, she comes to Chicago with Gretchen, the woman's daughter, who had been separated from her mother for five years before Anna claimed to be her (214-15), and obtains work with Dr. Geis. After the death of Geis's first wife and the marriage of Geis and Gloria, McGee's friend, Anna concocts her blackmail scheme with the help of Perry and Saul Gorba, her "daughter" Gretchen's latest husband. Although Anna's target is apparently more accidental than Grizzel's, both Esterland and Geis possess money, and the latter's effects, apart from its owner's knowledge or control, comprise its dangers. Strong characters though they are, neither Esterland nor Geis can divert the troubles that seem to rush toward money's possessor.

If one says a word frequently enough, it loses any sharp sense of meaning, taking on profound if elusive connotations. Contemplate money as idea or object, and it too begins to lose distinct significance and acquire immense possibilities. Among the many concepts in MacDonald's fiction, money touches most of them and acts as a crucial element in the social structure of his work. Though only a vehicle for society's method of valuing material goods and services, money struggles to emerge as a daunting, personified force.

Chapter 12

Freedom and the Individual

The series presents few examples of specific oppressive social or political forces against which individuals struggle to develop and maintain their identities. Few large organizations appear on which to focus antagonisms and against which to rebel. There are no threatening religious groups, outside of the Church of the Apocrypha in *The Green Ripper,* or political parties or social or cultural organizations exhibiting enough power to galvanize opposition. What initially seems a despotic police force in *The Long Lavender Look* turns out to be a largely honest, well-run organization in which Sheriff Norm Hyzer, struggling with his own past, attempts to apply the most modern law enforcement techniques with a minimum intrusion on individual liberties. And, most police forces in the series are hard-working and reasonably honest and competent. Continuous social changes, value shifts, and technological threats hover over and oppress MacDonald's characters but present no clear enemy. As a result, the individual's dilemma in American culture is how to achieve personal freedom amid multiple social and economic influences without clear standards.

As one among the few specific dangers, almost every novel in the series presents a criminal threat to the freedom of innocent citizens. This threat ranges from the depredations of the individual or outlaw to the organized criminal group with the victims either individuals or groups. The criminal threat runs as an underground, and sometimes not so underground, stream in the society and appears invulnerable to eradication. Some might argue that a commitment to individual freedom allows the existence of this threat and that is the price society must pay for freedom. MacDonald begins the series in *The Deep Blue Good-by* with a clear demonstration that there is no air-tight system of protection for people against those who would violate their freedom. Junior Allen's return to Candle Key to prey on Lois Atkinson could not be stopped by anyone. This is ironical when one considers the self-righteous attitude of Jeff Bocka, the realtor who thinks that Lois is not the proper type for their town (79-80). Where were the good citizens when Allen, one of the type whom Erling B. Holtsmark identifies as a "monster" (101), took over the vulnerable Lois's life? While one might argue that the Allens of the world will be ultimately deflected from their purposes, MacDonald's picture is not so positive. Allen apparently leaves Lois Atkinson's life when he tires of her, and Lois barely survives the visitation and departure.

Lois's fragile condition when McGee arrives at her home while searching for Allen underscores the danger and room for maneuver of the predator in a society that values individual freedom. In that type of community, law enforcement agencies usually are more reactive than interruptive. Police patrol a community but do not become involved unless they think a crime has been committed. Placing Tom Pike in *The Girl in the Plain Brown Wrapper* in such a context clarifies personal dangers even more than in Allen's case since Pike, as stated in Chapter Eleven, kills his own wife. As in the case of Allen and Lois Atkinson, could any society prevent Pike's actions toward Maureen, his wife? Ostensibly, Pike has "everything": a beautiful wife, a successful business, a prominent place in his community. Neither his business failure nor public disgrace would cause any government authority to rush to protect Maureen. Even Maureen's illness and progressive deterioration elicit only admiration for Pike's tender care from friends and acquaintances and from Bridget Pearson, Maureen's sister, who lives with them in order to help nurse Maureen and who McGee suspects has fallen in love with Pike (57). Thus, Maureen is alone and defenseless in the world, and only her death and McGee's hiding of the body force Pike into the open and lead to his belated death. Pike's sole apparent, but unintentional, usefulness in the novel comes from serving as a trap for Deputy Dave Broon, caught in the act of hanging Pike, and thus ending his own criminal activities. Even though one might read into MacDonald's work a remorseless and ultimate exposure of the guilty, the novelist is equally unrelenting in dramatizing the inevitable sufferings of the innocent.

While certain individuals play important roles in threatening personal freedoms, criminal groups also are a source of major danger. MacDonald is especially effective when he combines the lone outlaw and the criminal group. In *Bright Orange for the Shroud*, Boone Waxwell plays the dual roles of individual predator, discussed in Chapter Eight, and group member. McGee does not encounter Waxwell in his role as Calvin Stebber's enforcer; he only hears about that aspect after Arthur Wilkinson, one of Stebber's latest victims, comes to him for help. Wilma Ferner, a Stebber associate, chooses Wilkinson for her next victim, marries him, and alerts Stebber. The latter's organization subsequently defrauds Wilkinson of over a quarter of a million dollars (33-36). Even though the size of Stebber's group makes for a greater chance of police interference, in effect Wilkinson is as unprotected as Lois Atkinson and Maureen Pike. Once selected, Wilkinson's end is certain, and one may properly infer from MacDonald's scenario that nothing could prevent the process from unfolding. When Wilkinson confronts Crane Watts, the lawyer Stebber uses, in order to regain his money and threatens to expose them, Debra Brown, another Stebber associate, drugs him, and the police unwittingly arrest him for public drunkenness for which offense he serves thirty days in jail (44).

Wilkinson later arrives at McGee's boat, the *Busted Flush*, penniless, poorly clothed, and malnourished (6-7). One subsequently learns that he is also impotent (49). Waxwell, a relatively minor player in Stebber's con, looms as the major symbol of Arthur's humiliation. Wilkinson earlier traces Wilma to Waxwell's isolated shack and confronts him. As Wilma watches, Waxwell thoroughly beats him, and he almost literally has to crawl away (39). Stebber does not authorize the beating, and after McGee tracks Stebber down and offers him a profitable role in a scheme to trick Waxwell and recover some of the money the latter took from Wilma after accidentally killing her, Stebber declines the chance (129). He shows a proper caution in enraging Waxwell who cannot be entirely controlled. Waxwell's threat to individual freedom lies in his membership in a criminal group and in the violent acts he commits on his own.

The foregoing examples pit individuals against powerful criminal forces with which, knowingly or not, they struggle for their very existences. Of course, these are unusual instances in which the detective genre revels. Putting people *in extremis* allows for the action and suspense to build and creates an exciting novel. However, other characters raise the idea of personal freedom in more subtle ways and lead to speculations about the difficulty, or even possibility, of achieving an individual sense of self. After he is released from jail in *Lavender*, McGee begins his brief affair with Betsy Kapp. MacDonald first presents her as a woman with unusually large breasts (92) and then, almost sadly, as someone embodying romantic cliches (94, 102). He does not completely rob her of her separateness as a person, but through McGee, she does appear to be too easily summed up by her body and attitudes. However, several events lead McGee to an awareness of her as something more than a type even if she never completely transcends his initial impressions. This raises the puzzling question as to whether McGee grants her a sense of individuality or whether she possesses this quality even if it is never clarified. With the restrictions of a first-person narrative, this probably cannot be clearly answered. When Deputy Billy Cable makes a remark to her with obvious sexual overtones, she quickly rebuffs him (136-37). Cable fondled her breasts uninvitedly several years before (137). Her comments to Cable in McGee's presence make it clear that she is not an extension of his frustrations, fantasies, or desires. This action clarifies or sharpens her personality in McGee's eyes. In her home, McGee believes that she interjects layers of romantic make-believe between what they do and how she sees it. Essentially, he makes love with her the first night he meets her, and she has to transform this socially dubious practice into some deeper meaning. When he earlier reads her letter to Deputy Lew Arnstead, with whom she had an affair, warning him about Lilo Perris, McGee says that it "interested me mightily" (79), more for help on the case than for explaining her personality. Various interpretations could see her action in writing the letter as one of self-delusion, that it is only a pretended selflessness, but it is essentially a kindness done with little or no expectation of benefit. McGee later tells Sheriff Hyzer that "'it has that perfect ring of truth'" (221). Betsy thus appears to have a stubbornly persistent streak, an authentic quality, to be "a person entirely herself" (110) according to McGee, intertwined with common, predictable responses—something like listening to opera while drinking beer and eating pretzels.

Literature allows one to be privy to these hidden moments in which individuals act from profound motivations. At times, this is akin to making a choice that reflects one's truest sense of self, one's deepest values. While convention rules the lives of most people, the Betsy Kapps of the world sometimes fragment its hold. In contrast to this image of choice deepening, however infrequently, the awareness of one's individuality, MacDonald poses the person determined by his or her basic nature to act in a certain way. Paul Dissat's recognition in *A Tan and Sandy Silence* of his pleasure in torturing others separates him from most human beings (235, 237). What Paul lacks and Betsy has is an ability to make individual choices. In effect, Paul is a product of something akin to fate, progressively consumed by forces he cannot control.

The difficult choices that people make demonstrate MacDonald's contrast between the freely choosing individual and the determined being operating with few options. However, Dr. Varn's associates in *Nightmare in Pink* also show that people can make negative choices. MacDonald gives no indication that they were in any way forced to experiment illegally on people. Dr. Varn admits to McGee that his work concerns "'questionable ethical behavior'" (99). Dr. Moore specializes in "'hypno-therapy'" (97), and Dr. Daska is Varn's "'resident organic chemist'" (98). Someone named Wilkerson conducts studies in agility (110). However monstrous the activities in the Mental Research Wing of Toll Valley Hospital, the professionals involved freely participate. There is no indication of someone acting under the compulsion of fate, driven to do what society would abhor.

On the surface, Travis McGee, the only character who appears in all twenty-one novels of the series, represents the perfect case study for the idea of individual freedom. George S. Peek states that ". . . McGee, albeit in primarily sexual terms, argues for the development of an individual freedom and responsibility" ("Conquering" 90). MacDonald, who acknowledges his character's insistence "on saying lines consistent with his makeup rather than mine" ("How to Live" 16), has incorporated several factors in McGee's life that contribute to this notion. First, McGee slowly changes during the series, as MacDonald intended he should ("Introduction and Comment" 65), while maintaining a recognizable personality. His often poignant recollections of past incidents sparingly inserted in the series help create an image of stability. This mimetic device deepens his character by expanding reasons for his behavior and raising questions of choice and determinism regarding his actions. Second, McGee's lifestyle on the *Busted Flush* in Bahia Mar almost begs the question as to the idea of individual freedom. Yet, MacDonald continually leaches away McGee's sense of certainty as to the value both of what he does and his very existence. In a strong cross-current, McGee at various moments feels a clear sense of being alive which Mac-Donald afterwards renders problematic by the circumstances which call forth the feeling. The question that arises is, Is McGee's freedom more apparent than real? Finally, the context in which he lives ironically emphasizes McGee's separateness and freedom from entanglements: nearly everyone in the Bahia Mar boat and yacht basin, at least among the regulars, leads a largely unattached life. As Raymond D. Fowler observes: "There is no doubt that

McGee has a narcissistic, egocentric life-style and no continuing obligations or responsibilities for anyone but himself" (42). While the Alabama Tiger's floating house party may be an extreme example of the single life, rarely does one get married and settle down to raise a family in Bahia Mar. Referring to Gretel Howard, whom McGee meets in *The Empty Copper Sea*, MacDonald states in an interview with Charles Oberdorf while writing *Green*, his next novel, that "'I just killed her'" (61).

MacDonald has, thus, created a cautionary atmosphere in which to investigate through McGee the idea of individual freedom. McGee's sense of curiosity is one aspect of his character that clarifies him. Keeping in mind the demarcation between the person who makes choices based on some set of private values and one whose actions seem determined, the idea of curiosity matches well with the above description of McGee. He displays a sense of curiosity about people he meets in his work as well as about his own emotional life. However, one might question his interest in the emotional lives of other people. McGee knows Meyer well and enjoys his company. If he has a best friend, it is Meyer. They talk and share ideas and feelings, but McGee seldom wonders about Meyer's inner life. He does notice his periods of irritation and his moments of joy and sorrow. Essentially, Meyer is present in McGee's life and sufficiently fits with his likes and dislikes so that they maintain a friendship through the periods of strain. His familiarity with Meyer might explain this meager degree of reflection except in periods of reaction to some event in their relationship, e.g., in *Cinnamon Skin*, when his thoughts are situation-oriented. However, his lack of curiosity about Connie Melgar in *A Deadly Shade of Gold* reveals a certain flatness about his emotional responses to other people which appears connected to the sense of remoteness in him noticed by Anne Renzetti in *Cinnamon* (106). Connie's personality is like a smack in the face, and MacDonald does not depict a McGee in any way unaware of her or unwilling to relate to her. But the brief pairing of these two characters does reveal McGee's emotional limits. And, Thomas Doulis observes that immediately prior to Connie, McGee loses Nora Gardino, whom he barely has time to mourn (43). After his recovery from the gunshot wound and before they part, McGee and Connie become lovers and combatants—arguing and fighting, thus exchanging exuberant physical and emotional energy but not understanding one another. They essentially wear themselves out and separate in stalemate. While Connie might live in his memory,

McGee will not spend any time thinking about why she is the way she is or why she said or did any specific thing. When McGee's memories resurface in the series, they sharply impinge on him for only a brief time and then slip away.

In his critical biography on MacDonald, Edgar W. Hirshberg notes that "The moral implications of what happens to the characters in his stories [have] been a primary consideration in MacDonald's fiction" (*MacDonald* 62), and David A. Benjamin states that "The McGee novels (and in fact almost everything written by MacDonald) are morality plays . . ." (31). Being a moralist implies that one has a set of values that determine how one views life, how one makes choices in the difficult circumstances that arise. McGee's moral concerns help define the possibility and nature of individual freedom. In his everyday life and in the more dramatic conditions when he is on a case, McGee struggles with what to do or say and with what he has done or said. In opposition to T. Frederick Keefer's belief that McGee "is a genuinely Existentialist hero in his actions and his philosophical stance" (33), Thomas D. Lane asserts that McGee does not believe that man's actions are ultimately meaningless ("Criticizing" 45). While not arguing for McGee's belief in a transcendental being with whom he can establish a personal relationship (*Gold* 96), one can demonstrate that he thinks that his ideas, feelings, and actions matter in this world, both to him and others. This is not to say that he loyally adheres in every situation to what he thinks is right and proper, and Hirshberg observes a "blurring" of the moral context in the series (*MacDonald* 71). However, when McGee demeans George Brell in *Blue*, Carl Abelle in *The Quick Red Fox*, and Tom Collier in *The Turquoise Lament*, he regrets his actions. McGee in fact is too often susceptible to the idea that the ends determine and justify the means even though at times, as in the case of Collier's knowledge about Pidge Brindle, something needs to be done quickly to ensure a person's safety. Yet, he occasionally feels a sense of disgust at his actions, as if he has betrayed some image of himself. In an article on McGee's Calvinist traits, Frank L. Vatai states that

The only time Travis is free from the pangs of self-reproach is when he is battling evil. Only then does he feel saved, for only then does his inner image of himself connect with what he is actually doing. It is a state of grace and inner integrity where our emotions are not artificial but genuine. (19)

MacDonald will also use a character with a purer moral record, such as Dana Holtzer in *Red*, partially to absolve him. She notes that he takes no pleasure in what he did to Abelle and that he regrets the necessity of the action (75).

Given the number of people who die after interacting with McGee, one might well pause to sort out his degree of blame for their deaths before granting that he attempts to live a moral life. However flawed his character on examination, McGee does seek to abide by some set of values. And more to the point, what defines him as an individual is his acknowledgment and judgment of his own behavior and willingness to continue matching ideals and actions. Bill Ott's distinction between McGee's "conformist impulses" and Marlowe's more extreme "individualism" clarifies McGee's sense of connection to others (5). After McGee puts drugs into the coffee urn in *Pink* while still suffering from Dr. Varn's drug experiments on him and causes the deaths of several people, he later realizes that he was not in complete control of his actions, but he also acknowledges that what he did led to the deaths of innocent people (123-24). McGee's concern for the lives of others even calls forth some awareness of such a responsibility in Terry Drummond, the wealthy socialite who aids him (133). MacDonald is always careful not to overdo the knight in shining armor image as is shown by the many kinds of self-deprecatory references McGee makes to this very idea. Michael J. Tolley remarks that "The Quixote is one of the few acceptable hero types for this cynical age" ("Color" 7). McGee's self-deflation through Don Quixote references of any idealistic pose while still functioning under its influence deflects criticism while allowing him some freedom of action. As noted in the previous chapter, in *Darker than Amber* McGee sends to the victim's family money recovered from his killers, the murder gang to which Vangie Bellemer belonged before she lost the ability to lure men to their deaths (185, 37). Something akin to a moral conscience awakens in Vangie, and as MacDonald has her describe it, she flounders to a withdrawal from that life which subsequently leads to her death (37, 50, 64). At one level, Vangie's moral revulsion at what she has done for so many years speaks to McGee's sense of ethics. Lane observes that ". . . it is only the inability of Vangie . . . to continue with the scheme that causes McGee and Meyer to put a stop to it" ("MacDonald's Villains" 24). It sparks their pursuit of the killers, more fully discussed in Chapter Three, and leads McGee, unprompted, to return the money. Neither McGee nor Meyer pauses long before deciding on this latter action: it is an inevitable result of who they are as people.

MacDonald may have had a vision of a society closing in on individual freedom and through standardization, environmental pressures, and a general loss of personal control and awareness, making it harder to believe that one could and that some do make a difference and/or think independently. In a curious 1967 essay, MacDonald remarks that "McGee resents being processed, programmed, fed through the machinery by experts trained in handling people rather than persons" ("Everybody" 23). In analyzing *Green*, Joseph Marotta, echoing Meyer (*Green* 112-13, 283-84), argues that "It takes time to exorcise the demons of hate and violence, but time is the one thing neither McGee nor the rest of the world is allowed. The apocalyptic pot is already beginning to simmer" (109). Yet, in contrast, his last two Travis McGee novels, *Cinnamon* and *The Lonely Silver Rain*; his last two mainstream novels, *One More Sunday* (1984) and *Barrier Island*; and *Reading for Survival*, his monograph on reading, belie this image of failing hope. He might have said, in *Red*, the fourth novel of the series, that this was the last period in which "offbeats like me" could live independently (96), but in *Silver* and in *Reading*, McGee looks forward to a new salvage job and plans to read more, respectively. Action and thought, hope and curiosity underlie these final pictures of MacDonald's fictional hero and his belief that individual freedom is attainable—still.

Chapter 13

Resilience and Hope:
Political Communities

The functions of the many political communities that exist and overlap in the series provide clear examples of MacDonald's careful integration of plot and theme, the latter both cause and effect of the novels' conflicting tensions and resolutions. Bahia Mar, Travis McGee's home in Ft. Lauderdale, Florida, an archetypal political community against which others are measured and judged, forms and reforms over the series. In *The Scarlet Ruse*, the residents of Bahia Mar, literally a floating community, fear that they will not be permanently allowed to live on their boats, a fear that proves unfounded (9, 316). An initial focus on Bahia Mar as a political community clarifies MacDonald's most basic political ideas and leads to a broader examination of this theme. A general definition of the word *political*, extending beyond merely governmental structures and political parties and movements, would be: people combining together for a common purpose. Terry Eagleton, in his chapter on political criticism in *Literary Theory: An Introduction* (1983), states: "I mean by the political no more than the way we organize our social life together, and the power-relations which this involves . . ." (194). Although this raises difficult questions of origin and tradition in the formation and maintenance of political communities, it will serve as a working definition. From this, several ideas arise, e.g., the means of identifying fellow "citizens," the roles of stability and change, the relationships between supportive and exploitive political communities, and the effects of the past on political structures. In the Travis McGee series, the fragile but elastic nature of the multiple political entities serves as a paradigm for MacDonald's complex view of American society, a society that bends but has not yet broken.

Bahia Mar is at once the most resilient and fragile political community in the series. At the beginning of *The Deep Blue Good-by*, McGee wonders whether or not it is time to move the *Busted Flush*:

I was sprawled on a deep curve of the corner couch, studying charts of the keys, trying to work up enough enthusiasm and energy to plan moving the *Busted Flush* to a new mooring for a while. She has a pair of Hercules diesels, 58 HP each, that will chug her along at a stately six knots. I didn't want to move her. I like Lauderdale. But it had been so long I was wondering if I should. (6)

However, at the end of *The Lonely Silver Rain*, McGee and Meyer discuss the accomplishments of his daughter, Jean, at a party attended by many Bahia Mar regulars and other friends (277). Whatever his travels or experiences, McGee always returns to Slip F-18, Bahia Mar, a permanence in a state of impermanence. The major symbol of this impermanence is the water itself, for McGee's home rises with the tides and can be moved by casting the mooring lines. But, however tenuous the surface, the water does support his home, and with the aid of lines, buffers, and walkways, some stability and connection to others and the outside world are available. Although T. Frederick Keefer states that "Travis McGee . . . conveys his awareness of existential aloneness in images like those in Camus" (37), he later draws a parallel between McGee and Dr. Rieux and others in Albert Camus's *The Plague* which emphasizes McGee's compulsion to respond to people's troubles (44-45), a response drawing him deeper into the human community. As McGee notes the many people from Bahia Mar who, along with other friends, have come to Gretel Howard's funeral in *The Green Ripper*, he says: "My village and my people. They seemed to know what I needed most, a sense of place, the feeling of belonging to some kind of resilient society" (45-46).

The Alabama Tiger's floating house party also represents the seeming tenuousness of the Bahia Mar community. However, the very nature of a party, an event separated from the everyday realities, becomes inverted in this case. Until the Alabama Tiger's death in *Silver* (172), the party stretches from *Blue* to his physical removal. People come and go, occasionally including McGee, but the party seldom even slows. The image of the Tiger sitting and smiling benignly, barefooted and with a drink in his hand presiding over the festivities, the host encouraging the guests to stay in his very rootedness (*Pale Gray for Guilt* 130), centers the permanent in the impermanent. What the Tiger reveals is that the intention to stay in one place is more important than the apparent greater solidity of land versus water or house versus boat. Continuance, if not all, is at least part.

It is somewhat paradoxical to speak of the strength of communal bonds in such a setting that is much like a floating trailer court, but just as many residents of trailer courts settle in and establish permanent homes, so do the inhabitants of Bahia Mar. Of course, several groups associate themselves with the marina in the series: those who live and might also work there, those who visit and/or have friends there, and those who work but do not live there. Chookie McCall, a member of the second group, first appears in *Blue* and returns in later novels, especially in *Bright Orange for the Shroud* when she marries Arthur Wilkinson, another visitor and friend. Meyer lives on the *John Maynard Keynes* near McGee. Others operate boats from the marina and work at the gas dock or marina offices. Transients occasionally play an important role as is the case with Jillian Brent-Archer in *A Tan and Sandy Silence* who offers to make a "respectable" man of McGee, but the latter cannot see himself in the role of the anxious hoverer, ready with a light for his rich lover's cigarette and desperate to please her and thus continue his allowance (32).

Aside from McGee, Meyer is the most central figure in Bahia Mar's communal image. Meyer is stability itself, living in Bahia Mar from early in the series to *Silver*. Even after Cody T.W. Pittler—Evan Lawrence blows up his boat in *Cinnamon Skin* along with Norma Greene Lawrence, Meyer's niece, Captain Hacksaw Jenkins, and Pogo, a temporary deckhand (54), Meyer buys another boat and names it the *Thorstein Veblen* (210). Although McGee never reveals how he and Meyer became friends, Meyer's presence in McGee's life and in Bahia Mar gradually forms from two sources. First, McGee refers to Meyer's wisdom and knowledge. In *The Turquoise Lament*, he describes Meyer as "a transcendent warmth, the listening ear of a total understanding and forgiveness, a humble wisdom" (84). In addition, Meyer's kindness and tolerance pervade the book. Not only within the community but without, people react well to these qualities. They tell Meyer things that they would hesitate to say to other people (*Dress Her in Indigo* 76). On the beach near Bahia Mar, Meyer attracts people who, by some instinct, relate to him in a crowd rather than someone else (*Scarlet* 50). In *Indigo*, McGee states that people do not bore Meyer (76). Meyer's inclusiveness is the essence of that community which, threatened by violence and vulnerable to the human predators that occasionally invade it, survives in its flexibility and openness.

Bahia Mar is the model against which other political communities are explicitly or implicitly measured. The qualities of

openness, friendliness, flexibility, tolerance, and supportiveness last
throughout the series, providing a core of attitudes from which to
analyze and evaluate the outside world. As David Geherin notes,
MacDonald "displays an anthropologist's curiosity about man and
the various structures of his communities" (173). When McGee
ventures from Bahia Mar in *The Quick Red Fox* at the invitation of
Lysa Dean, a prominent Hollywood actress, to recover photographs
of her and stop repeated blackmail attempts, he explores another
type of community, contrasted with Bahia Mar in its short
existence, limited focus, and deadly outcomes. While having an
affair with Carl Abelle, Lysa becomes involved in a four-day orgy
(21) at a beach house near Point Sur, California (19). One of the
participants has hired a photographer to catch his wife, whom he
accompanies to the party, making love with women (120). Lysa,
thus, unknowingly opens herself to blackmail, first from the
photographer (102-03, 105) and then from his assistant (106). The
limited nature of this brief community lies in its focus only on
physical pleasure experienced through drink and sex (19-21).
Although communities have been known to last for much longer
periods focused primarily on the physical, Lysa's group has no other
interest and functions as a *reductio ad absurdum* of that
dehumanization of the individual when no other experience than
physical pleasure matters.

As the novel develops and McGee traces the whereabouts of
the people involved in the orgy, he uncovers death, destruction,
and changed living patterns which resulted both from the orgy and
from their previous lives. Aside from Lysa Dean, he traces Nancy
Abbott to a Florida center for alcoholics (51); learns that Sonny
Catton was killed in a motorcycle accident (55); finds Martha
Whippler in a lesbian community in a Las Vegas trailer court (117);
discovers that Vance M'Gruder's second wife has killed him and
Patty, his first wife and the blackmailing photographer's original
subject (120, 144-46); and follows Carl Abelle to Mohawk Valley,
New York, where Abelle poses as a German ski instructor (68).
Although McGee subsequently learns that Abelle is innocent of
blackmail, he initially attacks him to discover the truth and
consequently lessens Abelle's sense of himself (70-73). MacDonald
structures the outcome of this community so that the inadequate
nature of its purposes and social bonds propels it inevitably along
the path it takes, i.e., a moral failure contained in the idea of an
orgy which objectifies the intimate self and decenters each
individual from whatever core values he or she possesses.

Bahia Mar and Lysa Dean's "party" in *Red* are at opposite ends of the spectrum of political communities and may be classified as supportive and exploitive, respectively. However, an analysis of the constitutive elements of the series' political communities that fit into each category reveals not only broad differences but also sometimes disquieting overlaps. The supportive political groups reflect noncoercive and generally long-standing relationships, a respect for independence, tolerance, varying degrees of friendship, a sense of play, a diffused power structure, broad communal purposes, and a respect for and use of reason. In both contrast and occasional similarity, the exploitive groups reveal coercive though generally long-standing relationships, little respect for independence, a near total lack of tolerance, mutual dependency but no real friendship, a twisted sense of play, a concentrated power struct.re, a narrow, limited purpose, and the sometimes quite efficient use of, if no respect for, reason. The overlaps especially occur in the length of the relationships and in the use and value of reason.

The initial contrast between Bahia Mar and the party in *Red* posits length of relationship as a qualitative measure of the community: the longer the association the more valuable for the participants. However, frequently illegal and/or immoral groups exist for years, if nearly always with a narrow purpose, and some relatively short-lived communities reflect both narrow and broad purposes with admirable moral aims. In the first instance, Calvin Stebber's organization in *Orange* has successfully operated for years and comes into conflict with McGee after Wilma Ferner's marriage to Arthur Wilkinson draws him into Stebber's web. Generally harmonious because of Stebber's control, the group exists only to extort and con money from the naive and unwary. As an example of a short-lived community, Travis McGee, Puss Killian, Meyer, Janine Bannon, Judge Rufus Wellington, and Connie Alvarez form an ad hoc group in *Gray* to reverse the financial and political maneuverings by means of which Tush and Janine Bannon come close to losing their waterfront property in Shawana County. Once the community achieves its purpose and after Tush's death, they disband. Since Puss Killian leaves halfway through the novel, only McGee and Meyer remain in contact. An important element in the above two examples from *Orange* and *Gray* is that not only McGee but also Bahia Mar functions as an opponent to the exploitive communities and as a source of new supportive political communities. By contrast, the exploitive political communities have few direct ties or offshoots though new ones form separately in other novels. Realistically described and delineated, the exploitive communities represent a necessary negative force in the series and are in dialogue and conflict with positive, supportive communities.

The other functional overlap between the two categories is in the use of and value assigned to reason. Somewhat paradoxically, both types of communities see reason, on occasion, as an efficient tool to achieve desired ends. For the exploitive political communities, there is hardly a novel without some group banding together and thinking through, at some level, the problems they should avoid for success. Only loners like Junior Allen in *Blue*, Paul Dissat in *Tan*, and Cody Pittler in *Cinnamon* abstain from discussions with others as to how they should achieve desired ends. Starting with Dr. Varn and Baynard Mulligan in *Nightmare in Pink* and continuing with Griff and Nogs in *Amber* and Brother Titus and the Church of the Apocrypha in *Green*, MacDonald demonstrates the harmful use that people make of reason. In opposition, McGee generally combines with others as with Dana Holtzer in *Red* and Arthur Wilkinson and Chookie McCall in *Orange* to use reason in positive ways. The series has many more parallels between the exploitive and supportive groups in which reason's utilitarian value reveals little moral imperative and in which observation and logic work to achieve planned goals.

From first to last in the series, Travis McGee employs observation and logic to help solve his cases. But the question arises, Is there any other value placed on the mind than a utilitarian one? In addition, is there any pleasure in or appreciation of the intellect or the activities of the mind? And if so, does either type of political community predominate in the belief that the use of reason can lead to a higher quality of life? An analysis of the exploitive political communities in terms of their use of reason shows an almost total lack of appreciation of the intellect beyond the practical. The other negative qualities of the exploitive groups usually impede even an awareness that the mind can focus on more than predatory and calculating activities. However, two groups exemplify the distorted fashion in which reason moves beyond merely functional purposes. In *Green*, aside from learning about armaments and guerrilla tactics, the Church of the Apocrypha's guerrilla group has another educational task; they are to absorb the twisted beliefs of the Church propounded especially by its leaders, Sister Elena Marie and Brother Titus, the man whom Gretel had recognized in Florida as one of the people she had seen in California. McGee remarks in regard to Stella, one of the Church's assassin trainees, on the near complete withering of a critical intelligence, of the evaluation of experience in any larger context than prescribed by the Church authorities (183). No one in the camp even has the appreciation that Frank Sprenger in *Scarlet* shows for his bond business sideline. Sprenger at one point complains to McGee that he has grown to enjoy the intricacies of his front business and says, "'It's what I really want to *do*'" (295). Mental pleasures, however limited their scope, ironically seduce Sprenger, tantalizing him with a world he cannot enter.

In the supportive community of Bahia Mar, McGee and Meyer best exemplify the range of possibilities associated with the mind. As discussed in Chapter Five, McGee occasionally reads and enjoys good music. These activities occur before, during, or after working on a case in which he frequently forms some other, more temporary community to help him complete his salvage operation. However, Bahia Mar is nearly always where he reads. At a more social level, McGee also likes to discuss ideas. Admittedly, he is not an intellectual even though he reveals an intellectual curiosity about the world (Ecenbarger 24). McGee's curiosity is not limited to passing observations, e.g., seeing or hearing of something and responding to it at a low level of abstraction, but rather it leads him to speculate on why some things occur as they do and the possible consequences if they continue unabated. This curiosity leads to informed opinions which he is most likely to share with friends or acquaintances at Bahia Mar. Geherin describes him "as a bright and knowledgeable man whose active intelligence is as important as his fists, and as much responsible for his successes as are his more physical attributes" (166). And to a certain extent, the speculative aspects of his intelligence by necessity operate separately from his more violent activities; they need a stable environment in which to grow.

Since McGee narrates the series, one never sees Meyer alone on the *Keynes* or later the *Veblen* involved in his research and writing on economics. And yet, Meyer personifies for Bahia Mar the intellect as value. Although McGee admires as well his kindness and concern for others, he consistently appreciates Meyer's ability to think clearly through a problem. McGee cannot judge his professional work, but he can understand Meyer's conceptual reach either in a general discussion or when he brings Meyer a problem to solve in relation to his salvage work. The opposite end of the intellectual spectrum, at least in moral terms, would be Dr. Varn's inhuman drug experiments in *Pink*. In that novel, Dr. Varn sees the mind divorced from human concerns and values; Meyer never does. Professor Ted Lewellen in *Turquoise* resembles Meyer in the value placed on the intellect. Although Lewellen, like Meyer, has a practical purpose in his researches of lost ships and their treasures, McGee describes his scholarly inquiries as springing originally from broader motives (10). In the same fashion, Meyer's researches benefit his investments but also reveal an intellectual curiosity. The articles he writes and the papers he presents at conferences testify to his deep interest in economic and financial problems.

MacDonald creates a mixed legacy of past influences that interact in a variety of ways with the series' present political communities. In *One Fearful Yellow Eye*, McGee's previous friendship with Gloria Geis and Anna Ottlo and Perry Hennigan's evil past and long-range scheme to enrich themselves at the Geises' expense are just one example of opposite currents meeting and resulting in a positive future with Gloria, Janice Stanyard, Susan Kemmer, and her siblings creating a healthy new community. Even if Anna and Perry were *not* killed, McGee is able to help Gloria and the others join together, using her home as a base for their future life. MacDonald seems to argue in *Yellow* that good past motivations and actions produce good future results. *The Girl in the Plain Brown Wrapper* moderates this position somewhat since McGee does not figure out Pike's plan to inherit Maureen's and Bridget's fortunes before he kills Maureen, his wife, but McGee does prevent his harming his sister-in-law, Bridget. It is McGee's past friendship with Helena Pearson, Maureen and Bridget's mother, that brings him into her daughters' lives and leads him to work with Al Stanger and Ben Gaffner to help thwart Pike. *Pink* reveals equally positive past associations in McGee's friendship with Mike Gibson. Unable to help his sister because of Korean-era war wounds, he calls on McGee who establishes a close relationship with Nina in the process of discovering the source of money she found in her apartment after her fiancé's death. Only Mike's trust in McGee convinces Nina to confide in him and alleviate her doubts about the man she loved.

If anything, MacDonald is aware of man's capacity for evil. *A Deadly Shade of Gold* is a paradigm for the negative effects of past evil and corruption. Carlos Menterez, after enriching himself under Batista, flees Cuba when Castro takes over and settles in Puerto Altamura, Mexico. The political community he establishes, seemingly modeled on Batista's, places him at the center, controlling all wealth and power. The stroke he suffers leaves him unable to talk or move but conscious enough to experience fear and no ability to protect himself. This symbolic resolution to an ill-spent life is a clear converse to the above pattern in *Yellow* and *Brown*. However, *Purple* represents a more complex effect from the past. Jass Yeoman is at the center of two past currents that converge in the present, one killing him. Jass, Walter Ruppert, and Cube Fox did not keep within the tax laws, and Yeoman realizes that their past associations betrayed to the IRS by Ruppert, as discussed in Chapter Eleven, threaten to hit him doubly hard since he both married Mona, Cube's daughter, and looted her inheritance. The other current involves Amparo, a woman who bore him a child, Dolores, whom Jass takes into his home and later drunkenly rapes. Jass's current political community of business associates and Sheriff Buckelberry appears threatened when McGee enters Jass's life, and McGee has little time to understand the dynamics of Mona's murder and prevent Jass's death. If nothing else, MacDonald's novels clearly show that the marks left by the past do not easily disappear.

Although the Travis McGee series reaches no solution to the contest between exploitive and supportive political communities and even, as Keefer suggests (45), shows some contamination of the latter by the former, MacDonald demonstrates the breadth of those communities which nurture their members and sustain them without expecting monetary return. As McGee states in *Turquoise* after Prof. Lewellen dies in a traffic accident and the Bahia Mar community rallies around his daughter, Pidge, "The semipermanent population of Bahia Mar takes care of its own. Sympathy may not be long-lasting, but when it is focused, there is a lot of it. Pidge got a lot, and it helped her through the worst of it" (40). Such incremental restorations in MacDonald's fiction hold at least an imaginary line against dissolution and despair.

Chapter 14

Race, Ethnicity, and Class

MacDonald intertwines race, ethnicity, and class in his series to create one of his most important thematic focuses. No novel is without one of these ideas affecting the ultimate outcome. Occasionally, females, in the novels set in the United States, are from a racial minority. In *Darker than Amber* and *The Girl in the Plain Brown Wrapper*, MacDonald depicts black women as maids, thus employing the idea of class as well but partially inverting it in each case. Further, Noreen Walker in *Amber*, turns out to be not only a university graduate but secretly working for CORE, allowing MacDonald to reflect the current Civil Rights Movement. Although these two novels are special with their emphasis on modern United States race relations, other works in the series bring in American Indians, Cubans, Mexicans, Venezuelans, Peruvians, and descendants of the Mayans. In at least seven novels, important scenes occur outside the United States, and these different environments complicate the racial, ethnic, and class aspects for an American reader, but in those novels that unfold in the United States, MacDonald uses class within the larger white community and race and class as divisions between whites and other racial or ethnic groups to explore social tensions and add range to the possible outlooks and choices for action. Ultimately, the three themes represent division and allow MacDonald through the multiple permutations in the twenty-one McGee novels to explore the imperfect solutions possible in the tensions of his characters' lives.

As responsive as MacDonald's fiction is to the world around him, it is not surprising that he would include minorities as characters in his novels. In *Amber* and *Brown*, black women play small, if necessary, roles in the developing plots. While men and women from other races appear at important points in various novels, few black men do. Noreen Walker in *Amber* provides McGee with significant information about Vangie Bellemeer after the latter's murder. As usual, McGee's motivations in investigating the latter's death are mixed: he wants both money and vengeance

133

on those who killed her, a woman whom he saw as morally tainted even if possessing a rudimentary bad conscience about her own participation in the novel's murder ring. McGee obtains Noreen's address from a woman at Howard Realty, which manages the apartment complex where Vangie lived, phones, and drives to Arlentown after Noreen returns from work at six. There, after cautiously waiting at the gate, McGee learns from Noreen's mother that she has returned from work and is "'[c]hanging her clothes'" (87). MacDonald uses this stylized and careful exchange for two possible reasons. One, he distances McGee from the type of white man who assumes that blacks have few rights, feelings, or desires about the way that strangers approach their homes. Second, McGee's carefulness reflects his unsureness about how to deal with blacks. Not that he kicks in people's doors as a rule but he seldom acts so circumspectly when there is so little obvious danger. McGee says, "I parked in front of her place in the evening slant of sunshine, aware of eyes watching me from up and down the block" (87). This parallels the people watching him pay a daytime visit to Dolores Estobar, who is part Indian, in A Purple Place for Dying (90-91). McGee does not know the steps to the minority dance in the series and never really learns.

Noreen is a complex of appearances, attitudes, and desires, and it is with regret that one sees her disappear from the novel even though she no longer has any legitimate role to play when McGee acquires her information about Vangie. For Noreen, deception appears essential to living her life with some degree of control. David Geherin remarks that ". . . the woman turns out to be as much a master of the charade as McGee is" (77). The first element of her disguise is language. She approaches McGee's car parked in front of her mother's home and enquires, "'Askin fo' me, mister?'" (Amber 88). Noreen subsequently admits to being "'a University of Michigan graduate. I taught school before I got married'" (90). She explains her suspicion by saying that "'I hope you do understand that the standard disguise is . . . pretty imperative'" (89). Her job as a maid is another disguise since she is "'one of the regional directors of CORE. . . . Working as a maid gives me more freedom of action, less chance of being under continual observation'" (90). Noreen checks McGee out with a black lawyer named Sam B.K. Dickey, learns that she "'can trust [him] a hundred percent, which is something Mr. Sam would not say too often about our own people'" (89), and arranges to talk with him later that evening. From that talk, McGee acquires much needed information about Vangie and her girlfriends, especially a hint in regard to where Vangie hid her money (94).

As Geherin observes (78), Noreen also provides MacDonald with an opportunity to make two distinct statements about race, one from McGee's perspective, the other from hers. Largely ignoring the black male, McGee sees Noreen as one who has "that slightly forced elegance of the educated Negro woman" (*Amber* 92), a representative of those who "carry the dead weight of all their deprived people" (92-93). Even though educated and, according to McGee, knowing that the mass of blacks are not ready for the "realities of Now" (93), she cannot admit her knowledge and demands racial equality for all. This places her in a dangerous position and, evidenced by her reliance on Dickey's word to trust a white man, ". . . it meant she had a vulnerable streak of softness in her, which could guarantee martyrdom sooner or later" (93). McGee, "conceived," as Charles Oberdorf reports, "to embody all the fleshy fantasies of middle-aged, middle-class North American men" (61), acknowledges his own instinctive human awareness of difference but "would cherish the ones who came through as solid folk, and avoid the slobs and fools and bores as diligently as I avoid white slobs and fools and bores" (93). Stating that "My intolerance is strictly McGee-type" (93), McGee manages to maintain a distinctive, if not wholly original, voice in the explosive area of race relations.

Noreen Walker's position, hardly confirmatory of McGee's ideas about her, is one ultimately filled with contradictions. Speaking of her two boys at one point, she states, "'My boys are two and a half and four. What am I doing to their lives if I let them grow up here? We want out'" (*Amber* 96). Earlier she stated that she came back after her husband died of cancer and that she worked for CORE. These statements render her later comments about leaving ambiguous. It is possible with her education that she can get out at any time but that she stays because she works in the Civil Rights movement. Another contradiction lies in her racialist statements leading to a position close to separate but equal with blacks doing the separating. Noreen does not want white friends (96), socialization with whites (96), or any sexual contact with them (96). In *A Friendship*, MacDonald comments in a 1972 letter on this separatist phenomenon:

How about the fact that the colleges which made a maximum effort to recruit bright black students on the grounds that the interracial mix would be beneficial to both races, now find that the blacks refuse to mingle with the whites, forming their own closed enclaves? This is sad and funny. (200)

In addition to the "bitterness on her face" (96) observed by McGee, she reveals a physical aversion to whites: "'You know how white people look to me? The way albinos look to you'" (96). What she wants is equal treatment before the law and "'our share of the power structure of this civilization'" (96). Ironically, she states this world will be one in which "'. . . a good man will be thought a credit to the *human* race'" (96) though what will make a connected world in her view is not clear. A further irony is that she has armed herself with a switchblade knife for her walk home through "'the ghetto'" (95). Though not developed further, a possible "martyrdom" for Noreen is an inability to fit into either the black or white worlds or believe in one in which both races together create a third possibility.

Lorette Walker's role in *Brown* is more extensive, more integrated into the plot and McGee's life than Noreen's. While she has fewer outward accomplishments such as Noreen's university degree and work with CORE, she reveals a wide range of emotions to McGee, even tentatively crossing that invisible line that sometimes inhibits sexual relationships between the races. Both Lorette and Noreen are maids and share the same last name, and since *Amber* and *Brown* are the seventh and tenth novels in the series, respectively, it is unlikely that MacDonald connects them in this way accidentally. Although McGee knows Lorette for a longer period of time, he never meets her outside the motel setting where he stays and she works. In contrast, he meets Noreen only after work at her home and later the same evening when they drive to a friend's house to talk. Lorette always wears her uniform when with McGee, and Noreen appears in two sets of clothing. Yet, Lorette relates far more to McGee as a woman than Noreen does. Lorette has the requisite rejection of the aggressive white male who takes advantage of motel maids, yet she acts almost flirtatiously with McGee when he does not behave in any stereotypical way. On one occasion, she talks with him apart from the other maids in a service alley behind the motel kitchen (*Brown* 148) and even spends some time with him in his room with the door closed. Noreen is more ideological than Lorette regarding race if not more suspicious of whites, witness her diatribe against the two kinds of law meted out to blacks and whites (*Amber* 95-96), an acknowledgment also made by Detective Stanger in *Brown* (173), but Lorette reveals a fuller range of character traits, and at the end of the novel MacDonald temporarily withholds the name of the woman in his bedroom on the *Flush* before revealing it is Mrs. Janice Holton (256) and not Mrs. Walker whom McGee speaks of appreciatively as she leaves his Ft. Courtney motel room only a few pages before (254).

In *Amber* and *Brown*, race determines class, and while blacks were not limited to the lower class in the 1960s, MacDonald's Travis McGee novels reflect few American blacks that hold positions that imply a middle-class existence. For a wide range of class positions for people other than non-Hispanic whites, one must turn to his novels set in Mexico. MacDonald spent some years there in the late 1940s and came to appreciate the land and its people (MacDonald, *House* 70-72). *A Deadly Shade of Gold, Dress Her in Indigo, Cinnamon Skin,* and *The Lonely Silver Rain* expand his perspectives on race, ethnicity, and class, giving a greater understanding of his views on the dynamics of those concepts.

Gold describes a world of social and emotional extremes that derive their power from several dichotomies: North, South and light-skinned, dark-skinned. With the move to the almost inaccessible Puerto Altamura, Mexico, MacDonald can portray a world free from "civilized" constraints and yet, through expensive boats, a modern hotel, and villas, possessed of its services and products. The flawed and possibly lower-class, if to Nora Gardino attractive, Sam Taggart is, paradoxically, the human symbol of the primitive world from which he escaped only to be killed in Florida by Ramon Talavera, the brother of Maria Talavera, murdered by Sam and Miguel (*Gold* 272-73, 214); Talavera is from that world, i.e., the South, but, equally paradoxically, not representative of it. And the gold statues which are a ruse to get near Sam are a cultural symbol of the subterranean darkness in that area bracketed by the sea and the jungle. Sam from the North combines with Miguel to murder four Cubans who have come to kill Carlos Menterez, a former Batista official and Sam's employer. While Miguel is connected to the darker-skinned passions of the South, the four victims have family and political reasons for killing Menterez, reversing part of the image MacDonald creates through their superior moral concerns.

McGee and Felicia Novaro, a part-time prostitute and Sam's lover in Puerto Altamura, continue MacDonald's conflation of his two dichotomies. McGee has warned Nora, whom he accompanies to Mexico to avenge Sam's death, that part of his reason for going is to get a line on the gold statues that Sam lost. The objective white northerner engages the passionate, ungovernable southerner only to have the images reversed. For while Felicia attacks him when he asks about Sam, thinking he was like the others who tortured her to get information about him, she reveals herself as a self-indulgent, emotionally shallow figure. In contrast, McGee, after threatening Almah Hichin with torture and death, feels a deep revulsion for his actions. Even though Almah confesses that she, on Carlos's instructions, urged Sam to kill the four Cubans (Gold 166-67), McGee's response is to get drunk and defeat the image of the broken woman in the jungle clearing (176).

Connie Melgar, "'Very rich and very difficult'" (Gold 224), according to Paul Dominguez, McGee's acquaintance, brings geography and ethnicity to her relationship with McGee as she nurses him back to health after he is shot at Cal Tomberlin's party. An upper-class woman from Venezuela (224), Connie exercises few controls over her desires and emotions. Living in the United States, she has freed herself from most inhibitions:

I am the complete bitch, and it doesn't bother me a bit. I have a very rational approach to my needs and desires. I am thirty-five years old, darling, and I shall never marry again, and there is no reason why, with my looks and my money, I should settle for an empty bed. (228)

However, the threat that Tomberlin might entrap her by drugging and filming her making love alarms her (256). Yet, Connie is no more passionate and emotional than McGee as he recovers from his wound in a cabin "'near the San Bernadino National Forest'" (269). Both represent the ideas of control and passion, and through MacDonald's leveling of boundaries, mental and physical, the assertion of human complexity across all areas of experience becomes dominant.

Few novels in the series have as complicated a plot as Gold, yet Indigo challenges it. If not completely generating the sense of the exotic, Mexico at least enhances it in MacDonald's fiction. Several of his non-Travis McGee novels take place in Mexico, e.g., Please Write for Details, The Damned, and The Empty Trap, and while they may not always surpass the exotic qualities of the McGee novels set in the United States, they have an air of release, of possibilities for experiencing life differently if not better. The subtropical climate of Florida has a similar flavor in the series. Something in the mixture of the heat, water, animals, and wilderness areas speaks of a dark, unknown quality that can erupt in people's lives. An archetypal image of this is *Bright Orange for the Shroud's* Boone Waxwell and his swamp retreat. The statements that he and Cindy make about the fauna and flora of the nearby swamp (94, 136-37) and his flight and death at the end of the novel have an almost un-American quality about them. Hovering to the south and west with the Yucatan peninsula jutting into the Gulf of Mexico, that source of great power and terror in *Condominium* and *Murder in the Wind*, Mexico itself beckons to MacDonald's imagination equally with Florida and much of the rest of the United States.

Yet, *Indigo* is subversive of this picture of the exotic South. *Gold* has the orderly Mr. Arista as hotel manager and the banking and financial centers of Mexico City in the background as well as the efficient, experienced policeman in Colonel Marquez. But *Indigo* foregrounds this middle class Mexican existence, and except for the Indian culture in the nearby mountains and Jerry Nesta's tales of the Mexican peasants that his group encountered, the most apparent lower-class life is the generally former middle-class Americans who traveled with Bix Bowie to Mexico. The pattern is a downward movement in class behavior. Backspin and Jeanie, her drugged-out friend, two other young Americans, set the tone for McGee and Meyer as to what they will encounter when they find or learn about the members of Bix's group. Backspin's desire to leave Oaxaca with her friend reveals a wish to recapture her life and place in American society (*Indigo* 106-07). Contrasted with the failures of the above Americans, Enelio Fuentes, a Stanford Business School alumnus and the owner of a Volkswagen agency in Oaxaca (79-80), and the three young Mexican women, Lita, Elena, and Margarita, on vacation from Guadalajara where they work in an insurance company (135), look the picture of success and well-directed energy. In addition to his Volkswagen agency, Fuentes belongs to the Commercial Club set atop a building near Oaxaca (134-35). MacDonald's portrait of Fuentes and other well-to-do, hard-working Mexicans is in sharp contrast to the disintegrating youth who come south with Bix.

MacDonald returns briefly to Mexico in *Cinnamon* and *Silver*, the last two novels in the series. *Cinnamon* continues the image of the positive, healthy Mexican and Indian cultures while *Silver* presents a more complex picture of the debilitating drug culture represented by El Brujo, a Mexican with "'a degree in business administration from Stanford'" (138-39), and Ruffino Marino, the son of a Miami crime family leader (143). In *Cinnamon*, Barbara

Castillo, a descendant of the Mayans and Toltecs (227), helps McGee and Meyer kill Cody Pittler after she learns that he killed her lover, William Doyle (230). Pittler, a man with some college experience, destroys loved and promising young women and dies partially at the hands of a representative of a people with the furthest to travel in rising socially and economically in the 20th century. At the end of the novel, Barbara is with McGee in Bahia Mar, in one sense having completed the circle begun by Pittler's violence. Symbolically, the darker-skinned South partially replaces the lighter-skinned North in terms of energy and purpose.

Marino murders Howard Cannon and two young women after Howard, aka John Rogers, pays El Brujo, the Mexican drug dealer with whom Marino trades (138), with counterfeit money (139-40). The confluence of these three men raises interesting issues in terms of class and ethnicity. Can money bring class standing? Probably not when its source is so obviously known to be from illegal activity even though "'[Marino, Sr.] bought respectability and he wants to keep it'" (143), according to Browder, the American drug agent with whom McGee goes to Mexico. El Brujo, probably Mayan (135), "'uses his education'" according to his employee Martin. "'He's a very serious man'" (142). Howard Cannon, "'from trashy stock'" (14), probably thinks his clever plan to cheat El Brujo and force Marino to include him in any deal will lift him from his dead-end life (144). El Brujo is the only one who seems to profit from the triangular relationship and the only one with any possible future. It is not that MacDonald has presented them as representatives of their classes or countries but that in their interrelationships he depicts the Mexican-Mayan, as the most successful. All three men struggle in difficult circumstances, but one survives, however precariously, thus indirectly emphasizing the even greater instability of American society.

As in so many other areas, *The Deep Blue Good-by* (1964) presents a broad spectrum of MacDonald's views on class. From Lois Atkinson, one of Junior Allen's victims, to Corry and Deeleen, Allen's acquaintance and lover, respectively, MacDonald dramatizes a largely female cross section of American class attitudes. The class status of the characters, never very high and frequently below or even outside the concept, aids in defining their pasts, presents, and various futures. Junior Allen and Fancha, the Haitian whore, do not count in terms of either class or race. They are too extreme to represent any but a personal order. However, they do matter in contrast to the more refined Lois Atkinson, setting off her ability to appreciate a world in which civility, kindness, and nonaggression are admired qualities. Even though Lois has a potential weakness in her ability to be dominated and exploited, this does not lessen her value as a person. Patty Devlan, another and younger target of Allen's, is a less-experienced version of Lois, both examples of the middle class. Part of the good they represent lies in the sense of the future they suggest. Lois recovers from Allen's depredations with her humanity intact, and Patty's character suggests a life of private experience and feeling in sharp contrast to the more vulgar, if socially and economically middle class, Molly Bea Archer from the same novel. Both Lois and Patty exemplify the type of woman that McGee describes in *Blue* who demands commitment by the male in exchange for intimacy (26-27).

Cathy Kerr and Chookie McCall, ostensibly lower middle class, perform a peculiarly American action in the same novel in reducing the importance of class. Since class is so very clearly a relational concept, the foregoing is seen when they are contrasted with Corry and Deeleen. The latter two women are primarily physical in their orientations. Working as waitresses, posing for photographers, or moving toward a professional status in their sexual experiences, Corry and Deeleen endure hopeless lives from McGee's perspective, attracting men like Pete who reflect their lack of a future direction (178-79, 181). Pete's rejection of Patty in favor of Corry, the woman whom McGee has fastidiously avoided, symbolizes his poor taste (195, 206). Events act on them rather than the reverse, emphasizing their class limitations. Cathy, however, even though Allen also uses her and even though McGee initially senses some aura of defeat about her, transcends her circumstances in her love for her family and her hard work as a dancer in Chookie's troupe. Chookie, involved with Frank Durkin whom she calls "'my Junior Allen'" (25) and whom she will jettison in *Orange* (188-89), leads her dance group with a dynamism that impresses McGee. For these latter two women, the layers of their individual selves continually surprise, leading one to evaluate them from a more individual than social perspective and thus resisting categorization.

America has produced no national upper class, and this allows a continued redefinition of what it means to be socially above the upper middle class. The idea is flexible enough to accept foreigners such as Jillian Brent-Archer in *A Tan and Sandy Silence* and Lady Vivian Stanley-Tucker in *The Green Ripper*. Wealth and privacy are the expected ingredients of upper-class life. Its regional variants frequently mix power and family with the above two qualities as indicated in *The Dreadful Lemon Sky* with Jane Schermer's uncle, a judge and political player in Bayside, Florida. Even though they possess wealth and privacy, it would be difficult to place such figures as Judge Rufus Wellington in *Pale Gray for Guilt*, Jass Yeoman in *Purple*, or Millis Ingraham in *Silver* in the upper class. These characters are regional but would probably be labeled upper class only by default. Lacking social graces, another upper-class trait, they emphasize the absence of any national model for an American "aristocracy," leaving one with many upper classes. Possibly this leads to the vulnerability displayed by such characters as Linda Featherman in *The Long Lavender Look* to a type like Lew Arnstead, a decidedly lower-class figure, or less obviously by Jane Schermer to social climbers like Frederick Van Harn. These latter two women resemble Joanna Armister in *Nightmare in Pink*, one of the first upper-class women in the series, though each has different experiences. Linda presumably commits suicide rather than be controlled and/or exposed by Arnstead (*Lavender* 164). Jane Schermer reluctantly acknowledges Frederick Van Harn's weakness to McGee before Van Harn dies from fire ant bites in *Lemon* (243-44, 245, 253). And Joanna accepts her mentally impaired husband after Dr. Varn's plot fails. Not even the upper class can find a sanctuary in America as Terry Drummond, Joanna's sister, in *Pink* discovers when Dr. Varn and Baynard Mulligan's minions come close to capturing her as she aids the drug-weakened McGee.

The thematic struggles for dominance with character and plot in the McGee series; ideas struggle with formula. Yet, even though McGee changes throughout the range of novels, he is still a series character. Plot demands, as in any mystery/detective work, are vital; however, as the action shifts and alters him through aging, loss, love, friendship, violence, and regret, MacDonald employs similar devices found in his novels of manners and morals. He tells the stories with strong thematic focuses that twist and turn from *Blue* to *Silver* but nonetheless persist. Ross Thomas speaks of the McGee books as "a brilliant and often searing analysis of the '60s, the '70s and the beginning of the '80s" (D12). And for those decades, race, ethnicity, and class were, and still are, significant areas of contention for both novelist and society which find their place in the McGee series.

Chapter 15

Sexuality, Love, and Character

Probably in no area more than the sexual does the character of Travis McGee reveal itself in all of its complexity, diversity, self-delusion, and capacity for change. The reserve that Anne Renzetti in *Cinnamon Skin* sees in him possibly stems from his recurrent self-doubt about his sexual motives so clearly stated in *A Tan and Sandy Silence* (*Cinnamon* 6, *Tan* 250-51). This portrayal supports Michael J. Tolley's view that ". . . MacDonald is one of the important novelists concerned with the critique of sexual morality" ("Color" 7). His statement at one point to Cindy Birdsong in *The Dreadful Lemon Sky* that too many women are dying on him and his reaching out for her demonstrate a need to fill a void within himself that only the sexual act can accomplish (162). On various occasions, McGee has been both healer and healed through the act of love, and these positive encounters, as well as his apparent love for Gretel Howard in *The Empty Copper Sea* and *The Green Ripper*, portray a personality that, despite the seemingly permanent self-doubt, can experience real (if temporary) growth and depth of feeling in a world containing both loss and gain.

One of the most important roles that McGee plays in the areas of sexuality and love is that of the healer. MacDonald establishes this relational framework in *The Deep Blue Good-by*. McGee, trying to discover the whereabouts of Junior Allen for Cathy Kerr and recover what Allen took from her, encounters Lois Atkinson, another victim of Allen's sexual and emotional manipulations. When McGee appears at her Candle Key home, Lois assumes that Allen has passed her on to him (58). She soon collapses, and McGee, after nursing her back to health as discussed in Chapter Nine, continues to pursue Allen. Although McGee and Lois later become lovers (156), this occurs only after she once again assumes some responsibility for her life and can voluntarily engage in a sexual liaison with him. Carol Cleveland states that

Only when he is dealing with a person nearly restored to mental and physical health does a physical affair begin. Lois Atkinson . . . who has just survived the ministrations of Junior Allen, literally needs her life and sanity saved. These things accomplished, she makes the first advance to McGee. (408)

In essence, McGee, even granting the reservations about motive voiced in Chapter Nine, functions as a positive source of caring that allows Lois to find herself, reflecting John Feetenby's sense of the "genuine depth of human concern that MacDonald manages to evoke" (6) in the series. Though McGee is frequently skeptical about his intentions toward women, he usually sees them as more than extensions of himself. As Edgar W. Hirshberg has noted, "Despite his reputation, McGee does not simply take everything he can get by way of sex . . ." ("Social Critic" 132). His awareness of the possibility that his aim is only manipulative and self-seeking allows him to avoid the solipsistic trap.

Although McGee becomes involved in serious romantic relationships, as in the case of Nora Gardino (*A Deadly Shade of Gold*) and especially Gretel Howard, he occasionally attempts to change the sexual behavior of women, resulting in a more problematic association. This occurs with Isobel Webb (*A Purple Place for Dying*) and Heidi Geis Trumbill (*One Fearful Yellow Eye*). Isobel's brother, John, has reportedly run off with Mona Yeoman, the woman who hired McGee to retrieve some of her inheritance from her husband. However, McGee knows that Mona has been killed and helps to prove that John is also dead. After the case is over, Travis takes Isobel, discussed in terms of illness in Chapter Nine, to the islands, promising her that in his attempt to arouse her sexually he will stop whenever she says no (*Purple* 147). Eventually, he helps to free her sexually (154). As John Wiley Nelson remarks on McGee's role as a healer, putting it into a clear perspective, "The wisdom of the body is its own source of healing grace" (191).

When in *Yellow* McGee offers to help Heidi Trumbill achieve a full sexual experience and move from "ice-maiden" (47) to a fuller sense of her own life, Heidi derides his "'terrible sacrifice'" (147). While it is true that Heidi would benefit emotionally and physically, as she does at the end of the novel, and while McGee does attempt to defend his offer, he cannot quite efface the sense of his benefit weighing at least equally with hers. One key to McGee's attitude lies with remarks he makes to Heidi:

I guess I would say that I want to be friends. A friend wants to help a friend. I want to peel away that suspicion and contention because I don't think it's really what you're like. If we can get friendship going, then maybe we can get a good physical intimacy going, and from that we can fall into a kind of love or fall into an affection close to love. (148-49)

The difference between the two episodes is that McGee attempts to examine his motivations more closely with Heidi, revealing what Erling B. Holtsmark calls his "defined amatory code" (100). He admits that his desire to relieve her of her repressions is not completely disinterested (*Yellow* 147-49), a thought not only agreed with by Heidi but also by Isobel: "'I'm alive once more. And that is a gift from you, of course. But certainly not because you were being terribly terribly generous about everything'" (*Purple* 155).

Two interesting aspects of McGee's explanation to Heidi need consideration. One is that he willingly explores the ambiguity in his intentions. He knows that Heidi is desirable, but another less obvious motivation is his role as a healer. It possibly connects with his job as a salvage consultant, essentially a dangerous service job that benefits others as well as himself. Another and less favorable aspect lies in the psychological stance toward Heidi. McGee objectifies her if not exactly depicting her as an object. If it is a positive quality not to view people merely as extensions of oneself, one can see them as too much divorced from the cares and needs of the self. This stance could become manipulative. McGee is saved from this, saved from what Chookie McCall, as noted in Chapter Three, wonders about when she says that maybe Boone Waxwell is Travis "'gone bad'" (*Bright Orange for the Shroud* 103), by creating a sexual and emotional union with the one healed.

For all that McGee functions as a healer in many relationships, as Peggy Moran notes, ". . . he is more healer than healed" (86), he is nearly as often the one healed. Cleveland remarks, "For every woman McGee helps and heals, almost two do the same for him" (409-10). Whatever the exact number, MacDonald builds complexity into his character and avoids sexual stereotyping that, with McGee's life-style, might seem nearly unavoidable. Women heal McGee at two levels, physically and emotionally, although the levels are seldom completely distinct. Sometimes a woman from one level will function on the other as well. Connie Melgar, in *Gold*, is the best example of a woman who heals McGee physically. Shot by George Wolcott, the government undercover agent, while escaping from Calvin Tomberlin's house with the gold statues (262), McGee, as noted in Chapter Fourteen, is taken by Connie to a cabin in the California mountains (269). After he heals sufficiently, Connie slips into his bed and accelerates his convalescence (277). As observed in Chapter Twelve, they are both too independent and stubborn, and little emotional sympathy develops between them. Earlier in the same novel, McGee makes love to Junebug, the woman who helps him find a place to stay that allows him to avoid hotels. She makes it plain that she wants to sleep with him, but McGee avoids her and then almost indirectly reaches out for her:

I left it to chance. I put a robe on and let the Junebug number ring once before I hung up. I left the door ajar and sat in the dark living room. She pushed the door open cautiously and said, "Was that you?"
     And she was a warmth to cling to, to keep from drowning. (232)

It is obvious that Travis, emotionally isolated and still recovering from Nora's death, needs the healing contact of someone. While not providing much emotional support, Junebug's humanity and closeness are essential and represent more than the merely physical ministrations of Teddie, one of the crew on Mickey Laneer's *Hell's Belles* in *Tan* that rescues him from the Caribbean after he escapes from Paul Dissat (202-03).
     McGee experiences several other instances of emotional healing. After facing the horror and violence that the seemingly innocuous Wally McLeen commits in *Dress Her in Indigo*, McGee turns willingly to the emotionally and morally healthy Elena, an example of what Nelson terms "MacDonald's good girl [who] respects sex for the human sharing of the act itself . . ." (172). Further, Nelson terms Elena "the perfectly natural woman, uninhibited by complex social rationalizations" (189). Of course, McGee's need of her is as much an indication of uncertainties in himself as a revulsion over what he has witnessed, not only with regard to Wally but also between Eva Vitrier and Beatrice Bowie, the woman whose presumed death he had come to Mexico to investigate. Elena is a symbol, robbed of some complexity, of a positive, benign life force as well as a desirable woman. David Geherin says that McGee's "clouds of uncertainty [are] dispersed by the sunshine of her sex" (105). Elena and her sister Margarita glow with health, desire, and a confident energy that reflects well on them and a vibrant generation of Mexican youth (135). In a more complex fashion, Cindy Birdsong (*Lemon*) offers a physically and emotionally healing relationship. When Harry Hascomb plants a bomb in a package delivered to Joanna Freeler, McGee is injured

and moves from his partially destroyed boat to a room in Cindy's motel. By then, Jason Breen has killed her husband, and when McGee, recovering through Cindy's aid, reaches out for her, she responds (162-63). David K. Jeffrey, referring to this event, states that "Such sexual relationships have a regenerative function, healing the wounds of violence" (78). However, McGee, even needing the emotional help offered, cannot give of himself sufficiently to maintain the relationship (167-68). And, Cindy also asserts her emotional independence by not responding to McGee's offer for her to stay with him for a while on the *Flush*. Rather, she chooses to rebuild the motel and boat business that her husband had partially ruined (271-72).

At certain moments when McGee is in need of emotional healing, this need has been sharply stressed only to be deflected and at best only ameliorated. At the end of *Tan*, McGee complains to Meyer of a deep sense of disgust towards himself and his motivations with regard to women:

I just can't . . . I can't stand the thought of ever again hearing my own sincere, manly, loving, crap-eating voice saying those stale words about how I won't ever hurt you, baby, I just want to screw you and make you a more sincere and emotionally healthy woman. (251)

As noted in Chapter Two, Meyer refuses to let him further unburden himself, but Jeannie Dolan, with whom McGee has had some contact while unraveling Harry Broll's financial disasters, appears on Travis's boat. Meyer ironically questions Jeannie as to her inner conflicts; she, of course, has none (254) and thus represents a figure emotionally opposite to McGee with whom he can temporarily relate and neutralize his identity problems. Similarly, after McGee returns from eliminating the terrorist organization in *Green*, he eventually goes sailing with Lady Vivian Stanley-Tucker (277), and her healthy approach to life helps to complete the healing process that has taken "five months" (284).

In two later novels, McGee goes through what is now a discernible pattern, moving from a gradual withdrawal from meaningful human contact to a revulsion and disgust with self to a partial purgation and healing in a love relationship. When Ron Esterland asks McGee to investigate the circumstances of his father's death in *Free Fall in Crimson*, McGee is still recovering from Gretel's death (12). He says that, "I had tried to fit myself to somberness, to a life of reserve" (13), but he knows that he can stand apart from life only "For the healing time" (14). In the process of finding out how Ellis Esterland died, Travis meets and falls in love with Anne Renzetti, a relationship that steadies him at the very least. In *The Lonely Silver Rain*, McGee and Meyer's friendship undergoes some strains: ". . . we had gotten into a game of surly. Old friends do that from time to time. To loosen the bonds, I guess" (175). Eventually, McGee makes his "peace with Meyer" (183), and at the end of the novel, after he has established a relationship with his daughter, Jean, McGee recovers his spirits. Meyer's response is, tolerating McGee's effusive pride in his daughter, "'Welcome to the world'" (277).

McGee's love relationships are varied and complex, involving many aspects of his personality. Ministering to Heidi (*Yellow*) or being helped by her (*The Long Lavender Look*) surely portrays a McGee giving and receiving but not a McGee in love any more than when he tells Betsy Kapp he loves her after they make love (*Lavender* 108). After going with Anne Renzetti (*Crimson* and *Cinnamon*) for months, their relationship becomes strained. As McGee is ready to return to Ft. Lauderdale from visiting her at Eden Beach, the hotel she manages near Naples, Florida, Anne says:

But . . . I sense a kind of reserve about you. You seem to be totally open with me, but some part of you is holding back. Some part of you doesn't really believe that you are not going to lose me also. So you cut down on the amount of loss by not getting as deeply involved as . . . as we could be involved. Do you understand? (*Cinnamon* 6)

McGee replies that "'I'm not holding back. . . . I tell you I love you'" (6). Anne's direct quality senses some of the remoteness in McGee remarked on above.

In *The Turquoise Lament*, McGee goes to Hawaii in response to Pidge Lewellen Brindle's cry for help. After attempting to mediate between her and Howie, her dangerous husband, McGee and Pidge become lovers (74). But, their relationship is flawed. As a teenager, Pidge had attempted to lure McGee into a sexual relationship, and while they make love in Hawaii, McGee remembers the "wistful lust" (74) he had felt as he returned her to her father years before, this memory mixing with the "sweet and immediate realities of her" (74). When they part later, McGee thinks that their kisses "had the slightly sour flavor of betrayal" (77) and recalls Pidge saying that ". . . she would decide whether to marry me or merely keep me" (77). At the end of the novel, McGee remarks on the termination of their affair: "Two people, totally, blissfully, blindly in love. And gradually it became apparent that there was only one person in love . . ." (255). Surprisingly, or not so surprisingly, McGee reveals little in the novel that would connect them in a love relationship of any depth or power. MacDonald, it appears, shows a McGee worried about only being in love with the past (254-55) and feeling unworthy of having a real relationship (255). But, failure comes when McGee sees her with her psychiatrist with whom she has fallen in love (256), Pidge's seeming betrayal symbolic of what McGee cannot give.

However, McGee is capable of love, of that feeling for another that places her foremost in his thoughts or concerns or to be more exact, allows her successfully to compete for attention, care, and interest with the self. For McGee, loving someone appears to mean that he moves from an appreciation of that person to a valuing of her. Taylor Alderman states that what "distinguishes McGee's encounters as a lover . . . is his sense of attachment and devotion to the lovers" (20). As for Pidge, Anne, and the many other women whom he has helped or who have helped him, McGee has cared for them and sometimes deeply, even, in the case of Pidge and Anne, seemed to love them, but he does not experience the kind of love which erodes his sense of apartness. Although with Nora and possibly even Dana Holtzer (*The Quick Red Fox*), McGee is moving toward a deeper relationship, Puss Killian (*Pale Gray for Guilt*) represents the first commitment by McGee to a love relationship in his home environment. Certainly, McGee is seriously involved with Lois Atkinson in *Blue* before her untimely death, but after rescuing her and bringing her to the *Flush*, most of his efforts focus on finding Junior Allen. McGee meets Puss on the beach when she commands him to help her after she steps on a "sea urchin" (32). She and McGee eventually become lovers, and later Puss helps McGee in his efforts to aid Janine Bannon. After a joyous New Year's Eve alone together, McGee awakens to find Puss gone. His reaction reveals the depth of his feeling for her:

Why such a big hang-up over another promiscuous broad? Town was full of them. Go whistle up another one. Be the jolly old lover-boy, and be glad the redhead left before she turned into a drag, before she started bugging you about making it something legal and forever, and a-crawl with kids.

I like last year's McGee better. (98-99)

McGee's ironic dismissal of Puss, disclosing the possibility of the thought of marriage and children, indicates how deeply his feelings were committed. His response to her last letter, written shortly before her death ("I could feel my heart fall. It dropped a certain distance and there it would stay" [222]) shows even more clearly the profound effect she has had on him.

Jean's appearance completes a cycle begun by McGee's falling in love with Gretel Howard in *Copper*, bringing him out of his "isolation" (Oberdorf 61), and her subsequent death near the beginning of *Green*. After John Tuckerman, Gretel's brother, dies at the end of *Copper*, McGee and Gretel travel to Ft. Lauderdale aboard the *Flush*. At one point, Gretel refers to their relationship: "'To review the proposition you made me, you want me to share your life on any basis I choose, just so long as I understand it's permanent'" (*Copper* 254). When Gretel says, in making what Moran calls her "counter proposal" (87), that she must maintain some independence in order "'to take complete charge of my life'" (254), McGee eventually accepts her terms with the statement, "'But you'll be nearby'" (255). This awareness of another as a real, whole person is a sign of McGee's love for her, a love that Geherin terms "regenerative" (143). Even earlier, shortly after McGee first kisses Gretel on the beach near her brother's house, McGee contemplates his feelings for her:

There would never be enough time in all the world for us to say to each other all the things that needed saying, time to tell all that had happened to each of us before the other had appeared—a sudden shining in the midst of life. In so many ways she was like a lady lost long ago, so astonishingly like her—not in appearance as much as in the climate of the heart—that it was like being given another chance after the gaming table had already been closed for good. She had a great laugh. It was a husky, full-throated bray, an explosion of laughter, uncontrolled. And she laughed at the right places. (182)

The "lady lost long ago" is an apparent reference to Puss Killian. MacDonald thus ties in an earlier love relationship that involved McGee in ways that would have led to permanent links just as in the case of Gretel. The latter's death in *Green*, of course, ends this possibility and sends McGee to California seeking vengeance. If there were a need to emphasize McGee's hope for the permanence with Gretel, his statement in the hospital after Gretel falls ill that he is her "'Common-law husband'" (*Green* 36) confirms it.

McGee has other relationships with women that involve manipulation, a recreational attitude toward sex, and even, though rarely, revulsion for some of them. After Billy Ingraham's death in *Silver*, McGee goes to bed with Millis, his wife, and afterwards feels some shame for his action (89). An even earlier relapse occurs in *Turquoise* when McGee has sex with numerous women, most notably with a nurse, Marian Lewandowski, in a storeroom in the hospital where Meyer recovers from an illness (100, 85, 87). Meyer later remarks to McGee that he has an "'infinite capacity for self-deceit'" (99). To McGee, these episodes represent a dark side against which he struggles and towards which he must constantly be on guard. However, they do not define him. David Black observes that "What is remarkable about McGee is how he changes. In the early books his attitude toward women is one of blind assurance; they are there to please him. In the middle books he falls in love—once deeply, only to lose her to death. And in the later books, this loss transforms him" (1). This capacity for growth, however problematic (see Chapters Five and Six especially on his limits), occasionally lifts him from a state of weakness to emotional strength, surprising even him with its appearance.

Chapter 16

Family and Marriage

Family and marriage are unusual themes to explore in the series, and yet McGee occasionally alludes to personal family incidents in ways that show their importance to him. McGee, whom Erling B. Holtsmark suggests is "basically a loner" (99), concerns himself with people who need help but not only for themselves; he frequently aids their husbands, wives, children, or parents who have also suffered harm. Although not unselfish, McGee's actions on the part of clients and friends and his self-mocking references to these actions as examples of knight-errantry imply a strong sense of human relatedness, of actions formed on behalf of the human family while ostensibly helping specific individuals. The other half of this combined theme, marriage, would not appear to be a strong force in one who plainly states in *Blue* (92-93) and again in *One Fearful Yellow Eye* (149) that he does not want the settled life that either marriage or some lasting relationship would entail. And yet, McGee comes close to committing himself in some permanent fashion to several women. Marriage creates an immediate family of at least two, and whether or not his clients also have children, it is because of the bonds created and the joys and problems that grow from them that McGee most often is called into their lives. Thus, the themes of family and marriage develop powerful tensions that embroil McGee in situations that reverberate at deeper levels than merely solving a case and portray the many facets of MacDonald's artistry.

Although Travis McGee never marries, he frequently reacts to deterioration in families by attempting to heal breaches in affection and love and to shore up, if possible, any meaningful relationships that appear threatened, acting, as John Wiley Nelson states, as a "deliverer" (184). Thus, throughout the series MacDonald creates a thread of core values which McGee instinctively returns to, gropes for in moments of stress, and lives by, however haphazardly. Appropriately enough, one sees this operating in *Blue* as McGee first brutalizes George Brell in quest of information about Sgt. Dave Berry's World War II smuggling activities and then offers advice to

Mrs. Gerry Brell on how to reach Angie Brell, her stepdaughter, and salvage something from a disintegrating family situation. Angie saw Mrs. Brell with another man and in retaliation for this betrayal of her father begins the process of giving herself to Lew Dagg (138). McGee accidentally walks in on them in the Brell home as Lew, if not actually prepared to make love to Angie there, is at least getting her ready for that step (120-21). McGee's suggestion to Mrs. Brell to talk to Angie, even though he has doubts about the family's ability to survive, is a reflexive movement on his part; given the choices of speaking or doing nothing, he speaks, thus moving to hold together this core social unit as if it were as essential to him that they stay together as it is to them.

McGee also performs his gratuitous role as family healer in *Bright Orange for the Shroud*. Ostensibly helping Arthur Wilkinson recover some of the money that Calvin Stebber's con operation stole from him, McGee reacts sympathetically to Vivian Watts, the wife of the lawyer whom Stebber used to defraud Wilkinson in his complicated land scheme. McGee learns that Crane Watts, his law business failing, is drinking and gambling away whatever assets remain (69-71, 74). McGee also learns that Stebber gave Watts less than what he had promised for his close-to-illegal services, knowing that Watts could do nothing in retaliation (74). The contrast between the healthy and, as he learns, honest Vivian Watts and the weakly corrupt Crane Watts pulls McGee into an unintended relationship with them. Several days after helping Vivian remove the drunken Crane from their country club, McGee reveals to Vivian what she dimly suspects Crane has done. Further, McGee urges her to get Watts to leave Naples and start over somewhere else. She reveals a possible job offer that could help restore Crane's self-respect and bring some balance to their marriage. Boone Waxwell's unhappy return to their lives that very evening precipitates a tragic end to the Watts family with the wounded McGee unable to do anything but frame Waxwell for the murder-suicide. However, McGee's paradoxical response to the Wattses reveals a care for the ideas of family and marriage that transcends any profit for Arthur or himself and would only have benefited Watts, who had harmed Arthur.

McGee's actions as healer in *Orange* reveal a mind which appears to support the idea of a positive force in the world, not triumphant over evil but at least there, which he can use or further. This could degenerate into maudlin sentimentality, but MacDonald is careful to restrain such impulses with the counterpoises of loss and pain which the characters suffer. Nelson says:

Life itself bears a restorative power about which McGee knows, upon which he draws, and in which he truly and completely believes. It is the life-invigorating power of the health of the natural physical body. It is, if we could give it a philosophical tag, McGee's "naturalism." (187)

After Dana Holtzer recovers consciousness in the hospital from a blow to the head by Ulka M'Gruder in *The Quick Red Fox*, McGee soon realizes that the blow has both cancelled their burgeoning relationship and thrust her back into her role as wife to a comatose husband and mother to a severely retarded child. McGee quickly intuits what has happened to her emotionally and lets go, releasing her to family imperatives that she had been redefining to fit a life with him. Earlier, in an attempt to put them both at ease as they traveled together to solve Lysa Dean's blackmail problems, McGee joked with Dana as if they were an old married couple, thus risking a reminder of her old obligations (65). However, this act reduces any tensions they might have had with its implications of trust, affection, and shared memories. When Lysa Dean in *Free Fall in Crimson* answers McGee's question about Dana that she has remarried after the death of her husband, and "'. . . she's still making babies'" (115), McGee's response is brief but positive as if creating another family were one of the most natural answers to life's misfortunes.

This impulse to nurture families and thus heal and protect human beings from their own and others' actions takes its most bizarre form in *Yellow*. From the most disparate elements, McGee suggests the formation of a family that is, in truth, new. After Anna Ottlo's depredations have resulted in the loss of part of Dr. Geis's fortune, the near death of his widow, and the deaths of Anna's "daughter" Gretchen and Saul Gorba, McGee talks with the people who are soon to be a family and lays out a possible solution to their recent traumatic experiences: Gloria Geis, blessed with a good heart and a large home on Lake Michigan, will join with Janice Stanyard, former nurse and mistress of Dr. Geis (the latter relationship before his marriage to Gloria), and Susan Kemmer, Gretchen's oldest daughter, to raise and care for Susan's younger brothers and sister in Gloria's home. Along with part of the recovered money and their own hopes and energies, McGee sees a viable life for them, a family structure that will give new meaning to their lives.

In some instances, McGee thus successfully functions as a healer, similar to his role in the areas of sexuality and love referred to in Chapter Fifteen, or at least makes positive attempts to deflect negative forces that work to destroy families, marriages, and love relationships. The latter do not have the same legal status as that of family or marriage, but they do, if they last, resemble those generally more socially permanent unions, leaving the reader to answer yes to MacDonald's question whether or not it was good "to give [McGee] reasonably meaningful emotional relationships within the accepted practices of our social order, and consistent with his character and needs" ("How to Live" 16). In contrast to those above instances in which McGee feels called upon to act as healer, other family or marital situations explode from powerful disruptive forces that render McGee an onlooker or at most a participant in their dissolution. In one sense, McGee sometimes is a disruptive force in his own love affairs, gradually relating in more positive ways as he ages. From Lois Atkinson in *Blue* to Nora Gardino in *A Deadly Shade of Gold* to Puss Killian in *Pale Gray for Guilt* to Pidge Lewellen in *The Turquoise Lament* to Gretel Howard in *The Empty Copper Sea* and *The Green Ripper* to Anne Renzetti in *Crimson* and *Cinnamon Skin*, McGee changes and develops in that he seeks more permanent relationships. However, the paradigmatic interior disruptive force in the series occurs in *A Purple Place for Dying* in which all of the conflicts arise from actions within Jass Yeoman's marriage and family. Mona Fox Yeoman, Jass's wife-"daughter" (33), calls in McGee to recover the money from her estate which Jass, the executor and her father's old friend, has appropriated over a number of years (10-11, 13, 84). As the violent murders of Mona and Jass Yeoman discussed in Chapter Nine show, old hates fester and explode. In her confession, Dolores reveals her love-hate for this father-rapist who could not discern what she felt for him as her father and who in that moment of rape treated her as an object to plunder rather than someone to cherish (152).

Inevitably, money, discussed in broader terms in Chapter Eleven, destroys other families as well, not so much as an outside pressure distorting values and relationships but rather as someone's goal reached through the lives of relatives or loved ones. In *A Tan and Sandy Silence*, Paul Dissat kills his first cousin Lisa Dissat after she has become expendable in a plot to rob Harry Broll. More than cousins, Paul and Lisa have become lovers, and her murder is the more striking because of the closeness that Lisa believes exists between them (128, 139). But even more startling, Broll accepts his wife's murder at the hands of Paul Dissat. He weakly cries in the living room of their home after learning that Dissat has tortured and then murdered his wife in their bedroom (130). Ostensibly hoping to profit by her death and thus recover from a financial difficulty, Broll later becomes another of Dissat's victims (237, 239). The image of Broll's ultimate indifference to his wife resonates throughout the text. Tom Pike in *The Girl in the Plain Brown Wrapper* sees his wife Maureen as merely a way to control the money left to her and her sister, Bridget. Using drugs to alter her personality and faking her "attempted" suicide on three earlier occasions (227-28), Pike finally shoves her during a celebration party from the twelfth floor of his new building. Pike's actions imply that he sees Maureen merely as a river or conduit down which he can flow toward the money he desires. The blankness in his personality where one might imagine a care for the loving, beautiful wife is more effectively demonstrated in what he does than in any analysis that McGee brings, for in truth in McGee's response MacDonald shows there is no answer to some evil:

Perhaps because nothing anyone could do to Pike would ever mean anything to him in the same sense that we would react to disaster.
    He was a thing. Heart empty as a paper bag, eyes of clever glass. (238)

Pike's actions resemble the disruptive forces in the families of two other characters. Examined in Chapter Four as the model of the amoral character, Howie Brindle almost off-handedly destroys his family in *Turquoise* and epitomizes the image of evil buried in the human psyche that bursts forth in unexplainable terror and death. Brindle's essentially unprovoked murder of his immediate family and his grandparents, murders carried out before he was out of college, probably overstates MacDonald's argument for the tenuousness of family relationships and his seeming belief that there is no certainty or sanctuary in this world. Though not in quite so dramatic a fashion, Lilo Perris, in *The Long Lavender Look*, symbolizes a teleology of destruction in families if one gives in to forces that pull one away from the relationships that matter. MacDonald intertwines Lilo's life in the dissolution of three families: the Hyzers, the Hatches, and the Perrises. As Sheriff Norm Hyzer later reconstructs it, he and Wanda Hatch Perris conceived Lilo around the time his wife and daughter died in a car accident (229-30). Johnny Hatch later divorces Wanda, knowing that Lilo is not his daughter. Henry Perris, married to Wanda, sleeps with Lilo (206) and participated with Lilo, Frank Baither, Orville, and Hutch in the armored car robbery several years previously which set the stage for the novel's present action (207, 237-38). McGee eventually kills Henry Perris and indirectly causes Lilo's death at the hands of Deputy King Sturnevan when he leaves her tied up in the trailer which was to be the scene of his own death and where Henry killed Orville and Hutch as Lilo made love to them (207-08). Lilo, who also killed Frank Baither (214), is thus a true storm center which, unlike the meteorological analogy, is not quiet. Similar to her prototype, Fancha in *Blue*, Lilo is strong, sexually resilient, and completely amoral. Sheriff Hyzer, generally a model policeman, comes close at the end of the novel to giving up his profession partly because of what he acknowledges as a failure to act with regard to Lilo when he knew she was involved in illegal activities (230). Thus, even after her death, Lilo's actions continue to affect her father and make it difficult for him to make any balanced judgment on his life and career.

Disruptive or evil forces arising from within families frequently destroy them or so fragment them that a continued dissolution is the only possible outcome. As an opposite image, the power of the outside world to affect families and marriages in the series is equally striking. McGee attempts to help Shaja Dobrak and her husband in *Gold* and, as noted above, Crane and Vivian Watts in *Orange*, in one case with success and in the other not. However, the difficulties these people face, at least in part, originate in unforeseen and unstoppable events outside themselves. In *Gold*, the 1956 Hungarian uprising draws Professor Dobrak into political conflict and ultimately prison. For the Wattses in *Orange*, even though Crane's own weaknesses have made them vulnerable, Boone Waxwell, discussed more fully in Chapters Eight and Eleven, bursts into their lives, a dark force rising from his native swamps, and precipitates the family violence. As David Benjamin notes, Vivian "is ravaged not only sexually, but also psychically, a cruel abasement that leaves her no choice but suicide" (31). The Russian military and its Hungarian fellow-travelers operate on a much larger stage than the primeval Boone Waxwell, but both novels present a strong image of penetrative forces thrusting into futilely resisting lives. Rape, both metaphorical and literal, becomes the key to explaining their respective calamities.

Only after Tush Bannon's death in *Gray* does McGee begin to understand the dynamics which crush him and his family. After seeing Bannon at Miami International Airport and hearing of his difficulties (22-27), he decides to visit Bannon in Shawana County and learn more. When he arrives at the abandoned boatyard, a telephone repairman informs McGee that Bannon committed suicide the day before (36-37). McGee traces Janine Bannon and her children through the local sheriff and others to Connie Alvarez, an orange grower in Frostproof, Florida. From Janine and Judge Rufus Wellington, Janine's lawyer, McGee learns more about the Bannons' difficulties and Gary Santo's and Preston LaFrance's plans for the Bannons' property on the Shawana River. From a future with possibilities, forces against which they could not protect themselves and for which they could not plan overwhelm their lives, killing Bannon and leaving Janine unable to cope. Deputy Sheriff Freddy Hazzard's accidental killing of Bannon is an event set in motion by actions and decisions far removed from either Hazzard's or Bannon's life. Indeed, the contrast between the giant, hardworking Bannon, who formerly played football with McGee (9-10) and labors in the concrete world of boats and machinery, and Santo and LaFrance, who see Bannon's land as a segment of a map to be consolidated with other segments and sold to Calitron Corporation (92), illustrates MacDonald's vision of a world in which both man and nature grind inexorably toward a dangerous and dirty end. Just as some people survive the devastating hurricane and tidal wave in *Condominium*, so do Janine and her children, with help, attempt to reconstruct their lives. But MacDonald's image is of a world in which, for all these minor successes, characters in both novels are left just a little more vulnerable than before. The picture of Janine at the end of the novel, after she helps McGee dispose of Freddy Hazzard's body, is of someone coping but not quite whole (213).

McGee theorizes that Deputy Hazzard is sexually sick, dexterously using his blackjack, reminiscent of Deputy Donnie Capp in *Deadly Welcome*, to immobilize Janine and yet afraid to make love to a grown woman (*Gray* 193, 199, 208). And this blackjack is earlier the point of transference of the world's destructive power to Bannon who cannot protect himself against it. In contrast, Mary Alice McDermit in *The Scarlet Ruse* appears sexually whole but is both the originary and delivery source of the power that kills Jane Lawson and deprives her two daughters of a mother. When Jane confronts Mary Alice with the theft of the Sprenger stamps from Hirsh Fedderman's store where they both work, Mary Alice kills her and wrecks the house to make the police think some young dropouts trashed it (146-47, 272-73). Mary Alice's plan to switch stamps by substituting others of less value (28-29) and sell the originals begins the process which leads to Jane's death. And, McGee's impotence as he and Mary Alice attempt to make love not many days after she kills Jane casts doubt on her sexual wholeness, for McGee senses something wrong with her (218, 246). The image of the healthy, vibrant woman fades as her essentially corrupt nature surfaces, and at the end it is not Mary Alice but only a part of her wardrobe, her hat, which becomes the scarlet ruse (281, 286) that tricks Sprenger into boarding the *Flush*, jammed into the mangroves on No Name Island (280, 291-92). The parallel with Freddy Hazzard continues to Mary Alice's burial after Sprenger shoots her when Meyer, just as McGee and Janine had done with Freddy, drops her weighted body along with Sprenger's and Davis's into the sea (310-12). Although her death is a significant corrective action against those destructive forces which intervene in people's lives, just as McGee and Meyer's interventions create Santo's financial embarrassment and LaFrance's presumed bankruptcy, families and marriages continue to suffer unmerited assaults, fragilely holding on in this almost unequal combat.

MacDonald provides two other striking instances of the tenuousness of marital and family relationships in the face of outside forces. In *Green*, Gretel and McGee have established a permanence equal to a marriage, with McGee no longer seen by the woman with whom he is involved as, in Thomas Doulis's view, "unsuitable for marriage" (43), but they could have no possible protection against the events leading to her death. Although Gretel had seen her former sister-in-law at the Church of the Apocrypha's camp near Ukiah, California, some years before, she apparently did not know of its activities (22-23). She and her husband had gone to the camp in an attempt to liberate his sister from what they thought of as a religious cult. Through Meyer's connecting Gretel's symptoms to those of Markov, the Bulgarian defector assassinated earlier in London (94), MacDonald emphasizes the distance between her and McGee's life together and the forces which kill her. As Joseph Marotta remarks:

[I]ts simple formulas reveal in exaggerated fashion some of the more compelling concerns of recent American fiction, including the heightened sense of mystery stimulated by the fear of global dissolution, random violence, conspiracy, and the feeling of powerlessness in the face of that mystery. (109)

International intrigue invades the life of a woman working for a Florida resort whose principal ambitions are to find a balance between love and work. McGee's later reversal of the order of violence in which the individual now strikes at the impersonal outside forces proves somewhat ineffective when he learns that "At best it will push the target date further into the future. Maybe it will begin to happen a year from now" (282). And in heightened irony, McGee suffers emotionally from the retribution he takes (282-84), stressing even more the individual's vulnerability in trying to form relationships. While it is true that real people make up the Church of the Apocrypha and its various arms, their use of their own members and others as a means to an end dehumanizes everyone they touch. In contrast, Gretel and McGee balance ends and means as they try to give and receive love, nurturing one another in their attempts to establish a new life for themselves.

Focusing in part on *Cinnamon*, Chapters Two, Eight, and Eleven discuss different aspects of McGee and Meyer's connection to Cody Pittler through the latter's murder of Norma Greene Lawrence. Adding to this reason for their search for Pittler, MacDonald invests Meyer's loss with extraordinary significance. While McGee may find another love, Meyer cannot find another niece, especially one who represents his entire family (16). This is a loss that cannot be remedied. Compounding this sense of loss is the picture of her emotional healthiness, willing to love and give and her ability to contribute something in life through her skills as a petroleum geologist. As in Gretel's case, chance puts her in danger, raising the specter of a world in which the good find it ever more difficult to survive. For Meyer, he can either despair or act against a malignant chance which endangers that actuality and symbol of value, the family. Meyer's killing Pittler, though it does not bring back Norma, is hardly ineffectual. However illogical it might seem, MacDonald seems to imply that the greater danger would be to do nothing and that Meyer nurtures a sense of life by his actions, reconciled if not consoled.

MacDonald ends his last novel, *Barrier Island*, with an awareness of the family's centrality and the dangers it faces. Wade Rowley and his family, along with the wife and daughter of his dead real estate partner, picnic on Bernard Island, the center of the conflict in the novel. Rowley, from the core of the family group, looks out to the Gulf of Mexico:

He looked south. The wind out of the north, once it was past the islands, began to pick up the seas, and far far out, the horizon was jagged. Better to be here than there. Here on the sunny beach like a tribal family from long ago, vulnerable to all the forces of the world. (259)

Throughout the Travis McGee series, MacDonald has presented family and marriage in a similar, exposed position but a position from which people continue to hope. As in *The Lonely Silver Rain* in which McGee does not have Jean as a daily part of his life, MacDonald presents a partial solution, a partial success against what threatens people in their most intimate relations.

Chapter 17

Youth and Aging

MacDonald portrays a world of experience, sometimes hard and tragic, sometimes rewarding and fulfilling, in the series. He seldom employs very young children, but the youths who do appear are often at risk in a society full of predators. From Patty Devlan in *The Deep Blue Good-by* to Angie Casak in *The Lonely Silver Rain*, adults manipulate and seduce the young into harmful activities. Too often, neither parents nor the legal authorities can step between them and those who use them. Frequently, it is not only a matter of age but a certain quality of innocence that prevents someone from perceiving the danger that older people represent. Tom Pike in *The Girl in the Plain Brown Wrapper* deceives Bridget Pearson while he plans and carries out the murder of Maureen, his wife and Bridget's sister. Of course, not every older person betrays the trust of the young. Meyer, even more than McGee, knows the difference between his desires and the use of other people to satisfy them. Even the Alabama Tiger, given to pleasure as he is, does not prey on others. Many people come to his boat, and MacDonald does not even hint that anyone too young to know better has been harmed there. Wilma Ferner's use of the Alabama Tiger in *Bright Orange for the Shroud* stresses the distinction between the experience of age and an age-old view of others as objects. Ultimately, MacDonald combines youth and age in ways that reveal the hard edges the former must beware in order to participate, share, and survive in a world that offers few easy paths to happiness.

The image of innocent youth struggling against the depredations of wicked older people obviously over-simplifies MacDonald's concepts of inter-generational contacts. Some youths are generally negative and some adults usually positive in their relationships with others, both caught, as MacDonald observes in *Pale Gray for Guilt* (noted by T. Frederick Keefer 39), on a "long, shallow bar of sand and gravel . . . washing away at the upstream end [the old] and building up downstream [the young]" (87). The source of socially negative behavior on the part of the young may go largely unexplained. In *Blue*, Fancha cooperates with Junior

162

Allen in debasing Lois Atkinson. Fancha is young, strong, and apparently indifferent to the devastating effects of their behavior on Lois. Except through Lois's descriptions of her, Fancha does not appear in the novel. MacDonald never discusses her origins or what happens to her after Allen abandons Lois. Lilo Perris's sudden appearance at the beginning of *The Long Lavender Look* personifies a certain untamed force that seems more an accident of nature than a product of familial and social development. As McGee later pieces together information from Lilo and then reconstructs the events, Lilo crouched beside the highway in the Florida night waiting for a car to drive by so that she could cross in front of it and thus elude Frank Baither (200-01, 207). Traditional explanations for social conduct, however subtle, or forecasts of future actions, however carefully weighed, do not seem to include Lilo within their analytical frameworks, and she remains a female example of the "other," out there, as MacDonald observes in writing about natural evil, in all its frightening complexity:

In our real world we have, for example, a two hundred and thirty pound teenager who roams the streets, mugging children for the pleasure of gouging out their eyes. For me it is less satisfying to say that this is the action of a sad, limited, tormented, unbalanced child than it is to see that this is a primordial blackness reaching up again through a dark and vulnerable soul, showing us all the horror that has always been with mankind, frustrating all rational analyses. ("Introduction and Comment" 69)

Some older people are positive examples of decency, of people coming to the aid of their fellow human beings. When Sam and Leafy Dunning pick up the sick Arthur Wilkinson in *Orange*, they have little to offer besides food, shelter, and the chance to work (40-41). They take him into their home out of kindness even though they know nothing about him. Although it is more common in MacDonald's work to encounter people like Cal Stebber and Boone Waxwell, both also in *Orange*, the Dunnings are not isolated examples. They may even make up the bulk of a society coping with the predators. When Janine Bannon leaves her husband, Tush, in *Gray*, she goes to Connie Alvarez, an older woman friend, owner of some Florida orange groves, who shelters Janine and her children. After Janine learns of Tush's death and after McGee tracks her down, Connie, as noted in Chapter Thirteen, brings in another older person, Judge Rufus Wellington, to balance the maneuverings of Preston LaFrance and ultimately Gary Santo.

Aside from kindness, Connie's and Judge Wellington's actions emphasize another trait of older people, i.e., their capability. After her husband's death, Connie learned the business of fruit growing. Her resilience and toughness of spirit combined to help her cope and make an unexpected success (56-57). Years of legal experience and knowledge of the local power structure make the judge's discussion of Janine's financial problems with Whitt Sanders, the banker who holds the Bannon's mortgage, more effective than a younger attorney's would be. Sanders's reaction when Judge Wellington appears with Janine, and before the judge takes any action, reveals respect for his abilities (56).

And finally, Meyer is the consistent example in the series of an older person's almost disinterested kindness to younger people. McGee frequently alludes to Meyer's far greater rapport with the young than his own. Meyer has the ability to gain their confidence for their own good. Although he and McGee initially embarrass Backspin in *Dress Her in Indigo*, later Meyer offers the incredulous girl and Jeanie, an even more endangered friend, an escape from the drug environment in Mexico that so frightens her (106-07). Even the hardened Vangie responds to his kindness in *Darker than Amber* though he cannot ultimately help her (21,23). In *Gray*, McGee says to Janine Bannon, "'You should see the wolf pack of little kids . . . following this character up and down the beach, listening to his lies'" (190). Meyer is the nonthreatening figure that reassures from the adult world.

Some younger people either are old before their time or events thrust them into confronting harsh experiences before they can assimilate them. Since she is in her middle twenties, Nina Gibson in *Nightmare in Pink* is close to the chronological limit of youth. McGee describes her as "my very last bitter-sweet girl" (57), and behind her public persona, he discovers that she is a troubled young woman (14-17). On the surface, her life seems complicated enough when McGee comes to New York. Mike Gibson, her brother, lies dying in a North Carolina VA hospital from Korean War wounds; her fiancé, Howard Plummer, is dead; and Nina is left with 10,000 unexplained dollars she believes Plummer stole from his employer (9, 17). Before the novel ends, Nina comes of age emotionally. While McGee functions as a conduit for this maturing process and New York serves as a backdrop to it (the city's dangers giving it an urgency), Nina represents a clear example of MacDonald's understanding of the struggles to grow up mentally and emotionally.

Some characters are not as fortunate as Nina. *Blue* presents three different categories of the young who have difficulty in coping with the adult world; they range from the coarse to the delicate. Corry, Dee, and Pete are acquaintances of Junior Allen; however, McGee's observations of their physical and emotional makeups and life prospects reveal their possibly bleak futures (178-80). This bleakness lies partially in their personal deficiencies but also arises from the pressures of a world with which, unknowingly, they cannot cope. Allen thus acts as a fierce symbol of forces that will unmercifully crush them. Angie Brell, in the episode discussed in Chapter Sixteen concerning the infidelity of her stepmother, Gerry, reveals a degree of coarseness as she urges Lew Dagg to beat McGee when he stumbles on their love-making. Angie's hurt partially explains her desire for violence, but this desire also depicts her teetering on the edge of a destructive self-indulgence. Patty Devlan, Pete's former girlfriend and Allen's ultimate prey on his planned trip to the Bahamas, cannot cope with the world into which she is drawn. McGee sees in her a delicacy that makes her vulnerable to predators, and only his intervention saves her from Allen (*Blue* 192-93, 220). Her youthful innocence and the dangers she faces with Allen symbolize MacDonald's view of the gauntlet the unprotected young run in a harsh world.

The above examples from *Pink* and *Blue* exemplify the many forces both external and internal that affect young people. The external forces either act very suddenly or as part of gradual, systemic influences that make the young behave as if they had choices. Karen Hatcher in *Free Fall in Crimson* commits suicide with James Revere, her boyfriend, after being forced to participate in Desmin Grizzel and Linda Harrigan's violent pornographic films (211). Set partially in Iowa and drawing on images of wholesome middle America, *Crimson* depicts Grizzel filming himself raping Karen, a young girl completely unprepared for the horror she suffers (195). The town's belated attack on the people at the film location only underscores the previous brutality. It provides no answers to the eruptions of the Grizzels of the world or rather, a reflexive, if terrible and indiscriminate revenge. Ruffino Marino's savage actions against Howard Cannon, Karen McBride, and Gigliermina Reyes y Fonseca in *Silver* (46,55) are a similar invasion of a larger world that the three youths could hardly expect existed (138-46, 168-69). Although working on his own, Marino, the son of an organized-crime figure, symbolizes the organization's use of extreme violence to further its ends. The subsequent killings among the criminal figures, initiated by McGee's revelations to Jornalero of Marino's role in the youths' murders, especially Reyes's, only emphasize how extensive and unrelenting the violence could be (179-82, 208). Young people do operate in a maze as they grope toward maturity, and sometimes a wrong turn can lead to unforgiving results.

In addition to the external forces in *Crimson* and *Silver* that suddenly overwhelm the partially responsible but inexperienced youths, other social influences divert young people from healthy life-styles. The idea of a healthy life-style is a normative one and thus open to question in its details, but MacDonald leaves little doubt that events manipulate some youths more than they realize. Commenting on Jimmy Gerran in MacDonald's "The Big Blue," Edgar W. Hirshberg notes:

It deals with a young man's assertion of his victory over an evil influence in the form of a corrupt and strong-minded older man who has been trying to dominate him. He gains his freedom by demonstrating his superior strength and skill in fishing, which symbolizes his superiority over his enemy. (*MacDonald* 33)

However, not all youths face such clearly defined antagonists. Arlene and Roger Denn in *Gray* are a young couple who live at the Bannons' boatel and occasionally babysit for them. McGee describes Arlene as "a soft, doughy, pallid girl with a long tangle of dark blonde hair, wide, empty, indifferent blue eyes, a little sing-song voice and a mouth that hung open" (17). After she accuses McGee of killing Bannon and after her accusation falls apart, she describes the drug parties in which she and her friends, some in their early teens, indulge (153-54). Her description of straights as all looking alike (153), a parody of a racist ideologue, and her justifications of her and her friends' actions (153-54) demonstrate the thinking of someone pathetically controlled by a social philosophy whose implications and directions she does not understand.

Judy, Jane Lawson's younger daughter in *The Scarlet Ruse*, is another example of the adolescent stridently certain of her own ideas but who does not comprehend what compels her and her friends' conduct (95). Hirshberg describes her as "utterly undisciplined, in constant trouble, and disrespectful to her mother and everyone else in a position of authority" (*MacDonald* 96). For a time, the police even suspect her of being responsible for her mother's death (139, 144-49), and only that event shifts her out of a negative life-style into one in which she appears to have some awareness of what is happening to her (159-60). Judy is a good example of Norman A. Brittin's statement that MacDonald's ". . . handling of characters in later adolescence reflects his concern over the national problems of alienation and violence among the young and his psycho-sociological analysis of familial conditions fomenting such problems" (25). Finally, Stella in *The Green Ripper,* older but even more childish than Arlene and Judy, represents someone so manipulated and directed by the Church of the Apocrypha that she can see and discuss the planned violent acts but can no longer discover a position from which to evaluate them independently of the Church's. She has lost what Joseph Marotta calls "the child's nightmarish fear of death" (108). As McGee talks with her, she gives the impression of someone emptied of personal content and refilled by the sinister Brother Titus and Sister Elena Marie (178-81, 182-83).

The foregoing examples of external pressures, whether sudden or systemic, might be preventable; however, other internal pressures, resembling those of Fancha in *Blue* and Lilo in *Lavender,* seem fated, unavoidable, requiring both the individuals and society to endure their unravelings. Vangie in *Amber* can legitimately claim early experiences that harmed her but nothing that explains her part in the murder ring which she ultimately betrays (38-39). Calling her old before her time might possibly obscure more than clarify her motivations, but the phrase does evoke the nonchildlike childhood she went through. Howie Brindle in *The Turquoise Lament,* discussed earlier in Chapter Four, is a better example of an uncaused evil than Vangie. McGee uncovers no reasons in Howie's childhood for his killings. Howie is such a chilling figure because he is old before any conceivable influence that would lead to murder. Killing his immediate family at eleven or twelve years of age and grandparents when he is about twenty-one or twenty-two (169, 174-76) strains one's credulity but does raise the logical question as to how early evil will operate if it exists as a natural force in some people. Deputy Lew Arnstead in *Lavender* is probably about Howie's age when he commits his destructive acts (76), but when McGee talks with Arnstead's blind mother (74), she describes someone who only harmed himself and others after his army days (76). His drug-taking comes when he is a young adult, and his abusive behavior toward others seems to spiral out of control before Sturnevan murders him (248). Like Vangie and Brindle, Arnstead lives out an inevitable scenario but without the cunning that Brindle employs.

If the future of America, MacDonald's frequent concern, lies in its youth, then his picture of the country's direction is decidedly ambiguous. The prospects are bleak, dangerous, and only occasionally optimistic. Meyer, especially in the latter novels, broods about the alarming conditions in the country, and McGee also reflects on the difficulties the culture faces, especially in the largest cities. In *One Fearful Yellow Eye*, Gretchen Gorba and Susan Kemmer, her daughter, emphasize the troubles with which young people cope and the different directions their lives take. When McGee comes to Chicago after Gloria Geis's plea for help, Gretchen, who might already be dead, is in her mid-thirties (34, 38-39). McGee learns that growing up at the Geises' Gretchen was a good-natured, if not very bright, child whom Anna physically abused (129, 37, 157). Saul Gorba, Gretchen's second husband, probably kills her (157) and then beats and attempts to rape Susan (155). When McGee first meets Susan, her courage and resilience impress him (158). Dr. Fortner Geis, Gloria's husband and Susan's father, had kept track of her and had given Gretchen money through the years to help with Susan's expenses and future education (38-40). Surviving the variegations of Gretchen's many relationships with men, jobs, and family disruptions, Susan grows up to be a strong, healthy seventeen-year-old with more promise than one could have expected from such a background (38-40). Gretchen and Susan, mother and daughter, thus represent two different directions of young lives. Gretchen matures into a life of meaningless jobs and futile relationships, and while the novel ends before one can learn the course Susan's life will ultimately take, she shows great promise in controlling, rather than being controlled by, events that confront her.

As many of the examples show, youth must frequently struggle with older people (and sometimes not very much older) in order to have a future, and even if the struggle is not always deadly, it can be serious. In *Orange*, Boone Waxwell's relationship with Cindy Ingerfeldt, noted in Chapter Eight, is at one level comic. He is approximately thirty-five to forty years old and she is about fifteen (92); he calls her "my nearby girl this year" (93) and she sees him as something to get out of her system, like an illness (92, 137). Cindy is in a struggle with Boone for some control over her life, and when McGee questions her in order to locate where Boone has buried Arthur Wilkinson's money, she cooperates willingly even while acknowledging his effect on her (135-37). The scooter on which Cindy rides away after McGee first sees her at Waxwell's shack belongs to Boone; he has given it to her to come to him when he wants her. Boone's method of communicating his desire is to drive by her home, blow the horn, and then return to his shack to wait for her (93). Cindy's attraction to Boone lies partly in the danger he emanates, but she realizes that she must move away from him to have a future. McGee represents the way for her to turn in her scooter.

While Cindy successfully rids herself of Boone, Bix Bowie's future in *Indigo* is far more problematic. Her struggles lie with a once indifferent father and self-destructive actions from which she barely escapes. Bix is the perfect-looking daughter who can achieve perfection neither in her father's eyes nor in her own (15, 251). Hindsight says that willingly putting her money and body under the control of Walter Rockland and Jerry Nesta (166) would inevitably result in the violence done to her, Carl Sessions, and Minda McLeen discussed in Chapter Eleven. Her need for degradation could lead nowhere else, and she is only alive by accident when McGee rescues her in Mexico City from the drug and lesbian fantasies of the wealthy Eva Vitrier (246-47). At that point, Bix has no personality or sexual orientation; the most that can be said is that she likes her pills, knows Eva's name, is still beautiful, and compliantly accompanies McGee to the American embassy (244-47). Back in Florida and off drugs, Bix's irritation with her father's newly discovered responsibilities may symbolize a healthy assertion, but MacDonald does not explore her possible futures with or without her father. To discover a mental health, Bix would have to relive her childhood and adolescence, a struggle that Harlan Bowie might not himself survive (251-52).

Of course, MacDonald displays a proper awareness of the resilience of American youth, even if most of his examples are women. Again *Indigo*, one of MacDonald's novels most extensively focusing on young people, introduces several people who demonstrate a positive outlook and a confident sense of the future. In addition to Jerry Nesta, Mike Barrington, and Della Davis, McGee meets Ben and Laura Knighton and learns of their encounter with Rockland. Before Wally McLeen ends Rockland's contamination, the latter confronts Ben and Laura Knighton in a trailer park near Oaxaca. Rockland is looking for drugs and attacks Ben who promptly grabs a wrench and knocks him out. Ben, a young professor from Texas Central University, is writing a historical novel and seems to have little doubt about who he is and why he should be left alone (122-26). He projects an independence of mind and action that sustains him and symbolizes a positive force counter to Rockland's image of death and decay.

Throughout the series, MacDonald balances the examples of failed and even sadistic youth against exuberant, confident, and positive youth, frequently in the same novel. In *Amber*, Merrimay Lane counter-balances Vangie Bellemer and Del Whitney. Merrimay's name evokes her sense of joy in life. McGee needs someone to act the part of the dead Vangie so as to spook Ans Terry, Del's lover. Ans, more muscle than brains, believes he sees the real Vangie, even though he helped on the first attempt on her life and thinks she is now dead. McGee has unsettled Ans by his actions on the *Monica D.*, and when the boat docks in Port Everglades, Florida, Merrimay waits for Ans behind the dockside barrier dressed and acting like Vangie; this completes his derangement (172-73). Merrimay, a model, is so convincing that her agent later gets her a screen test. However, she fails it, but it is clear that she has not failed life. Whatever the source of her positive outlook, Merrimay bounces back and meets what life offers (189-90).

MacDonald is probably right not to question too closely the origins of her youthful hope any more than he does for Jeannie Dolan in *A Tan and Sandy Silence*. When McGee first meets her, she is trying to sell condominiums for one of Harry Broll's collapsing ventures (46-47). McGee does not become involved with her then though he likes her spirit. After Broll's and Paul Dissat's deaths, Jeannie comes to the *Busted Flush* before returning to Columbus. McGee invites her on a cruise, but before they begin to discuss it in any detail, Meyer, as noted in Chapter Fifteen, interrupts and puts her through a mock grilling. Meyer's ostensible motive is to satisfy himself that she has no neurotic hangups that might further contribute to McGee's self-pity (253-54). At one level, Jeannie's uncomprehending answers reveal someone too shallow to be believable, but it is possible that MacDonald wishes to contrast the gloom of the older McGee with Jeannie's energetic, joyful outlook (252-54). Inexperienced relative to McGee, Jeannie nonetheless represents the potential for a different savoring of life when that greater experience comes.

Younger than Jeannie when she comes to Ft. Lauderdale to confront McGee, Jean Killian in *Silver* is MacDonald's last portrait of someone moving from adolescence to maturity. Jean is only 16, but she has lost her mother and has been rejected from an early age by Paul, Puss's husband, after he learned that Jean was not his daughter (272). She is inventive in using the colored pipe cleaners twisted to resemble cats which she leaves on McGee's boat to remind him of her mother and argumentative in refusing to accept his explanation of his and Puss's relationship (257, 260-63). However, he shows her the letter Puss sent him (reprinted from *Gray*) after mysteriously leaving Florida, which convinces her that he did not know that Puss was pregnant with her or dying (267, 272-73). Although young, Jean realizes that she must settle the issue of her parentage. McGee represents an idea of her past that needs clarification before she can have any healthy future. After they establish a close relationship, she returns to live with her Aunt Velma in Youngstown, Ohio, and plan her life (272-73, 277). Out of Puss's sickness and death from cancer, Jean rises to a life of health and possibilities. Tall and attractive (258), Jean appears as the generational development that promises hope while Marino, in the same novel, the murderer and child abuser, loses his freedom and maybe his life (246, 255). And, McGee bores Meyer and other friends with Jean's news of what she wants to do in life though Meyer, the honorary uncle, only feigns boredom with this unlooked for participation in what is to come (277, 276).

MacDonald's death in 1986 cut short the series, and while *Reading for Survival* dramatizes the dangers America and its youth face if they lose contact with their literary heritage, it is fitting that Jean should be MacDonald's last youthful character. Just as McGee says that he feels some stirrings to reenter life's struggles at the end of *Silver* (277), Jean is a link to the other portraits of young people struggling with dangers and surviving.

Chapter 18

Thematic Synergy:
MacDonald's Travis McGee Series
and His Post-1964 Fiction

In any detective series, the author struggles against the reduction to formula: characters, especially the central, repeated one, plots, and themes must continually move away from formula while, paradoxically, existing in it. It is this incremental movement from some restrictive formulaic center that gives life and quality to the novelist's work. Contrasting the classical detective story with the hard-boiled formula, John Cawelti indicates some aspects of that tension: "Since he becomes emotionally and morally committed to some of the persons involved, or because the crime poses some basic crisis in his image of himself, the hard-boiled detective remains unfulfilled until he has taken a personal moral stance toward the criminal" (143). One way of measuring MacDonald's ability to function as a novelist within the confines of the series is to contrast it with his other, generally more traditional novels written during this same time period. The many novels MacDonald wrote before 1964 play an influential role in the direction of the series and in its critical examination, but the four novels written during the Travis McGee series reveal a depth and complexity, as well as an overlapping time-frame, against which the series, characterized by H.R.F. Keating as "our best example of the crime story as a novel of feelings" (195), can also be measured and understood. Analyses of these four novels show a consistent concern with a dominant group of themes that confirms MacDonald as a serious novelist who dramatizes difficulties plaguing modern American society.

In *The Last One Left, Condominium, One More Sunday,* and *Barrier Island,* the four novels written during the Travis McGee series, love and sexuality, the focus of Chapter Fifteen, are important themes interwoven with, among others, power and money. Although not in every case, some of the strongest aspects of sexuality link up with the predatory. Peggy Moran describes one category of "female villains" in the Travis McGee series as

"Predator-accessories" (82). Crissy Harkinson in *The Last One Left* and the Rev. Joe Deets in *One More Sunday* exemplify those who use sex to gain other ends than pleasure or the deepening of their relationships. Crissy, a former prostitute and mistress of a powerful state senator in Florida, uses her body to convince Garry Staniker to kill six people, including his wife, in a boat explosion for the over $500,000 Bixby Kayd has brought on his Bahamas trip for a business bribe (*The Last One Left* 165, 85-86). Before Staniker returns to Florida, shaken but successful, Crissy lures young Oliver Akard into a sexual relationship and convinces him to murder Staniker and thus enable them to continue their affair. Crissy has to finish the job Oliver starts and subsequently kills him as well. Self-absorbed and amoral, part of Crissy's motivation comes from the desperation she feels; in her late thirties, she uses her powerful sexual allure to achieve a security which has always eluded her. Even Vangie in *Darker than Amber* eventually recoils from the sex and murder ring in which she is involved. Unlike McGee, for whom, as David Geherin notes, "[his] relationships with women, and his constant assessment of their authenticity, comprise a key feature in the novels for they represent a significant measure of his ethical stance" (165), Crissy does not consider the people she harms and apparently feels no remorse for her actions. Later, the police trap Crissy during an interrogation by stripping her of any outward semblance of beauty. With prison clothes, no make-up, and uncertainty about what the police know, her sexual shell collapses, revealing a drab, unattractive woman with no internal resources on which to rely (*The Last One Left* 343-44). Del Whitney in *Amber* presents a similar picture when McGee confronts her in jail. After denying any involvement with her on board the *Monica D.*, McGee notes the changes in her appearance: ". . . her discreet tan had faded to paste, and all the life had gone out of the hair of cream, so that it hung in dulled strands. . . . There were deep violet smudges under her eyes" (186). If Howie Brindle, the casual murderer in *The Turquoise Lament*, had been confronted in a way that could have penetrated his shell, little more of an internal self would have been found. With no moral core, neither Crissy, Del, nor Howie could easily maintain their deceptive surfaces.

The Rev. Joe Deets, while no murderer, is driven by sexual urges beyond a mere desire for pleasure that make him almost as dangerous to the emotional stability of his partners as Junior Allen in *The Deep Blue Good-by*. Deets confesses to Annalee Purves, the mother of Doreen, his present mistress:

It's always been like a hunt. The right wind direction, camouflage, weaponry. All the right words. Walk lightly and move ever closer. Never be hasty. Never give up. It's been my avocation. And once they are caught, and when finally the novelty is gone, and the loving is getting too familiar, then I shuck them, as gently as possible leaving as few scars as I can. (*One More Sunday* 280)

Like Allen, Deets seeks out vulnerable and ever younger women. Unlike Allen, Deets's interest in and skill with computers and his susceptibility to positive change in his life allow him to break this dangerous cycle of seduction and abandonment. But while he is involved with Doreen, he enjoys his power in manipulating her sexually and emotionally. Possibly, this power springs from some great need and relates to that sense of light he experiences when Annalee prays for him, a light that would give his life "some kind of meaning that he could not even guess at" (*One More Sunday* 283).

Money represents a powerful theme in the four novels under discussion and finds significant echoes in the Travis McGee series as well. But as in life, it is not the physical possession of money but rather what it can be used for, the obstacles to acquiring it, and the business and social purposes it engenders that reveal its potency. Martin Liss, in *Condominium*, tries to decide whether or not to build Harbour Pointe Club on the vacant Silverthorn tract on Fiddler Key near the west-coast town of Athens, Florida. He has lined up the financing, contractors, and permissions; nothing remains but his decision to commit himself or pull back and retire on a potential investment income of $200,000 a year. However, he thinks: "And never have this feeling in the gut again? Never feel the queasy flutter of risk-taking, of high rolling, of doing things they said you'd never pull off?" (29) Clearly, the uncertainties from attempting to acquire more money outweigh the security that retirement will provide. The projected "$2.8-million net before taxes" (29) on Harbour Pointe only rates a passing reference and is not a determining factor in his decision to build or not. Although Edgar W. Hirshberg's characterization of the Golden Sands condominium, Liss's earlier project, accurately stresses one aspect of his dealings as it "seems to typify all that is dangerous and shoddy and contemptible in the motives and machinations of the men who built it" (*MacDonald* 84), money raises Liss into a milieu in which controlling others and experiencing danger exist and threaten in an ambience of fear, uncertainty, and manipulation. Liss's catalog of personal disasters, "a third wife he mistrusted and two grown children he despised" (28), hardly measures up to "that familiar hollow breathless feeling which meant it was decision time" (28) that money makes possible.

Although money is still "countable" in *Condominium*, the Eternal Church of the Believer in *One More Sunday* weighs on delicate scales the contributions it receives. So much comes in that it no longer is viable as a means of keeping score. Matthew Meadows, the founder of the Church, symbolizes money's lack of meaning with his progressive deterioration from Alzheimer's disease (47). Matthew resides in the manse as a crumbling center of a religious empire that continues to grow and expand. The Church gathers momentum from the huge contributions much as a rocket uses the gravitational force of the earth to spin into space. But whereas the rocket has some clear planning and thinking behind its trajectory, the Church's direction and purpose are only seemingly apparent, something to awe the thousands who attend the services at Meadows Center or the millions who watch on television. John Tinker Meadows's thoughts before beginning a sermon at the end of the novel reveal the state to which they have come:

One more Sunday, he thought. I will get through this one somehow, and there will be another. And another and another. Somebody accepted an award once and spoke of prevailing rather than merely enduring. God, if You are there and if You will ever listen to me again, I no longer want to prevail. It will be enough merely to endure. (311)

John, lacking the fervor of his father and now, with his sister Mary Margaret, in charge of the Church, increasingly withdraws from meaningful contact with other church leaders, thus paralleling the effect of his father's illness. John's life silently comments on the engulfing force of the money and power that invades the Church.

Chapter Eleven discusses money as a pervasive element which influences conduct and ruins lives. From the complicated financial dealings in *Pale Gray for Guilt* to the drug deal in *The Lonely Silver Rain*, MacDonald presents a vast panorama in which money functions as both cause and effect. Somewhat paradoxically, *The Dreadful Lemon Sky* demonstrates a closer connection to the role of money in *One More Sunday* than do the other novels in the series. On the surface, the difference in the amount of money in the two novels is so great that any connection appears tenuous. Yet, the disassociation between the money coming into the marijuana operation with which Carrie Milligan in *Lemon* is involved and the purpose for which it is used resembles the distance between the enormous contributions to the Church and its officials' lack of awareness of the money's connection to their religious mission. For *One More Sunday*, it takes the Rev. Tom Daniel Birdy, a backwoods preacher whom Mary Margaret and John hope to entice to revive the spirit of the Church, to show them how saving souls and expanding operations do not necessarily mix well. Birdy reminds them that the human element often gets lost in complex institutions: "'What this whole place does is separate you from your people, and that separates you from God and Jesus Christ.' . . . 'All your members are little numbers somewhere down inside machines'" (294-95). For *Lemon*, Jack Omaha's possibly accidental death precipitates an unraveling of the operation and several subsequent deaths. Fred Van Harn, an ambitious local politician, does not really need the money which the marijuana operation brings in since he is engaged to Jane Schermer, the niece of the wealthy and politically powerful Judge Schermer. Carrie Milligan and Cal Birdsong could benefit from the money in practical ways, but Omaha apparently plans to steal from Harry Hascomb, his partner in the building supply business where Carrie also works, and take off with the money from the business and the illegal marijuana sales (257-59). Walter Demos, the local dealer and apartment manager who enlists his tenants to sell the marijuana, has no awareness of the troubles the operation could attract from organized crime (124, 129-30). In sum, no one benefits from the money since they either could not or would not integrate its use into their lives. The large amounts of money raise similar questions in both novels about the world of illusion the money has created, for why should the marijuana leaves generate so much wealth and why should people pour such vast amounts of money into the Church merely because a minister asks them?

Work and professionalism come closest to being the two most pervasive themes in the Travis McGee series. For all that McGee types himself as a "boat bum" (*Blue* 28), he has developed a certain type of work as a salvage consultant that requires wide-ranging practical knowledge, the ability to act, and skill in dealing with people in a variety of situations. In *The Quick Red Fox*, he asks Gabe Marchman to analyze the photos of Lysa Dean's orgy in order to know who may have taken them and under what conditions. In the next novel, *A Deadly Shade of Gold*, before setting out with Nora Gardino to avenge Sam Taggart's death and track down the gold statues Sam had stolen, McGee goes to Prof. Warner B. Gifford at Florida Southwestern for a quick background on the statues (44). This pattern, discussed in Chapter Seven, repeats itself throughout the series as McGee supplements his skills and knowledge with those of others. A variation occurs when McGee is the professional as in *Bright Orange for the Shroud* when he tracks down Stebber's operation or in *The Green Ripper* as McGee relies on his past military skills and his natural ability to adapt to most situations. Ostensibly not as dangerous as his actions in *Green*, McGee's luring Frank Sprenger to No Name Island in *The Scarlet Ruse*, thus risking his life and Meyer's, shows a McGee experiencing what Larry E. Grimes calls "moments of full freedom and intensely pure action" (105). His general professionalism in his work, if not always in his aims and motives, and the risks arising from it are not merely MacDonald's efforts to flesh out his major character but rather function uneasily in McGee's mind as parts of his unexplored psyche.

In the non-Travis McGee novels written after 1964, work and professionalism also figure centrally. In *The Last One Left*, Sam Boylston, a lawyer from Harlingen, Texas, typifies those whose competence dominates the lives of people with whom they relate. Although Boylston's separation from Lydia, his wife, stems from a lack of discrimination when to apply his forceful character, his search for his sister, Leila, and her presumed murderer reveals an intensity bound up with his abilities and helps to define them. MacDonald also describes a professional thoroughness in *Condominium*, especially in the characters of Gus Garver and Sam Harrison. Garver, a former construction engineer, had frequently used Harrison in his work. When Garver begins to examine the dangers of living on the Gulf Coast Florida keys off Athens, he writes Harrison and hires him to do a proper survey of possible hurricane destruction. With money from LeGrande Messenger, a wealthy man living in the Golden Sands condominium apartments, Garver's home as well, they print and disseminate their study which forces some people to leave the key when the inevitable hurricane appears. Their thorough professional work can apparently either be accepted or rejected outright but leaves little room for argument.

MacDonald knows that work well done does not automatically reflect the person's deepest needs or moral vision. In *One More Sunday*, John Tinker Meadows's preaching differs from his father's because he has lost the latter's intensity. After the sermon which opens the novel, John points up what he has lost by replying to Mary Margaret's compliment: "'I had the feeling it was going well.

This time Fred Stubbs did the first draft and then Spencer McKay and I worked it over. We'll use the original long version in PathWays, I think'" (9). And during the sermon, his consciousness of a rhetorical trick reflects his over-analytical approach:

You could tell if you had them by the way some of them jumped. This was one of the good Sundays. Sometimes it worked better than other times. He had never achieved the consistency of the old man, who always made it work. (6)

Possibly, Matthew did not have to plan his effects but rather lived them, not unaware of them as effects but unaware of any distance between act and intention. Mary Margaret's emotional response to the Rev. Birdy's parable of the little girl who wraps herself in seaweed (292-93, 294, 296, 297), similar to McGee's rejuvenation at the end of *Silver*, reveals someone who might begin to unify work and self while John's response to Birdy's comments on the direction of their church are dismissive, a man cut off from his feelings, surviving but not truly living through performance (297).

    Barrier Island, MacDonald's last novel, opposes several aspects of work and professionalism which ultimately revolve around a moral position. Tuck Loomis develops a land scam to profit from the rumored government condemnation of any planned building on Bernard Island off the coast of Mississippi. Though not in MacDonald's usual Florida setting, the island, like Fiddler Key in *Condominium*, symbolizes a clear issue in its separation from the mainland. Isolation and division are contexts which MacDonald also uses in *One More Sunday* and *The Last One Left*, as well as in numerous McGee novels. In order to make his plan work, Loomis employs the services of the Rowley/Gibbs real estate firm to process some of the paperwork. Bern Gibbs responds more to Loomis's overtures than does Wade Rowley. Although both are competent, Rowley is more careful and more honest. He is willing to define limits, even though they are acting within the law, that reveal moral sensibilities which supersede legal ones. Admittedly, Rowley acts partially from a sense of self-protection when he goes to Gordon Hammond from the National Park Service to explain his doubts about Loomis's deal. Yet, the differences between his bases for action and Gibbs's with reference to Bernard Island resemble his insistence to Gibbs four years previously that their firm should inform the retired couple about to buy the Maxwell place that the ground water was contaminated. Then, Rowley says, "'We have a public reputation and we have a state license and we are not going to lose either or both'" (153-54). When profits are possible, Loomis and Gibbs choose them over the moral stance. Rowley chooses the morally correct course of action, and as in medieval morality plays, this course ultimately leads to deeper and more lasting benefits.

Family and marriage, discussed in Chapter Sixteen, might seem to be themes of minimal importance in the Travis McGee series. After all, McGee remains unmarried throughout the series although he does have intense love relationships. Yet in the novels, family and marriage are identified by both presence and absence. For McGee, marriage is a continual absence, but it is present in the lives of other characters in most novels in both positive and negative ways. However, family gradually looms as an important presence in the aging McGee's life until the culmination in *Silver* in which he gains a sixteen-year-old daughter, as discussed in Chapter Seventeen. McGee also alludes to various other members of his immediate family throughout the series although none ever appear. Of course, the initial focus on family for McGee is the introduction of Meyer. Not only a friend, Meyer represents that intimate relationship for McGee that family embeds in people's lives. They occasionally experience anger and frustration toward each other but develop a stronger friendship because of these episodes. At the end of *Silver*, McGee includes Meyer in his relationship with his daughter.

Although there are positive marital relationships in the Travis McGee series, e.g., Shaja Dobrak and her imprisoned husband in *Gold*, Chookie McCall and Arthur Wilkinson who marry in *Orange*, Gloria and Fortner Geis in *One Fearful Yellow Eye*, and Janine and Tush Bannon in *Gray*, MacDonald generally portrays destructive, crumbling, or inadequate marriages that reveal a troubled social institution. However, in *Barrier Island*, Beth and Wade Rowley represent the paradigmatic positive marriage that survives whatever problems arise between themselves or between them and their two children. Beth is a woman who, because of the break-up of her family as a child (124), cannot easily handle any threats to her security. When Wade tells her that he and his partner might dissolve their business, she becomes frightened. However, he calms her by saying that the problem will not immediately occur. What gradually develops is that Wade must take the lead in maintaining the sense of family security. When problems arise with their son, Tod, over his moodiness and withdrawal, Wade talks with him and manages to reach him (128-29). Later, Wade conceals from Beth the fact that

Bern's death occurred when he was beaten after he was mistaken for Wade (191-92). In "The Mythology of Crime and Violence," David K. Jeffrey states, "[T]he positive models for women [in the mythical world of crime and violence] are passive, the negative models, assertive . . ." (79). While not one-hundred percent true in MacDonald's paradigm, the man usually safeguards the family or makes necessary changes when problems between husband and wife arise. The woman is a barometer which reflects difficulties but which also shows ways out of the difficulties. In *The Last One Left*, Lydia Boylston leaves Sam because of his inability to relate to her in meaningful ways and only returns once he changes and, more importantly, understands the need for change. Subconsciously agreeing on their respective roles, they can only experience a good relationship when they live out these roles.

Wade and Beth Rowley and Sam and Lydia Boylston represent ultimately positive images of marriage, but these images are only possible if they function from some moral core. In *One More Sunday*, John Tinker Meadows's disintegrating family and ministry parallel one another. Meadows lacks energy or conviction both for the church and the affair with Molly Wintergarten, the wife of one of his employees. The listless manner with which he approaches life suggests a hollowness that nothing can fill. In one sense, Meadows symbolizes the decay that touches his family. In addition to Matthew Meadows's illness, Mary Margaret is thirty-eight years old, single, and according to John, guilty of gluttony, "'one of the sins of the gratification of self'" (58). Paul, Matthew's youngest son, "mutilated himself" (50) and "was put away" (50) where he died (46). Mary Margaret believes that

the three of us, and maybe Momma too, we had to kind of . . . push ourselves upward to fill up the big image he [Matthew] had of us. To be better people than we ever were. And it was too much, maybe. It was too much for Paul, certainly. And maybe in ways we can't quite comprehend, it was too much for you and me too. (56)

John's wife, Chris, died nine years before the novel begins (57), and when Mary Margaret suggests that he marry Tracy Bellwright, a member of the Church, John only vaguely remembers her but rejects the idea (57). His sister states that "'People are getting very wary of you'" (56) and says that "'Lately you've been so irritable and restless and remote, and it makes me wonder how vulnerable you might be to some sort of trouble'" (58). She knows of earlier affairs (57), and when he rejects her offer of help, she thinks, "He's going bad. . . . Like something rotting away underneath the shiny outer skin" (58). Her views parallel those of Finn Efflander, one of John's close assistants, who wonders if "John Tinker Meadows might be going mad" and feels, when John begins to talk "about the necessity for faith," "as though he were alone in a room with an animal that had no idea of what its next move might be, and cared nothing about the consequences" (28). Although Jonathan Yardley's observation on MacDonald's position on evangelicals "that they seek, out of whatever motive, to fill a genuine longing among their followers" (B8) might be true, the Meadows family and the Church of the Eternal Believer are twin shells waiting to topple and shatter like the statue John sees in a dream of himself in a Christ pose (11).

The four groups of themes are some of the most important ones in the MacDonald canon. In one sense, MacDonald's use of them in the non-Travis McGee novels is an attempt to explore them in different constructs, to rethink them outside of the developed limits of the series. To MacDonald, they represent a core of central concerns that reveal no ultimate solution but remain a continuing attraction to him. From his first novel, *The Brass Cupcake*, to his last, *Barrier Island*, MacDonald has dramatized these and other themes and over the 36 years of his novel production has demonstrated not so much a progression in his thought as a sense of fascination, a puzzlement as to what his imagination, focused on these ideas, will reveal to him about American society. Rick Lott observes, "As an American literary artist, John D. MacDonald has, like most of his predecessors [sic], found it necessary to explore the American Dream; and his view of this great myth is essentially dystopic" (14). Whether one accepts this as the direction of MacDonald's fiction, one cannot help being involved with his fictional exploration of American culture. For readers, his meditations successfully engage them to enter on the same fruitful and disturbing journey.

Works Cited

Abrahams, Etta C. "Cops and Detectives." *Clues: A Journal of Detection* 1.1 (1980): 96-98.

____. "Travis McGee: The Thinking Man's Robin Hood." *New Dimensions in Popular Culture.* Ed. Russel B. Nye. Bowling Green, OH: Popular Press, 1972. 236-46.

____. "Visions and Values in the Action Detective Novel: A Study of the Works of Raymond Chandler, Kenneth Millar, and John D. MacDonald." Diss. Michigan State U, 1973.

Alderman, Taylor. "Hedonist, Therapist, Lover: The Sexual Roles of Travis McGee." *JDM Bibliophile* 46 (Dec. 1990): 17-21.

Arnold, Matthew. "Literature and Science." *The Portable Matthew Arnold.* Ed. and intro. Lionel Trilling. New York: Viking, 1949. 405-29.

Benjamin, David A. "Key Witness: J.D. MacDonald." *New Republic* 26 July 1975: 28-31.

Black, David. "The Moralism of John D. MacDonald." *Boston Phoenix* 3 Aug. 1982: 1+.

Brittin, Norman A. "The Joys and Troubles of Children and Adolescents in the Work of John D. MacDonald." *JDM Bibliophile* 36 (July 1985): 19-25.

Carlyle, Thomas. *Sartor Resartus and Selected Prose.* Intro. Herbert Sussman. New York: Holt, 1970.

Cawelti, John G. *Adventure, Mystery, and Romance: Formula Stories as Art and Popular Culture.* Chicago: U of Chicago P, 1976.

Chesterton, G.K. "A Defence of Detective Stories." *The Art of the Mystery Story.* Ed. Howard Haycraft. Intro. Robin W. Winks. 2nd. ed. 1946. New York: Carroll & Graf, 1992. 3-6.

Christie, Agatha. *And Then There Were None.* New York: Washington Square, 1975.

Cleveland, Carol. "Travis McGee: The Feminists' Friend." *Armchair Detective* 16 (1983): 407-13.

Cook, Wister. "John D. MacDonald: A Little Ecology Goes a Long Way." *Clues: A Journal of Detection* 1.1 (1980): 57-61.

Culler, Jonathan. *The Pursuit of Signs: Semiotics, Literature, Deconstruction.* Ithaca, NY: Cornell UP, 1981.

Doulis, Thomas. "The Liabilities of Professionalism." *Journal of Popular Culture* 10 (1976): 38-53.

Eagleton, Terry. *Literary Theory: An Introduction*. Minneapolis: U of Minnesota P, 1983.

Ecenbarger, William. "Violence on Violet Nights." *Inquirer: Philadelphia Inquirer Magazine* 17 Mar. 1985: 20-25.

Feetenby, John. "Pigments of the Imagination." *Million: The Magazine About Popular Literature* 14 (Mar./June1993): 4-8.

Fitzgerald, F. Scott. *The Great Gatsby*. 1925. New York: Scribner's, 1953.

Fowler, Raymond D. "The Case of the Multicolored Personality." *Psychology Today* Nov. 1986: 38-40+.

Garrett, George. "Travis McGee in Hawaii or: MacDonald in the Big Time." Rev. of *The Scarlet Ruse* and *The Turquoise Lament*, by John D. MacDonald. *Richmond (VA) Mercury* 17 Oct. 1993: 9.

Geherin, David. *John D. MacDonald*. New York: Ungar, 1982.

Green, Martin. *Transatlantic Patterns: Cultural Comparisons of England with America*. New York: Basic Books, 1977.

Grimes, Larry E. "The Reluctant Hero: Reflections on Vocation and Heroism in the Travis McGee Novels of John D. MacDonald." *Clues: A Journal of Detection* 1.1 (1980): 103-08.

Hemingway, Ernest. *For Whom the Bell Tolls*. 1940. New York: Scribner's, 1968.

Hirshberg, Edgar W. *John D. MacDonald*. Twayne's United States Authors Series. Ed. Warren French. 1985. Boston: Twayne, 1986.

____. "John D. MacDonald." *Dictionary of Literary Biography Yearbook: 1986*. Ed. J.M. Brook. Detroit: Gale Research, 1987. 235-40.

____. "John D. MacDonald as Social Critic." *Clues: A Journal of Detection* 1.1 (1980): 129-34.

Holtsmark, Erling B. "Travis McGee as Traditional Hero." *Clues: A Journal of Detection* 1.1 (1980): 99-102.

Homer. *The Odyssey*. Trans. Robert Fitzgerald. 1963. *The Ancient World Through the Renaissance*. Vol. 1 of *Literature of the Western World*. Ed. Brian Wilkie and James Hurt. 3rd. ed. 2 vols. New York: Macmillan,1992. 262-580.

Hoyt, Charles Alva. "*The Damned*: Good Intentions: The Tough Guy as Hero and Villain." *Tough Guy Writers of the Thirties*. Pref. Harry T. Moore. Ed. David Madden. Crosscurrents: Modern Critiques. Gen. Ed. Harry T. Moore. Carbondale, IL: Southern Illinois UP, 1968.

Jackman, Mary K. "A Question of Survival: Feminine Narratives in John D. MacDonald's *The Deep Blue Good-by*." *JDM Bibliophile* 50 (Dec. 1992): 41-48.

Jackson, S.H. "The Enlightened but Earthbound Detective Hero in Novels by Ross Macdonald and John D. MacDonald." *JDM Bibliophile* 46 (Dec. 1990): 6-10.

Jeffrey, David K. "The Mythology of Crime and Violence." *Clues: A Journal of Detection* 1.1 (1980): 75-81.

Kaler, Anne K. "Cats, Colors, and Calendars: The Mythic Basis of the Love Story of Travis McGee." *Clues: A Journal of Detection* 7.2 (1986): 147-57.

Keating, H.R.F. "John D. MacDonald: *The Green Ripper.*" *Crime & Mystery: The 100 Best Books.* Foreword Patricia Highsmith. New York: Carroll & Graf, 1988. 195-96.

Keefer, T. Frederick. "Albert Camus' American Disciple: John D. MacDonald's Existentialist Hero, Travis D. McGee." *Journal of Popular Culture* 19.2 (1985): 33-48.

Kelly, R. Gordon. "The Precarious World of John D. MacDonald." *Dimensions of Detective Fiction.* Eds. Larry N. Landrum, Pat Browne, and Ray B. Browne. Bowling Green, OH: Bowling Green State University Popular Press, 1976. 149-61.

Lane, Thomas D. "Criticizing the Critics: A Reader's Response to Commentary on John D. MacDonald." *JDM Bibliophile* 46 (Dec. 1990): 42-48.

____. "MacDonald's Villains: Assumptions on Their Origin and Selection." *Clues: A Journal of Detection* 11.1 (1990): 21-29.

Lott, Rick. "Signs and Portents: John D. MacDonald's Apocalyptic Vision." *JDM Bibliophile* 44 (Dec. 1989): 8-15.

MacDonald, John D. "The 'Aging' of Travis McGee." *JDM Bibliophile* 20 (1975): 3-4.

____. *All These Condemned.* 1954. New York: Fawcett Gold Medal-Ballantine, 1983.

____. *April Evil.* Greenwich, CT: Fawcett Gold Medal, 1956.

____. *Area of Suspicion.* Rev. 1954. New York: Fawcett Gold Medal, 1961.

____. *Ballroom of the Skies.* New York: Fawcett Gold Medal, 1952.

____. *Barrier Island.* New York: Knopf, 1986.

____. *The Beach Girls.* Greenwich, CT: Fawcett Gold Medal, 1959.

____. "The Big Blue." *End of the Tiger and Other Stories.* 1966. New York: Fawcett Gold Medal-Ballantine, 1984. 23-35.

____. *Border Town Girl: Two Novellas.* Greenwich, CT: Fawcett Gold Medal, 1956.

____. *The Brass Cupcake.* New York: Fawcett Gold Medal, 1950.

____. *Bright Orange for the Shroud.* Greenwich, CT: Fawcett Gold Medal, 1965. Subsequent references to novels in the Travis McGee series will be by the color in the titles.

____. *A Bullet for Cinderella.* Greenwich, CT: Fawcett Gold Medal, 1955.

_____. *Cancel All Our Vows*. 1953. New York: Fawcett Gold Medal-Ballantine, 1985.

_____. *Cinnamon Skin: The Twentieth Adventure of Travis McGee*. 1982. New York: Fawcett Gold Medal-Ballantine, 1983.

_____. *Clemmie*. Greenwich, CT: Fawcett Gold Medal, 1958.

_____. *Condominium*. New York: Fawcett Crest, 1977.

_____. *Contrary Pleasure*. 1954. New York: Fawcett Gold Medal-Ballantine, 1985.

_____. "The Creative Person and Some Dangerous Streets." *Writer's Digest* June 1969: 58-61+.

_____. "Creative Trust." *Writer* Jan. 1974: 13-15+.

_____. *The Crossroads*. New York: Fawcett Gold Medal, 1959.

_____. *Cry Hard, Cry Fast*. Greenwich, CT: Fawcett Gold Medal, 1955.

_____. *The Damned*. New York: Fawcett Gold Medal, 1952.

_____. *Darker than Amber*. 1966. New York: Fawcett Gold Medal-Ballantine, 1982.

_____. *Dead Low Tide*. 1953. New York: Fawcett Gold Medal-Ballantine, 1985.

_____. *A Deadly Shade of Gold*. 1965. New York: Fawcett Gold Medal-Ballantine, 1982.

_____. *Deadly Welcome*. Greenwich, CT: Fawcett Gold Medal, 1959.

_____. *Death Trap*. New York: Fawcett Gold Medal, 1957.

_____. *The Deceivers*. Greenwich, CT: Fawcett Gold Medal,1958.

_____. *The Deep Blue Good-by*. 1964. New York: Fawcett Gold Medal-Ballantine, 1982.

_____. *The Dreadful Lemon Sky*. 1975. New York: Fawcett Gold Medal-Ballantine, 1982.

_____. *Dress Her in Indigo*. 1969. New York: Fawcett Gold Medal-Ballantine, 1982.

_____. *The Drowner*. Greenwich, CT: Fawcett Gold Medal, 1963.

_____. *The Empty Copper Sea*. New York: Fawcett Gold Medal, 1978.

_____. *The Empty Trap*. 1957. New York: Fawcett Gold Medal-Ballantine, 1983.

_____. *The End of the Night*. Greenwich, CT: Fawcett Gold Medal, 1960.

_____. "Everybody Knows *Something* Is Wrong." *Miami Herald Tropic* 15 Oct. 1967: 22-23+.

_____. *The Executioners*. New York: Fawcett Gold Medal, 1958.

_____. *A Flash of Green*. Greenwich, CT: Fawcett Gold Medal, 1962.

_____. *Free Fall in Crimson*. 1981. New York: Fawcett Gold Medal-Ballantine, 1982.

_____. *A Friendship: The Letters of Dan Rowan and John D. MacDonald: 1967-1974*. New York: Knopf, 1986.

_____. *The Girl in the Plain Brown Wrapper.* Greenwich, CT: Fawcett Gold Medal, 1968.

_____. *The Girl, the Gold Watch & Everything.* Greenwich, CT: Fawcett Gold Medal, 1962.

_____. *The Green Ripper.* 1979. New York: Fawcett Gold Medal, 1980.

_____. *The House Guests.* Illus. 1965. New York: Fawcett Gold Medal-Ballantine, 1988.

_____. "How a Character Becomes Believable." *Mystery Writer's Handbook.* Rev. ed. Cincinnati, OH: Writer's Digest, 1976. 113-22.

_____. "How to Live with a Hero." *Writer* Sept. 1964: 14-16+.

_____. "Introduction and Comment." *Clues: A Journal of Detection* 1.1 (1980): 63-74.

_____. "Introduction to *Slam the Big Door.*" *JDM Bibliophile* 38 (July 1986): 7-9.

_____. "JDM as an Art Critic." *JDM Bibliophile* 31 (Jan. 1983): 8-11.

_____. *Judge Me Not.* Greenwich, CT: Fawcett Gold Medal, 1951.

_____. *A Key to the Suite.* New York: Fawcett Gold Medal,1962.

_____. *The Last One Left.* Greenwich, CT: Fawcett Gold Medal, 1967.

_____. Letter. *JDM Bibliophile* 8 (Dec. 1967): 5-8.

_____. *The Lonely Silver Rain.* 1985. New York: Fawcett Gold Medal-Ballantine, 1986.

_____. *The Long Lavender Look.* 1970. New York: Fawcett Gold Medal-Ballantine, 1982.

_____. *A Man of Affairs.* Greenwich, CT: Fawcett Gold Medal, 1957.

_____. *Murder for the Bride.* Greenwich, CT: Fawcett Gold Medal, 1951.

_____. *Murder in the Wind.* Greenwich, CT: Fawcett Gold Medal, 1956.

_____. *The Neon Jungle.* 1953. New York: Fawcett Gold Medal-Ballantine, 1984.

_____. *Nightmare in Pink.* 1964. New York: Fawcett Gold Medal-Ballantine, 1983.

_____. *On the Run.* New York: Fawcett Gold Medal, 1963.

_____. *One Fearful Yellow Eye.* 1966. New York: Fawcett Gold Medal-Ballantine, 1982.

_____. *One Monday We Killed Them All.* Greenwich, CT: Fawcett Gold Medal, 1961.

_____. *One More Sunday.* New York: Knopf, 1984.

_____. *The Only Girl in the Game.* New York: Fawcett Gold Medal, 1960.

_____. *Pale Gray for Guilt.* Greenwich, CT: Fawcett Gold Medal, 1968.

_____. *Please Write for Details.* Greenwich, CT: Fawcett Gold Medal, 1959.

_____. *The Price of Murder.* Greenwich, CT: Fawcett Gold Medal, 1957.

_____. "A Public Lecture." *JDM Bibliophile* 35 (Jan. 1985): 8-14.

____. *A Purple Place for Dying.* Greenwich, CT: Fawcett Gold Medal, 1964.

____. *The Quick Red Fox.* Greenwich, CT: Fawcett Gold Medal, 1964.

____. *Reading for Survival.* Washington: Library of Congress, 1987.

____. "Report from the Ironic Underground." *Chicago Tribune Books Today* 24 Oct. 1965: 3A-4A.

____. *The Scarlet Ruse.* 1973. New York: Fawcett Gold Medal-Ballantine, 1983.

____. *Slam the Big Door.* 1960. New York: Fawcett Gold Medal-Ballantine, 1987.

____. *Soft Touch.* Greenwich, CT: Fawcett Gold Medal, 1958.

____. *A Tan and Sandy Silence.* New York: Fawcett Gold Medal, 1971.

____. *The Turquoise Lament.* 1973. Greenwich, CT: Fawcett Gold Medal, 1974.

____. *Weep for Me.* New York: Fawcett Gold Medal, 1951.

____. *Where Is Janice Gantry?* Greenwich, CT: Fawcett Gold Medal, 1961.

____. *Wine of the Dreamers.* 1951. New York: Fawcett Gold Medal-Ballantine, 1984.

____. *You Live Once.* Greenwich, CT: Fawcett Gold Medal, 1956.

Marotta, Joseph. "The Disorderly World of John D. MacDonald: or Travis McGee Meets Thomas Pynchon." *Clues: A Journal of Detection* 3.1 (1982): 105-10.

Matthews, Jack. Rev. of *The Dreadful Lemon Sky,* by John D. MacDonald. *Ohio Review* 16.3 (1975): 108-11.

Moore, Anthony. "Travis McGee as an Antimodern Hero." *JDM Review* Spring 1992: 43-48.

Moran, Peggy. "McGee's Girls." *Clues: A Journal of Detection* 1.1 (1980): 82-88.

Morris, William. *News from Nowhere. Three Works.* Intro. A.L. Morton. London: Lawrence and Wishart, 1986. 179-401.

Nelson, John Wiley. "Travis McGee, Tarnished Knight in Modern Armor." *Your God Is Alive and Well and Appearing in Popular Culture.* Philadelphia: Westminster P, 1976. 170-92.

Oberdorf, Charles. "The Dauntingly Prolific Beige Typewriter Keys." *MacLean's* 20 Nov. 1978: 61-62.

Ott, Bill. "Places in the Hearts of Hard-boiled Heroes." *Openers: America's Library Newspaper* Summer 1987: 4-5.

Pearson, Richard. "John D. MacDonald, Writer of Popular Mysteries, Dies at 70." *Washington Post* 29 Dec. 1986: B6.

Peek, George S. "Beast Imagery and Stereotypes in the Novels of John D. MacDonald." *Clues: A Journal of Detection* 2.1 (1981): 91-97.

————. "Conquering the Stereotypes: On Reading the Novels of John D. MacDonald." *Armchair Detective* 13 (1980): 90-93.

Phillips, Robert K. "Travis McGee—Androgynous Existentialist." *JDM Bibliophile* 46 (Dec. 1990): 29-33.

Rand, Ayn. *Atlas Shrugged*. Intro. Leonard Peikoff. 1957. New York: Dutton, 1992.

Sanders, Joe. "Science Fiction and Detective Fiction: The Case of John D. MacDonald." *Science-Fiction Studies* 7.2 (1980): 157-65.

Shine, Walter, and Jean Shine. "Charles Willeford." *Rave or Rage: The Critics and John D. MacDonald*. Gainesville, FL: U of Florida, George A. Smathers Libraries, 1993. 4.

————. "Snippets and Scoops from the Shines." *JDM Review* Autumn 1991: 19-26.

Stout, Rex. *In the Best Families. Triple Zeck: A Nero Wolfe Omnibus*. 1950. New York: Viking, 1974. 301-502.

Streitfeld, David. "Super Mac." *Washington Post Book World* 24 Jan. 1988: 15.

Svoboda, Frederic. "The Snub-nosed Mystique: Observations on the American Detective Hero." *Modern Fiction Studies* 29 (1983): 557-68.

Thomas, Ross. "Mastery of the Mystery: John D. MacDonald's Rare, Insightful Prose." *Washington Post* 29 Dec. 1986: D1+.

Todorov, Tzvetan. *Poetics of Prose*. Trans. Richard Howard. Foreward Jonathan Culler. 1971. Ithaca, NY: Cornell UP, 1977.

Tolley, Michael J. "Color Him Quixote." *Armchair Detective* 10 (1977): 6-13.

————. "The Hero in Popular Fiction: John D. MacDonald's Travis McGee." *The Hero in Popular Fiction*. N.p.: U of Adelaide, n.d. 49-57.

Vander Ven, Karen. "Psychological Genesis of the Prototype Hero in Mystery/Detective Fiction as Embodied by Travis McGee: A Retrospective Analysis of His Development as a Child and Youth." *Clues: A Journal of Detection* 11.1 (1990): 31-56.

Vatai, Frank L. "John D. MacDonald and Calvinism: Some Key Themes." *Clues: A Journal of Detection* 11.1 (1990): 9-19.

Yardley, Jonathan. "Taking on Faith: John D. MacDonald's Superior Sermon." Rev. of *One More Sunday*, by John D. MacDonald. *Washington Post* 14 Mar. 1984: B1+.

Index

www.ingramcontent.com/pod-product-compliance
Lightning Source LLC
Chambersburg PA
CBHW060417100426

42812CB00030B/3221/J